PRAISE FOR *WORK LESS, DO MORE*

"Bravo Jan Yager for coming up with a "quick read" and m[...] and life under control so that you will accomplish more and enjoy doing so. I will definitely recommend *Work Less, Do More* to my clients."

—Nella G. Barkley, President, Crystal-Barkley Corp., Life-Work Design

"*Work Less, Do More* certainly will help those of us who struggle to make every minute in our days count for the very most!"

—Don Gabor, author, *How to Start a Conversation and Make Friends*

"*Work Less, Do More* is a fabulous resource for helping you. What is most significant about this book is the focus on you and your attitude toward time management, the habits you'll need to change to diminish stress and improve productivity and the decisions you alone are responsible for in order to create a more meaningful existence."

—Julie Jansen, author, *I Don't Know What I Want, But I Know It's Not This*

"Time . . . your most precious commodity! Yet time is often the most squandered of your possessions! Reclaim your rich inheritance of time now. Jan's words will bring you renewed peace and provide you with "found" time in which to live your dreams!"

—Glenna Salsbury, author, *The Art of the Fresh Start*

"Jan Yager understands the complexity of time management and how it intersects so many different aspects of our lives—intellectually, socially, and emotionally. The valuable information and exercises in this book will help us look at time management, ourselves, and our behavior in a whole new way. She gives us not only ideas but motivation to be more productive and more satisfied at the end of each day."

—Suzanne Vaughan, speaker, Suzanne Vaughan & Associates

"This is the path to a more rational and productive lifestyle! Jan Yager provides the prescription for success. For anyone looking to continuously grow, both personally and professionally, here is your tool! *Work Less, Do More* is a great read. Very useful, practical, and well-written."

—Matthew B. Kiger, music producer/media executive

WORK LESS, DO MORE

The 14-Day Productivity Makeover

Jan Yager, Ph.D.

STERLING

New York / London
www.sterlingpublishing.com

For my husband, Fred, and our sons, Scott and Jeff

STERLING and the distinctive Sterling logo are registered trademarks of Sterling Publishing Co., Inc.

Library of Congress Cataloging-in-Publication Data

Yager, Jan, 1948-
    Work less, do more : the 14-day productivity makeover / Jan Yager.
       p. cm.
    Includes bibliographical references and index.
    ISBN 978-1-4027-4837-0
1. Time management—Problems, exercises, etc. 2. Office management—Problems, exercises, etc. 3. Self-management (Psychology)—Problems, exercises, etc. I. Title.

HD69.T54Y348 2008
650.1'1—dc22

               2007052538

10 9 8 7 6 5 4 3 2 1

Published by Sterling Publishing Co., Inc.
387 Park Avenue South, New York, NY 10016
Copyright © 2008 by Jan Yager, Ph.D.
Distributed in Canada by Sterling Publishing
% Canadian Manda Group, 165 Dufferin Street
Toronto, Ontario, Canada M6K 3H6
Distributed in the United Kingdom by GMC Distribution Services
Castle Place, 166 High Street, Lewes, East Sussex, England BN7 1XU
Distributed in Australia by Capricorn Link (Australia) Pty. Ltd.
P.O. Box 704, Windsor, NSW 2756, Australia

Sterling ISBN 978-1-4027-4837-0

For information about custom editions, special sales, premium and corporate purchases, please contact Sterling Special Sales Department at 800-805-5489 or specialsales@sterlingpublishing.com.

Contents

Introduction

Each day is 24 hours long, which equals 1,440 minutes or 86,400 seconds. What did you accomplish with those seconds, minutes, or hours today? Yesterday? Can you even remember? If you can point to at least one thing you did, that's a good start. If that one thing was something you absolutely had to do, that's even better. But for many, the seconds, minutes, and hours are more of a blur, a frenzy of activity—responding to a phone call here, an e-mail there, or an unexpected request from a boss or coworker—without attaining the hoped-for results.

How much of your day did you spend in activities that were, in hindsight, a poor choice because those activities did not—and will not—move you or your career (or even your relationships) along as effectively as other activities that you may not have gotten to in time? Was it half your day? Ten percent? An hour or two? In today's competitive, results-oriented workplace, even half an hour is thirty minutes too many—and yet how many of us are wasting far more time than that?

How will you spend your time tomorrow? Will you be as productive as you want to be, as you know you could be, or should be, if you just had the tools to manage your time more effectively?

How to Use This Book

Before you turn to Day 1 of this time management program, I want to comment on the structure of this book. As you know, this is a 14-day plan, with each chapter representing another day in your self-improvement program. However, the idea of focusing on one chapter a day is only a suggestion. Read through each section at whatever pace is comfortable for you. You might prefer to jump around, focusing on those issues that are most pertinent and relevant for you. You may also choose to read the book straight through, like any other self-help or business book, and then go back, rereading it and completing the exercises and logs a chapter at a time or a section at a time.

Most important of all, this book is an interactive learning tool that depends on you to make it work. Of course you can still benefit from reading the book if you just read the prose, consider the concepts and the examples, and apply them to your own situation. But if you make the time to take the quizzes, fill in the worksheets, complete the logs, and do the exercises at the end of each chapter, you will get even more out of the book because you will be putting more into it. Congratulations on making time management a priority as you prepare to transform your career, your business, and your life. I wish you well and I welcome hearing about the improvements that you achieve!

How I Researched and Wrote This Book

In addition to my experience as an author, consultant, and speaker, I have been teaching Crisis Intervention, Interpersonal Communications, and the Sociology of Health at the college level since the 1980s, most recently at the University of Connecticut. I therefore bring to this time management book a unique medical sociology perspective, which includes a heightened awareness of the connection between stress and increased time pressures—and how work productivity impacts on our health, our work, and our personal relationships.

I developed the original 14-day plan that is the foundation of *Work Less, Do More* from the time management coaching, speeches, and workshops that I have delivered over more than two decades to a variety of audiences, including executives, administrators, entrepreneurs, authors, sales professionals, consultants, speakers, copywriters, mental health supervisors, human resource managers, career advisors, management consultants, development directors, working and stay-at-home mothers, small business owners, fundraisers, freelancers, students, and others.

This is my third book on the topic of time management, and I've attempted to highlight what's new in this area, in addition to covering the basics. There are many time management challenges that have remained consistent over the years, such as the need to prioritize, set goals, get organized, and deal with obstacles to effective time management. But there is also a lot that has changed; for example, technology and an escalation in the pace of society, compounded by the competing demands of a more competitive workplace influenced by global conditions, and the shared goal of working men and women to have a more balanced life. The widespread use of e-mail and cell (mobile) phones is turning practically every job into a 24/7 responsibility. (Remember when it was just doctors and therapists who got called or beeped outside of typical office hours?) This availability has created time management issues that are much more dramatic and pressing than they were even ten years ago. *Work Less, Do More: The 14-Day Productivity Makeover* provides powerful techniques to counter these challenges, such as the ACTION! System for optimum productivity; WOO (window of opportunity); RRA (respond right away); OTD (out the door); guidelines for establishing "me," "we," and "us" time; and tips for dealing with a superior who lacks time management skills.

As I discuss in greater detail in Day 10, a phenomenon is on the rise that I call *distractionitis,* the pulling away from one's primary focus by other disparate demands that often turn out to be low priority, especially through such behaviors as compulsively checking and rechecking e-mail throughout the workday, taking cell phone calls that interrupt meetings, and Internet surfing far removed from the original reason the search was initiated. The bombardment of 24/7 availability is making it harder and harder to concentrate and to stay focused for extended hours. Without help, stress levels are going to continue to rise to life-threatening amounts. We must take greater control of our time; our responsibility for dealing with distractionitis has to start now, and it has to come from within. This book will provide you with the tools to accomplish that goal in the face of increasing time, work, relationship, and technological pressures.

Author's Note about Sources: Quotes in this book not attributed to a secondary source are based on original research conducted by the author, in the form of either interviews or questionnaires, and are reprinted verbatim and, if necessary, excerpted. If minor editing was required for either sense or clarification, brackets indicate those additions or changes. If anonymity was requested, a fictitious first name has been provided; identifying details have also been changed to maintain that anonymity. However, care has been taken to preserve the integrity of each example. Secondary sources cited within the text have complete bibliographic entries in the book's List of Works Cited.

DAY 1

Getting Started

"I don't have enough time" is a common complaint heard in companies of all sizes, voiced by employees at all levels—from managers to administrative assistants, from vice presidents, lawyers, and professors to CFOs and CEOs. No type of company is exempt from this predicament, whether it's a huge corporation with tens of thousands of employees, a smaller business with a couple hundred employees, or a home-based business with just one entrepreneur, consultant, or freelancer at the helm. As companies across the board downsize, fewer employees are being asked to accomplish more tasks in even less time. The Internet has turned practically every business into a global operation, often with expanded work hours because of the different time zones that need to be serviced.

Cell (mobile) phones, portable laptop (notebook) computers, e-mail, fax machines, and handheld electronic devices (PDAs) also make it possible to do business from anywhere in the world, 24 hours a day. Therefore, in today's 24/7 work world, learning how to self-regulate has become more important than ever before. Self-regulating means that even though you can work around the clock, you decide how much time you will devote to work, whether at the office, during your commute, or in your evening and weekend leisure hours. For example, while your boss might expect you to be available from 8 a.m. until 6 or even 7 p.m., you may draw the line at working at home every evening and on weekends, except when it's absolutely necessary. Or, if you have a specific deadline that needs to be met, you may choose to put in 18 hours a day for as long as it takes, knowing the end is in sight. (If, on the other hand, you find yourself working 18 hours a day, every day, without taking even a one-week annual vacation, take heart. You will find help in this book to amend your grueling schedule and still get a lot done.)

How Are You Currently Handling Your Time?

Consider how much of your workday you spend productively, as opposed to how much time you waste in meetings that should not have been called in the first place, looking for something you misplaced, answering phone calls that could have been directed to someone else, or dealing with a low-priority project—when you could have been spending your time following up on a time-sensitive, hot lead for new work. According to a 2008 telephone survey of 429 men and women who are employed full or part time and think that something keeps them from getting their job done, on average, almost 1 hour (50.3 minutes), exclusive of lunch or commuting time, is wasted at work. The survey was conducted for me by CARAVAN® Opinion Research Corporation.

Successful business executives, leaders, entrepreneurs, and student handle their time well. They make choices about what to do, and when to do it, that accomplish their short- and long-term goals so that they finish what they start and meet their deadlines. Even more fundamental is that they have a way of figuring out what priority tasks to begin in the first place. If we add the adjective *happy* before successful, you will find that happy executives, leaders, entrepreneurs, and students tend not to be workaholics; work is part but not all of their lives. Their lives are balanced. They make time for the activities and relationships that matter to them in addition to the work that they need and, ideally, even want to do.

Yes, I have found that it is the successful business executives who take the time to send a quick e-mail or note or, if they are unable to personally do so, they at least delegate the task of getting back to others to staff members who will follow up on their behalf. They do not ignore someone because they "don't have time." They understand that connecting with an individual in a timely fashion, whether it is a potential business associate, client, customer, coworker, employee, or boss, is the cornerstone of a responsive and accomplished employee or business leader.

How to Accomplish More in Less Time

Time management is a systematic approach to the way you organize your work and free time so that you are in control of how you spend your time; time does not control you. Those who lack effective time management skills may, at the end of the workday, reflect back and wonder, "I was really busy today, but what did I actually accomplish?" They may also think or even blurt out, "Where does the time go?" Or, at the end of the weekend, they may be filled with regrets over the friends they did not find time to socialize with, the novels that remain unread, the day trips that got postponed yet again, the family time that didn't seem to happen, the exercise plan that got short shrift, or the flowers that still need to be planted.

The effective time manager uses such proven techniques as prioritizing, long- and short-term goal setting, planning, organizing, setting realistic deadlines, and delegating to accomplish what has to be done right now as well as making sure future projects are conceptualized and planned for adequately.

When and how do you learn these helpful time management skills? There are some who truly seem to be born organizers and natural time managers. They developed a knack for coordinating or organizing their school papers, books, and assignments early on, way back in elementary school. Certainly these natural organizers were showing their stuff by college or graduate school years. At work, they are systematic in how they respond to their boss's requests, meet deadlines, keep track of where things are filed, and pace themselves appropriately. When they become the bosses, they set an example in these areas for their employees.

Perhaps you recognize yourself in this description. Perhaps even more disparate demands on your time, as well as juggling multiple projects and roles (worker, parent, student, community leader, or volunteer)—or even just trying to keep up with the changing time demands caused by the Internet or the ability to communicate 24/7 through a handheld device or a cell phone—have pushed you over the top lately, so that you now need help with how you manage your time.

There are others, and you may be in this group, who, until now, got by without being all that organized or systematic about how they spent their work or leisure time. Unfortunately, for a variety of reasons ranging from downsizing and staff cutbacks resulting in increased workloads to wanting to accomplish more without working longer hours, these workers now want to—need to—improve their time management skills. If you fall into this category, you would be wise to put the time and effort into enhancing your time management skills on your own before your boss requires you to attend a time management course. Perhaps you have read one or two books on time management before, listened to a CD or tape on the topic, or have even attended a time management lecture or seminar. However, you want to take a refresher course, aware that having excellent time management skills and being well organized, able to multitask and to meet deadlines are traits that human resource managers and employers often emphasize as essential for a wide array of jobs. You are probably even judged by how well you handle your time in your periodic job performance review.

If you're a freelancer, a small business owner, or an entrepreneur, you have learned the hard way that the more work you can generate and complete without sacrificing quality, the more likely you will be to succeed; for you, especially, time truly is money. Whatever your current job situation, you have therefore decided that taking stock of how you are handling your time and becoming more effective at time management are excellent uses of your time. This will help you as you read, ponder, and complete the recommended exercises in *Work Less, Do More*.

Effective Time Management: Understanding the Benefits

Now consider some of the concrete advantages and potential negative consequences of how you manage or mismanage your time. In this chapter you'll discover the most obvious as well as the subtler benefits of improved time management skills. You will also consider the downside of mismanaged time. Some results, such as meeting deadlines, are obvious; others, such as missed opportunities or being passed over for a promotion, are just as real but less tangible. In this chapter you will have an opportunity to assess where your own time management skills are at right now. This will help you to chart the course of your self-improvement plan as well as to document your progress, reinforcing that the time you are putting into your 14-day productivity makeover is time very well spent indeed.

Although time management may not cut down on the volume of your work demands, it does offer useful strategies and techniques to help you get more done, in less time. By accomplishing more, you and your department, agency, or company are more

likely to be viewed favorably as your career also advances further, and faster. A 32-year-old paralegal shared with me: "We recently had a transaction with close to 400 different properties involved and a month to organize and review files, draft two documents for each site, and have them available for execution at close. Through the miracle of prioritizing the task and timely postponement of [the] close for five days, we were able to get our documents prepared ahead of schedule." Note that this time she was able to complete the task in a timely fashion because of a five-day extension; she might not be granted this grace period next time. Improving your time management skills will help you to meet and even beat deadlines, rather than relying on someone else to grant you additional time.

Knowing that we could do things faster and better inspires us to improve our time management skills. For example, as a 31-year-old executive secretary noted, "I typically underestimate the amount of time in which something is going to get done. So I leave work feeling like I didn't get anything accomplished." A 59-year-old health care administrator shared with me that he would like to learn how to plan and prioritize at work more effectively so he could spend more time with his family. A 37-year-old married woman, who maintains two positions—as the CEO of an online information service and as a consultant working an additional 30 hours a week, a total of 65 hours each week—is on the verge of becoming a workaholic (if she isn't one already). She notes: "[I] leave [work] at about 5 p.m. and come home and do more work after dinner and throughout the night."

By becoming a more effective time manager, you will have more time for the leisure activities and relationships that you enjoy, and your life will become more balanced.

In most jobs, time goes hand in hand with money as one of the most precious resources a company has. The more clients or customers you can service, the more money you will earn. The more efficiently you answer those e-mails, the sooner you will get to your other work, especially if those other pulls are more lucrative or creative. Generally, the more sales you can achieve, the faster you can complete projects, and the higher your income.

Yes, usually the early bird does indeed get the worm. By managing your time well, and being quick to respond to opportunities, you are more likely to get the job, land the deal, scoop up the new business, and set yourself apart from the more laggardly competition.

What Are the Consequences of Poor Time Management?

Conversely, what happens to those who do not handle their time well? A derailed career, being passed over for promotions, frustration, self-doubt, or even job termination can result.

- A 37-year-old newsletter editor, who is married with two teenagers, responded when asked to name the number one consequence of poor time management: "Lack of time for myself—to read, exercise, sleep. . . ."

- "I don't schedule time for selling into every business day," admits a 54-year-old speaker. However, making time to pitch his speaking skills to potential new clients could make a huge difference in how

ON THE PLUS SIDE

What are the benefits to improved time management in your particular job, school, or leisure-time activities? List the top benefits:

- _____.

- _____.

- _____.

ON THE NEGATIVE SIDE

Use the space below to note the consequences of ineffective time management that have affected you:

- _____.

- _____.

- _____.

much income he generates for the month, for the rest of the year, or even in the year ahead, since booking one to two years ahead is not unusual in his business.

- A 21-year-old college senior notes: "I procrastinated on a project that both did not interest me and presented a big challenge to me. I avoided putting any serious work into it until the week it was to be completed. Had I been using my time effectively, I could have completed the project much sooner and gone on to other things."

Poor Time Management Increases Your Stress Level

Here is another significant consequence of poor time management: stress. When you are stressed, you have an increase in your heartbeat, respiration, or perspiration, and your blood sugar level also rises. Failing to leave enough time—to get to the train station, to complete a work or school project, to buy and mail a card or present for your best friend's birthday—leads to additional stress. Researchers have found that too much stress has health consequences: Stress can make you feel exhausted; it can also cause severe headaches and heart irregularity. Some causes of stress, like a boss who is overly demanding or relationship problems, are complex and may not be solved overnight. But how effectively you spend your time is one potential cause of increased stress that you *can* control. For example, you can learn to get rid of your clutter, a major cause of disorder (and disorder is linked to higher stress levels).

Learning to pace yourself is another key time management technique that you can master. Poor pacing is tied to increased stress as well as to burnout, which occurs when your body and mind literally burn out, and you shut down and cannot function anymore. In Japan they have a term for it: *karoshi,* or death by overwork—when fatigue and chronic overwork lead to high blood pressure and hardening of the arteries, which proves fatal. In his book *Medical Sociology,* William Cockerham notes that of the 98 *karoshi* victims he studied, typically middle-aged men from Tokyo, 22.4% had worked 50 to 59 hours per week, 32.7% had worked 70 to 99 hours weekly, and 21.4% had worked over 100 hours a week.

You certainly don't want to be a victim of *karoshi!* Fortunately, by practicing effective time management techniques you can get more done in less time and with less stress, so you can avoid extreme exhaustion and the related physical or mental consequences of chronic overwork and stress.

Your Time Management Starting Point

Take this opportunity to gather more information about your current time management skills. Answer the questions in the accompanying quiz, How Do You Currently Rate Your Time Management Skills? honestly; this self-quiz, an edited version of the quiz that I've been offering at my website (drjanyager.com) and in my seminars for many years, will serve as a starting point on your time management excursion. If you know where you're starting from, you'll be better able to pinpoint where you need to go.

HOW DO YOU CURRENTLY RATE YOUR TIME MANAGEMENT SKILLS?

1. Do you make a conscientious effort to separate urgent matters from other demands?

Yes _____ No _____ Sometimes _____

2. Do you take the time to do enough background research and due diligence so you can make the best possible decisions?

Yes _____ No _____ Sometimes _____

3. Do you allocate at least one hour each day for uninterrupted time for thinking, reading, planning, daydreaming, or creative work?

Yes _____ No _____ Sometimes _____

4. Do you spend sufficient time initiating, cultivating, and maintaining business and personal relationships?

Yes _____ No _____ Sometimes _____

5. Do you work hard to do your best, rather than measuring yourself by a standard of unattainable perfection?

Yes _____ No _____ Sometimes _____

6. Have you been on time every time in the last week for personal or business appointments?

Yes _____ No _____

7. Do you take at least one week off from work each year and make sure your vacation is a memorable experience that offers you the chance to connect with yourself, your immediate or extended family, and/or your friends?

Yes _____ No _____ Sometimes _____

8. Do you regularly and carefully read through each and every professional or business publication or newsletter you subscribe to (print or online)?

Yes _____ No _____ Sometimes _____

9. Do you meet all your deadlines at work?

Yes _____ No _____ Sometimes _____

10. Do you return all phone calls within 24 hours (or delegate to someone else the task of dealing with those phone calls that should not have been directed to you in the first place)?

Yes _____ No _____ Sometimes _____

11. Do you reply to urgent e-mails immediately and to all others within a reasonable period, usually within a day or two (unless you are away)?

Yes _____ No _____ Sometimes _____

12. Do you take the time to regularly update your database or some other organized system for work and/or personal contacts?

Yes _____ No _____ Sometimes _____

13. Are you usually pleased with how you handle sending or receiving holiday cards or gifts?

Yes _____ No _____ Sometimes _____

14. Do you have a five-year career plan?

Yes _____ No _____

I'm working on it _____

15. Are you working at a job or pursuing a career that satisfies you on at least one or all levels—professional, intellectual, creative and/or financial?

Yes _____ No _____

If you answered yes to all 15 questions, at least on these issues your time management skills are excellent. If you answered no, "I'm working on it," or "sometimes" to one or more questions, you know the areas you can begin addressing to improve your time management skills.

How Will You Measure Your Progress?

The good news is that help is readily available. You have now pinpointed your most pressing time management work challenges. Fortunately, you will find help in this book for the most common time management obstacles, and then some.

I always recommend to those who want to improve how they handle their time that they create a way of quantifying their progress. This will be different for each of us. A salesperson might measure her achievements in terms of dollars or number of units sold. A vice president in charge of corporate communications for a major corporation might look at how many media interviews were handled and what reports were written and distributed. Some writers measure their time by how many pages they write each day; others focus on hours spent writing with less emphasis on the per-day page count. Someone who sells commercial real estate may measure his productivity by how many deals were brokered in any one day. There is no right or wrong when it comes to productivity measures; what counts is what guideposts are pivotal for you and your particular job.

Start now by taking the quiz titled Measuring Your Time Management Improvements. You may want to return to this quiz later on, since the standards by which you judge your time management improvements may change over time. As an example of how your standards may change, when you're single and working at your first job out of school, you may be okay with working late every night and then getting together with your coworkers at a local restaurant or pub to discuss the day and to connect, rather than rushing home. But as you age, or as there are romantic partners or dependent children counting on you, you may want to get out of the office by 5:00 so you can return home to make dinner or help your children with their homework. You may even want to find a way to become so productive that your boss allows you to work from home one day a week. For that reason, when you take this quiz, remember to date it. Use pencil so it's easier to erase and take the quiz again at a later date. Or make a photocopy of this blank page as a master version and put it aside, so you can retake this quiz when you want to. This is a good practice to follow for all the quizzes in this book.

QUANTIFY YOUR PROGRESS

I always recommend to those who want to improve how they handle time that they create a way of quantifying their progress.

MEASURING YOUR TIME MANAGEMENT IMPROVEMENTS

TODAY'S DATE: ⬜

Select from the list below three benchmarks that you will use as proof that you are managing your time more effectively. Rank them in order from #1 to #3. If none of the below applies to you, you may add other options on the blank lines below, but limit yourself to three, since trying to achieve too many goals at once may overwhelm you.

    Indicate whether your answers apply to work or school by marking those answers with a *W* or an *S*; if they apply to your leisure time or personal concerns, use a *P* for "personal."

TIME MANAGEMENT BENCHMARKS

_____ Leaving the office an hour earlier than usual, but getting as much work done.

_____ Leaving the office by 5 p.m., but getting even more work done in fewer hours.

_____ Not taking work home anymore.

_____ Not working on weekends.

_____ Increasing my company's revenue by _____ [amount] by _____ [specific date].

_____ Increasing the number of clients I work with so that I have _____ [amount] more by _____ [specific date].

_____ Feeling _____ about my work [fill in a positive adjective such as *happy, joyful, enthusiastic, inspired, proud,* etc.].

_____ Spending more time with my family. (If possible, pick a specific amount of time such as _____ hours daily or _____ hours on the weekend.)

_____ Taking _____ [amount of time] each week to exercise.

_____ Planning and taking a vacation this year.

_____ Attending a trade show in _____ [month and year].

_____ Spending _____ [amount of time] on my paperwork.

_____ Having a clear desktop _____ times a week.

_____ Meeting every deadline for every project or assignment.

_____ Taking more time to connect with my friends.

_____ Making the time to date (if you are looking for a romantic partner) or spending more time with my partner.

_____ (Write your own) _____

_____ (Write your own) _____

Review the three top ways you will measure your progress in your work (or school) and personal life. Now write those goals down in the space below. This process will offer you concrete evidence of your accomplishments because you will see the before and after: the written personal or professional goal and the achievement of it.

WORK TIME MEASUREMENT(S)

TODAY'S DATE: _____

1. I will _____

2. I will _____

3. I will _____

SCHOOL TIME MEASUREMENT(S)

TODAY'S DATE: _____

1. I will _____

2. I will _____

3. I will _____

PERSONAL TIME MEASUREMENT(S)

TODAY'S DATE: _____

1. I will _____

2. I will _____

3. I will _____

Assessing Your Current Time Management Behavior: Keeping a Time Log

Now we get to another activity for you to participate in, but this one will have amazing immediate and far-reaching benefits! Time, most will agree, can be a very amorphous thing. Unless you're one of those rare individuals who instinctively tracks what he or she is doing every single minute of the day, you may find a lot of your time unaccounted for, or you may look back on your day and you're in a bit of a fog about what you did when, why, or where. The time log technique will help you pinpoint both where your biggest wastes of time are occurring and when you're experiencing your personal energy highs and lows. Yes, there really are such things as morning and night people. If you learn what type you are, you can work with that information to achieve more in less time and feel even more energized doing it.

I like to give out time logs in advance of a seminar so participants arrive armed with this information. Filling out a time log works best if you keep the log handy and fill it out throughout the day and evening, rather than trying to compile it in hindsight or retrospectively. Fill in a time log for today. Note what kind of day it is: work/school or leisure. Write down everything you do, including starting and stopping points, from the time you wake up. This may include getting ready for work (or school), commuting, attending meetings, eating meals, traveling to appointments, and completing morning and afternoon tasks. Be sure to record when you leave work, what you do in the evening, and when you go to sleep. Make and work on a photocopy so you can use the original again later on. Since you'll be asked to keep a separate telephone log, in this basic time log just write down if you receive or place a telephone call, and how long the call lasts. The details of those calls will be recorded in the telephone logs that follow.

Just by filling out a detailed time log, you'll be giving yourself a good head start on improving your time management skills. Keeping, and reviewing, your Day 1 time log will help you to gain clarity about just when and how your time is being spent today, from the time you wake up till you go to sleep.

DAILY TIME LOG: DAY 1

TODAY'S DATE: _____   **DAY OF THE WEEK:** _____

TYPE OF DAY: _____ (Work? School? Leisure?)

TIME   **ACTIVITY**

Begin with the time you wake up:

_____   _____

_____   _____

_____   _____

_____   _____

_____   _____

_____   _____

_____   _____

_____   _____

_____   _____

_____   _____

_____   _____

_____   _____

DAILY TIME LOG, *continued*

TIME	ACTIVITY
_____	_____
_____	_____
_____	_____
_____	_____
_____	_____

End with going to sleep:

_____	_____
_____	_____
_____	_____
_____	_____
_____	_____

ADDITIONAL NOTES:

_____

_____

_____

_____

COMMENTS (Try to notice if there are any times when you are especially alert, or particularly tired, as well as any peaks of efficiency, periods of heightened concentration, and times when you pay better attention to details. At what times are you better or worse at working with people—both in person and over the phone?)

_____

_____

_____

_____

For now, put aside your time log. We will review this log at the end of this chapter, after you have completed additional worksheets.

PHONE LOGS

Two more pieces of information will empower you by providing you with specific data about just what you're doing with your time. The first is a phone log, with which you will monitor how you use both your regular phone line, if you still have a landline (the traditional phone that most still use at the office), and your cell phone. Track your phone usage for one complete work or school day, as well as one weekend or leisure day, noting who you call, who calls you, how long you're on the phone, and the purpose of each call. First do a log for calls received; then do one for calls placed.

PHONE LOG 1: CALLS RECEIVED (LANDLINE)

CALLS RECEIVED AT WORK

TODAY'S DATE: _____   **DAY OF THE WEEK:** _____

TIME	WHO CALLED	HOW LONG DID CALL LAST	PURPOSE OF CALL
_____	_____	_____	_____
_____	_____	_____	_____
_____	_____	_____	_____
_____	_____	_____	_____
_____	_____	_____	_____
_____	_____	_____	_____
_____	_____	_____	_____
_____	_____	_____	_____
_____	_____	_____	_____
_____	_____	_____	_____
_____	_____	_____	_____

CALLS RECEIVED AFTER WORK (AT HOME)*

TODAY'S DATE: _____   **DAY OF THE WEEK:** _____

TIME	WHO CALLED	HOW LONG DID CALL LAST	PURPOSE OF CALL
_____	_____	_____	_____
_____	_____	_____	_____
_____	_____	_____	_____
_____	_____	_____	_____

*You may prefer to log only those calls you receive at work here and to address calls received at home on another day, if at all.

PHONE LOG 2: CALLS PLACED (LANDLINE)

CALLS PLACED AT WORK

TODAY'S DATE: _____   **DAY OF THE WEEK:** _____

TIME	WHO CALLED	HOW LONG DID CALL LAST	PURPOSE OF CALL
_____	_____	_____	_____
_____	_____	_____	_____
_____	_____	_____	_____
_____	_____	_____	_____
_____	_____	_____	_____
_____	_____	_____	_____
_____	_____	_____	_____
_____	_____	_____	_____
_____	_____	_____	_____
_____	_____	_____	_____
_____	_____	_____	_____
_____	_____	_____	_____

CALLS PLACED AFTER WORK (AT HOME)*

TODAY'S DATE: _____   **DAY OF THE WEEK:** _____

TIME	WHO CALLED	HOW LONG DID CALL LAST	PURPOSE OF CALL
_____	_____	_____	_____
_____	_____	_____	_____
_____	_____	_____	_____
_____	_____	_____	_____
_____	_____	_____	_____
_____	_____	_____	_____
_____	_____	_____	_____
_____	_____	_____	_____

*You may prefer to log only those calls you receive at work here, and to address calls received at home on another day, if at all.

CELL PHONE LOGS

Now do the same thing for your cell phone. If you use your cell phone for both work and personal calls, you will have a combination of calls to sort through. Where the log asks for the "purpose of call," start by noting if the call was related to work (or school) or if it was personal, followed by more specific details.

CELL PHONE LOG

TODAY'S DATE: _____   **DAY OF THE WEEK:** _____

CALLS RECEIVED

TIME	WHO CALLED	HOW LONG DID CALL LAST	PURPOSE OF CALL
____	_____	_____	_____
____	_____	_____	_____
____	_____	_____	_____
____	_____	_____	_____
____	_____	_____	_____
____	_____	_____	_____
____	_____	_____	_____

CALLS PLACED BY CELL PHONE

TIME	WHO CALLED	HOW LONG DID CALL LAST	PURPOSE OF CALL
____	_____	_____	_____
____	_____	_____	_____
____	_____	_____	_____
____	_____	_____	_____
____	_____	_____	_____
____	_____	_____	_____
____	_____	_____	_____

Put these phone logs aside for now. We will review what you have learned about your phone use during Day 8, More Effective Ways to Use the Phone and Other Equipment.

INTERNET TIME

We come to the last time log that I will ask you to complete: Internet time. For some, the Internet has become, in the last decade, the source of the greatest increase in productivity; for others, it has become a productivity drain. Sadly, for some, the Internet has even become a new addiction, something that pulls individuals away from the activities or relationships in which they should be engaged. I call it an addiction because, for these people, it has become such a compulsion, such a need, that it is no longer something they choose to do. In my survey of wasted time, mentioned earlier, the fifth most common reason, given by 7% of those surveyed, was "using the Internet unrelated to work, including surfing the Internet and computer games."

I'll address Internet addiction again later on in the book. For now, let's gauge whether or not you're using the Internet as efficiently as you could be. To do this, please keep an Internet time log for 24 hours. You'll find in this section on Internet Time one blank log so you can track your Internet usage for an entire day—either a work, school, or leisure day. The key is to get clarity about how long you're really online, what you do when you're online, and whether there is something else that you should be doing at that time that you're not doing. Finding answers all starts with keeping a log of Internet time.

INTERNET TIME LOG

TODAY'S DATE: **DAY OF THE WEEK:**

TYPE OF DAY: _____ (Work? School? Leisure?)

TIME	INTERNET TASK*	LENGTH OF SESSION	PURPOSE	WHAT I SHOULD HAVE BEEN DOING INSTEAD

*Note: The task might be e-mail, surfing, research, for example.

LOG REVIEWS

Look over your various time logs from today. Are you starting to see some patterns in the way you're handling your time, hour by hour, as well as certain key tasks, including receiving and placing phone calls? What about time on the Internet? Did your log reveal a lot of Internet surfing? If you were surfing online, how much of it was related to your priority task for the day? How much of it was a waste of time? How many e-mails did you receive or send today? How many of those e-mails were crucial to your key job-related goals?

The information you gained about your time, phone, and Internet habits through these logs will definitely help you to see the point that you're starting from on your quest to becoming more efficient and effective. In the Appendix you will find additional blank logs if you would like to repeat this exercise tomorrow, next week, or even in another month or so to see how far you've traveled on your road to improved productivity and decreased wasted time.

You've finished Day 1 of your 14-day journey to enhanced efficiency and productivity. Congratulations! You've worked hard on this first day. Give yourself a reward. If you don't have time for a movie or a dinner out with friends, at least pat yourself on the back.

Now on to Day 2, as together we help you achieve your metamorphosis into a more efficient, joyful, productive, and successful you. In the next chapter, we will take a giant step toward getting your time management skills in order by looking at one of the cardinal principles of effective time management: goal setting. How and why should you set goals? What have we learned about goal setting that can help you to create, and achieve, your professional (or academic) and personal goals?

BEAT THE CLOCK

1. List one negative consequence you experienced professionally or personally in the last month due to poor (or less than ideal) time management.

_____

2. Think of someone you know who's an excellent manager of time. What does that role model do that makes you say that? Write down that individual's exemplary time management traits. Keep this role model in mind as you work on improving your own time management behavior. How would that person answer the phone? When you speak, how long is your typical conversation?

_____

3. Reflect on what you learned in Day 1. What is the most important idea that you learned that you will immediately apply to your own time management challenges? Write down that idea here:

_____

_____

Goal Setting

Yes, you're busy. But are you "good" busy? How will you know what good busy is if you have not taken the time to figure out what your goals are for today, this week, this month, this year, and even over the next five or ten years? Having a clear idea of what you want to do with your time is what goal setting is all about. Examples abound of just how powerful goals can be in shaping behavior. Bob Danzig, former Hearst newspapers executive who is now a motivational speaker and author, shared how goal setting words helped him when he was a child in foster care, on his journey to one day becoming a CEO: "The social worker simply told the 11-year-old foster child 'You are worthwhile' every time she met with him. Those three words invited that child—for the first time in his life—to see possibilities for his life. Goals, as it were. I never forgot her words—they were with me as I took my first job as a teenage office boy at the Albany, New York, *Times Union*. Her goal-inviting words were with me as I became publisher of that newspaper and remained as an ongoing incentive when I became nationwide CEO of all Hearst newspapers for twenty years. Early goal seeds can sprout to become a lifelong garden."

Here's another example of how goals can shape the way you spend your time: Three teenagers, childhood friends, from a tough part of Newark, New Jersey, decided that they would set their sights on attending medical or dental school, and they spurred each other on. Their goal setting, initially sparked by the visit to their high school by a college recruiter from Seton Hall University, is detailed in their bestseller *The Pact.* Coauthors Sampson Davis and Rameck Hunt, who became doctors, and George Jenkins, who became a dentist, have been inspiring others through their example of how setting shared goals helped each of them to realize his own ambition.

Goal Setting Basics: Why Set Goals?

If you have not been goal-oriented recently, it's not too late to start or rethink your career (or personal) aspirations. Goal setting goes hand in hand with another fundamental principle of optimum time management: planning. You need goals in order to plan better. Better plans usually lead to greater efficiency and improved results.

Of course, we've all heard about "The best laid plans of mice and men" and Murphy's Law, that anything that can go wrong, will. Goal setting and planning do not mean you can completely control the world or the outcome of your actions or the actions of those with whom you work. However, there is a greater likelihood that you will achieve your goal if you have a direction and a strategy in mind.

By setting goals, you know where you're going. Goals are necessary, at work or in your leisure time. Without goals you're more likely to flounder and react erratically to opportunities and problems, with too little perspective on the effects they will have on your personal and professional life.

How many goals should you have? One? Two? Three? How many can you handle at once? I coached a woman in her early twenties who was working full-time at a publishing company while pursuing her goal of being in a professional band, as well as getting her master's degree at night at a nearby university. She wondered if she should focus on just one of those goals. She was single, although she had a boyfriend, and she did not yet have children depending on her. I explained to her that working on those three ambitions simultaneously, and being very busy in their pursuit, was completely age- and situation-appropriate for her. Just because she was busier than most of her friends who were only pursuing one goal—whether it was working or going to school—was not her concern, as long as she was competently managing all three of her own without undue stress. Fortunately, one of those goals—getting her master's degree—would be achieved within a year, allowing her to pursue another goal, to devote more time to the other two aims, or just take it easier.

Ronald D. Brown, president and chief executive officer of Atlanta, Georgia based

Atlanta Life Financial Group, shared in an interview how having a clear view of what you need to do will help you in how you spend your time:

> In some people's cases, there is an inability or an unwillingness to actually make the distinction between what's important and what isn't: the "I'm busy" trap instead of the "I'm making a contribution" scenario. It's the same with all people who are immersed in being busy and how much they're able to produce . . . but they're not producing the right things or the important things. The whole e-mail scenario becomes just another way or a proof statement of "Oh I get 150 e-mails a day and I answer my e-mails before I go to bed." My puncturing question is, "So what? In the grand scheme of what you're trying to accomplish in your business, did it get you any closer to doing that?"

Deciding on Long-Term Goals

A crucial step in time management is to decide on your long-term goals. As speaker Brian Tracy puts it in his article, "5 Steps to Setting Goals": "Goals are the essence of a successful life characterized by a feeling of being in control of your own destiny. Think where you are and where you want to go. With clear goals, you will fly straight like an arrow toward your dreams."

The next all-important action is to write down those goals. By putting them down on paper (or doing so electronically, if you prefer to use your computer or your electronic handheld device), you are reinforcing those goals and your commitment to them. If you've written down your goals electronically, print out a copy. I'm old-fashioned enough to suggest that you even consider carrying around a journal with you, preferably one that does not allow you to easily tear out the pages. Date your list of long-term goals so you can review it from time to time; create a schedule to review your long-term goals, if you like, perhaps every December 31st, in time for the New Year, or, alternatively, on your birthday each year. Are you moving toward achieving your long-term goals? Have you reevaluated those goals? Do you want to substitute different ones?

At the end of this section are two lists for you to fill in, one for long-term professional goals and the other for long-term personal goals. Your career ambitions may include going back to school and getting an advanced degree within the next five years, or perhaps you want to become CEO within ten years. There might be a certification that you want to gain by the end of next year, or a sales volume that you are determined to reach. Your personal goals for the next ten years might include relocation for retirement. You might want to start a book club within the next year or, perhaps, by next month you want to start exercising three times a week. Be as concrete as possible in formulating your long-term goals. Avoid vague statements such as "I want to be rich," or "I want to be popular," or "I want to be more creative." The key is to establish specific goals that you can work toward in clear-cut steps.

DECIDING ON LONG-TERM WORK GOALS

TODAY'S DATE: _____

What do I want to accomplish by the end of:

Ten years?_____

_____

Five years? _____

_____

The next two years?_____

_____

The next year? _____

_____

Six months? _____

_____

This month? _____

_____

This week? _____

Deciding on Short-Term Goals

Now that you understand how setting long-term goals can help you improve how you manage your time, let's put that same effort into establishing your short-term goals. What do you want to accomplish at work, or in your personal life, in the next week? Day? Hour? Hopefully, there will be a relationship between your short-term goals and your long-term goals. If there isn't, you may have to reevaluate what you're doing, and why, as you attempt to bridge the gap between your goals, or dreams, and your everyday reality.

For example, if your long-term goal is to become senior vice president of a company in financial services and you're currently working for a company in the health care field, you may be sabotaging yourself, since it may be harder to switch careers or areas of specialization the further you progress down your current path.

Look over your long-term goals and ask yourself: What do I have to do now to make that goal happen? Work backwards from your goal.

Making a Difference with Your Time is another goal-setting activity that can help you to identify your goals—as well as any potential blocks to achieving them.

DECIDING ON SHORT-TERM WORK GOALS

TODAY'S DATE: _____

What do I want to accomplish by the end of:

This month? _____

Next week? _____

This week? _____

Tomorrow? _____

Today? _____

This hour? _____

MAKING A DIFFERENCE WITH YOUR TIME

WORK-RELATED GOALS

What is the one work-related activity you want to engage in that would really make a difference in your life? Do you want to write a report that is presented at the annual meeting? Get a promotion and a raise by the end of this year? Sell more products than any of your coworkers? Write down this goal:

_____

Create a realistic time frame for starting and completing this goal:

_____

What might stop you from realizing this goal? (Procrastination? Fear of success? Fear of failure? Disorganization? Devaluing your goal? Other blocks?)

_____

How are you going to overcome that block, or those blocks, so you will complete this goal?

_____

Date this sheet: _____

When will you look at this sheet again to see where you are in achieving this goal?

_____

Now go through the same exercise for a leisure-related goal, using the activity sheet on the next page.

PERSONAL GOALS

What is the one activity you want to do outside of work that would really make a difference in your life? Writing a book? Going on a trip? Visiting with old friends? Reading a novel? Write down this goal:

_____

Create a realistic time frame for starting and completing this goal:

_____

What might stop you from realizing this goal? (Procrastination? Fear of success? Fear of failure? Disorganization? Devaluing your goal? Other blocks?)

_____

_____

How are you going to overcome that block, or those blocks, so you will complete this goal?

_____

_____

Date this sheet: _____

When will you look at this sheet again to see where you are in achieving this goal?

_____

Setting Time Management Goals

Just as you've been recording goals for your career and your personal life—the grand scheme, such as getting married, having children, getting an advanced degree, finding a cure for cancer, publishing a book, writing a musical score, and the like—you want to commit to paper a concrete plan for how you would like to manage your time. For some, working on one task at a time is the ideal. For others, that would be lackluster and the boredom that ensued would lead to unproductive fidgeting. For those individuals, juggling several projects simultaneously, but effectively, is the key.

POSITIVE IMAGING: WHAT WOULD YOUR DAY LOOK LIKE IF YOU HANDLED YOUR TIME MORE EFFECTIVELY?

This exercise will help you to visualize just what a more productive and joyful work or leisure day would look like. Social science research supports the benefits of image work in helping us to create new possible patterns if what we have been doing automatically results in less than what we want. By creating, visualizing, and writing down, you concretize your ideal workday (followed by your ideal leisure or weekend day); you will have something to work toward. You will also be more likely to turn those ideals into a reality.

Remember, this is not a test. There are no right or wrong answers, nor does your coworker's or boss's ideal day have to, in any way, shape, or form, resemble the ideal workday *you* dream about. Similarly, the ideal leisure day or night that you aspire to does not have to look like the one that your neighbor, sibling, or best friend covets.

AN IDEAL WORKDAY AND EVENING

Use the space below to construct your ideal workday. What day of the week will you pick? When will you wake up? Get to work? Will you start the day by attending a seminar or business breakfast? Will you go to an office or will you work from another location? Will you take lunch? How long will your lunchtime last? Will you eat at your desk, or go out to a restaurant with a customer, client, coworker, or friend? What will you accomplish during this ideal workday? How often will the phone ring? Who will deal with the phone calls? How do you feel during this ideal workday? Is it calm and predictable, or chaotic and frantic? How late will you leave the office for home? Will you have evening work-related commitments? When will you go to sleep?

Day of the week: _____

Wake up: _____   Get to work: _____

Leave work: _____   Go to sleep: _____

Use this space to write about your ideal workday:

_____

_____

_____

_____

_____

Think back over the last few months. When did you come closest to realizing this ideal workday? _____

What are you going to do to try to make your ideal day an everyday occurrence?

_____

_____

_____

_____

_____

Pick a date when you will reevaluate your progress, comparing your actual workday to your ideal workday: _____ . Mark this date in your day planner or calendar.

AN IDEAL LEISURE DAY AND EVENING

Use the space below to construct your ideal leisure day (a day off from work). When will you wake up? Will you sleep later than on workdays, or get up at the same time or even earlier? How will you start off your leisure day? Making breakfast for the family? Going out for brunch with friends? Taking a jog in the neighborhood?

Will your day off be structured, unstructured, or some combination of the two? Will you do chores, go shopping, or go on a family trip? Visit extended family? Friends? This is your dream day off from work, so have fun creating an ideal leisure day that could become your goal.

Day of the week: _____

Wake up: _____   Go to sleep: _____

Use this space to write about your ideal day off from work:

_____

_____

_____

_____

_____

_____

_____

Think back over the last few months. When did you come closest to realizing this ideal leisure day? _____

What are you going to do to try to make your ideal leisure day a regular occurrence?

_____

_____

_____

_____

_____

Pick a date when you will reevaluate your progress, comparing your actual days off from work to your ideal: _____ . Mark this date in your day planner or calendar.

BEAT THE CLOCK

1. Think about the work habits of a few people you know intimately. It may be easier to see time being wasted by others than by yourself. Plan how you would restructure their workdays to increase their efficiency.

2. If you won the $10 million lottery, what would you do with your time? What would you do during the first week after you won? The first month? The first year? The second year? Would you work? Quit your job? Find a new job? What would you do during the workday? In your leisure time? What would you do with the money? Your answers might help you sort through the things that you do now because you love what you're doing and the things that you do because you need to earn a living. Is there a way to work toward achieving a lifestyle whereby you enjoy your work and get compensated for it? How would managing your time differently or better help you to move closer to achieving that ideal?

3. What is your goal for today? Why have you chosen that goal? What are the consequences if you achieve that goal? If you miss your mark? What can you do to increase the likelihood that you reach that short-term goal?

Dealing with the Five P's:

Procrastination, Perfectionism, Poor Planning, Poor Pacing, and Petulance

n 2007, I commissioned CARAVAN® Opinion Research Corporation, a Princeton, New Jersey based research company, to conduct a telephone survey aimed at finding out what workers feel are their main time management obstacles. (Based on my previous surveys, workshops, and research, respondents were given seven possible choices as well as the opportunity to provide an alternative answer if their top obstacle was not included.) Of the more than 350 working men and women surveyed, more than half listed their top three obstacles as either trying to do too much at once (22%), paperwork (21%), or procrastination (18%). The rest listed their top obstacles as perfectionism, e-mails, poor planning, or meetings.

For now, let's take a closer look at what I call the Five P's: procrastination, perfectionism, poor planning, poor pacing, and petulance. In later chapters we'll discuss other obstacles to efficient time management, such as doing too much at once (Day 5), paperwork (Day 7), and e-mail (Day 9). Time-saving ideas for conducting or attending meetings are explored in Day 13.

Procrastination

Whether you call it procrastination or resistance, it's the same thing: putting off doing something you have to do because you just don't want to do it! Unfortunately, those who procrastinate are very artful at denying it or concealing it. If you're one of those people, you can grow so busy doing everything but what you should be doing—and justifying the importance of these other tasks—that you're unaware that you're procrastinating about what's really fundamental to your success until you find your career in harm's way.

Labeling yourself a procrastinator isn't going to help. Trying to figure out what's behind your actions, and overcoming this common block to more effectively managing your time, will help.

There was an interesting finding in the CARAVAN® survey I conducted. For 18% of the sample, procrastination was the biggest obstacle to managing time more effectively at work, making it the third biggest obstacle overall. But when the sample was divided into two groups—managers, business owners, and professionals versus sales and clerical workers—the differences were more pronounced. While only 14% of the managers named procrastination as their biggest time obstacle, a whopping 31% of the sales and clerical workers reported it to be their number one challenge. Bottom line: If you

want to rise up the ranks, overcome your problem with procrastination now or it may derail your career. Here are some techniques for conquering procrastination:

- **Make whatever it is you're avoiding the very first task you do that day.** Start the day by working on that priority task—instead of checking e-mail, surfing the Net, or reading the newspaper—and move that job along or even finish it. Then go on to another priority task, or take a break and do some low-priority work that you enjoy more.

- **Try the reward system.** Pick a reward that will be a real motivator, something you truly want but have been denying for yourself. For example, as soon as you finish the report that's due at work, you're going to take a walk outside or go get a cup of coffee with a colleague in another department. Or you're going to order that new computer you've been promising yourself as soon as you finish a major project that will bring in the revenue that you need for the purchase.

- **Try what I refer to in my book *Creative Time Management for the New Millennium* as creative procrastination.** If you're finding your top priority to be too daunting, try tackling the second or third most important items on your to-do list. You will accomplish all your day's priorities, but in a different order. This is different from avoiding your priority task with a trip to the doughnut cart or a phone call to a friend (who is happy to hear from you but is now feeling guilty about talking during work hours).

- **Allow for delays.** Build delays into your schedule so you actually have some "goofing off" time that will still permit you to get the project done without the tendency to put yourself down or engage in the self-criticism that too often accompanies procrastination.

- **Procrastination provides information.** Why are you delaying something? What does the postponement provide? What will it take to get you to act now?

Perfectionism

The perfectionist may not even try to achieve his goals, because he expects to be disappointed, since his standards are unrealistic and unattainable.

Whether or not perfectionism is an obstacle to managing your time efficiently is a tricky concept. You certainly want your brain surgeon to be a perfectionist, but do you need to rewrite that memo eight times if you got the point across adequately the second time? If this is a memo that will determine if an investor will put $40 million into your company, then maybe all those rewrites are warranted. If it's a standard memo, and you've at least made sure it's free from typos and embarrassing gaffes, and it says what you need it to say, then maybe the perfectionism that is behind those extra rewrites is wasted time. Here are some helpful suggestions when dealing with perfectionism, both in yourself and in others:

- The effort and the task should have a good fit: If you're expending more energy than the task warrants, then your perfectionism is probably wasting time.

- If you have a problem with perfectionism, you might find that establishing a firm deadline for a project or task will help. Open-ended projects just give the perfectionist that much more time to do things again and again, and sometimes even ruin things by making them too long, too complicated, or too late to be useful.

- Consider if your perfectionism is covering up a fear of failure: If you don't finish, you can't be judged, and perhaps judged harshly. Work on building up your self-confidence and competence. Similarly, help others whose perfectionism is adversely impacting you to become more confident so they can let go. Saying something like, "This business plan is the most comprehensive one you've done so far. I know it's going to get an excellent reception at the bank," might help your business partner or employee to finish up a draft and submit it.

Poor Planning

The third of the Five P's that can sabotage your time is the doubly troublesome P of poor planning. Planning is the cornerstone of those who manage their time and their businesses well. You can still allow happenstance and serendipity to occur; you can and probably should "go with the flow" if ideas are being generated and new products and initiatives are evolving in a creative, unplanned way. But you need to plan enough so that you are in control of as many factors related to your success at your job, in your career, and in your relationships as possible.

What, after all, is a plan? A plan is a commitment to yourself and, once you make the plan public, to others, that you will do something. Often, plans include even more details, such as the date by which you will achieve that goal.

Why do you need to plan? By having a plan and making that commitment, you are increasing the likelihood that you will achieve your goal.

In Day 4, we will look at the value of the to-do list, one of the all-time favorite planning tools. A daily or longer-term plan helps to reinforce the goals you have set for yourself and your job.

Other plans that will help you to succeed include:

- Business plans
- Career plans
- Licensing plans
- Savings plans
- Retirement plans
- Educational plans
- Reading plans
- Menu plans
- Exercise plans
- Vacation plans
- Fashion, hair, and personal hygiene plans
- Leisure time plans

- Are there any other plans that could help you that are not listed above? Please list those plans here:

_____

If you rarely plan, or if your plans are inconsistent—for example, you plan in some areas of your career and life and not in others, or you plan every now and then, neglecting to update your plans as needed—here are some tips that might help:

- Create a planning schedule that is tied to a specific or recurring event. For example, pick a week each December to review what you have accomplished the previous year and to set goals for the next year. If you want to become more consistent about your vacation plans, choose a week six months to a year before the time you want to go away, and make that your vacation planning time. If you teach a course, or you're a student, carve out a certain number of days before the course begins, or after it has ended, to assess what you plan to learn, or to review what you have learned.

- Hire experts or coaches in the areas where you have failed to plan who can help you to create deadlines. Being accountable to someone makes your goal more likely to become a reality. For example, if you want to become a better speaker, working with a coach could help you to develop a concrete plan to improve your presentation skills, a plan you could then methodically implement.

HOW DO YOU THINK OF PLANNING?

What words do you associate with *planning*? Write those words down here: _____

_____

Are these positive or negative associations? If you see planning as something negative that could inhibit you, rather than help you, it will be hard for you to put the time and energy into planning. Work on figuring out why you might not see planning in a positive light. If you do see planning as something positive to do, try to explore what reasons from your past or current work or personal experiences might lead you to avoid planning.

Poor Pacing

Pacing refers to how you space out your work from week to week, from day to day, and even from hour to hour, including time at your computer, time on the phone, time spent taking efficiency or coffee breaks, and even time for lunch. Some workers have a frenzied pace that reflects their personality and approach to time. Others work at a slower overall pace but are able to gear up if they're faced with an imminent deadline or if they have not finished a task that needs to be done before they can leave for the night. Having a pace that suits your personality and the demands of a specific job or project is key to getting more done in less time and with less stress. Failure to pace yourself, including skipping efficiency breaks or not taking vacation time, can lead to physical and mental stress. As noted previously, there are even cases of poor pacing being linked to heart attacks and premature death.

Consequences of poor pacing include:

- Stress
- Exhaustion
- Depression
- Anxiety
- Frustration
- Short temper
- Failure (i.e., goals not reached)
- Failure to build and maintain relationships
- Burnout
- Physical or mental breakdown
- Lowered immunity to disease and greater likelihood of illness

PACE YOURSELF

The acronym PACING below emphasizes how you can use pacing to improve your productivity. Each letter has a pacing concept associated with it. Read this list over whenever you're feeling overwhelmed, reinforcing these suggestions.

P = Plan for efficiency breaks. Build into your day pacing that is healthy and effective.

A = Aim to please your family, your boss, your friends, your coworkers, and your clients. But most of all, aim to please yourself.

C = Concentrate and avoid distractionitis, which will make it harder to pace yourself properly.

I = I counts, so make sure to budget for personal time. (See Day 14 for suggestions.)

N = *No* is an okay word. Get comfortable saying it and hearing it. Saying no to requests that you do not have time for will allow you to focus on the priority tasks that you have to do.

G = Gear up by giving yourself downtime. In addition to taking vacation time, use your weekends to do something other than more work—catch up with family and friends, exercise, or take mini-vacations.

WHY EFFICIENCY BREAKS AND GOOD PACING HELP YOU SAVE TIME AND REDUCE STRESS

Efficiency breaks—taking time out from work (especially from working nonstop at a computer) to walk around, get a drink of water, or switch to a relaxing, nonwork task—can lower the turnover rate at a company, reduce the number of mistakes made by employees, and alleviate fatigue, stress, and boredom. The benefits of taking a break were proven back in the 1920s, in the Philadelphia textile mills. It was there that researcher Elton Mayo discovered that allowing workers who had to stand all day to take four brief rest periods throughout the day enabled the mill workers to become more productive, and this policy substantially reduced a 250% worker turnover rate. Those efficiency breaks had a more positive impact on the employees than the financial incentives that had been offered to them.

Fast-forward almost 100 years: The challenge today is how to get workers who no longer stand all day, but rather sit all day at their computers, to stand up and walk around, and improve their pacing by taking a break. After all, doing so could help these workers drastically cut down on mistakes. A 1999 Cornell University study found that those employees who had occasional on-screen notifications that they should give themselves a break, stretch, or sit upright, made 13% fewer errors.

Become attuned to your physical or mental signals that it's time for a break. Maximize your work performance by understanding when and for how long breaks can help you during the day. *Note:* Use discretion in some work settings if your coworkers or employer might misinterpret your break time

as goofing off. Consider an exercise break, running for twenty minutes around lunchtime as one lawyer in Washington, D.C., does, or taking a walk. If necessary, and if it's permitted at your workplace, find a way to take a brief nap. You'll find a discussion of vacation breaks in Day 14.

DAY 3

PREVENTING/DEALING WITH BURNOUT

Burnout occurs when an individual has too much to handle. There is no one set amount that everyone is able to manage. How do you deal with burnout?

- First, admit that you're burning or burnt out.

- Second, find ways to deal with burnout that work for you. Here are some suggestions: Connect to a few people who really care about you and your business; reach out to like-minded individuals on the Internet; have a cup of coffee with a friend or colleague; make time for regular exercise; listen to music; give yourself permission to enjoy your time away from your work activities (rather than taking a break and feeling guilty about it).

- Another possibility, as discussed in greater detail in Day 12, is delegating. If you don't have the funds to hire others to help, consider unpaid interns who are willing to help you, usually for credit, in exchange for the training they receive (and the ability to put assisting you and your company on their resume!).

WHAT IS YOUR PACING PLAN?

If you don't have one, create one now. Use the space below to monitor your pacing plan.

- How many breaks do you currently take each day at work? _____

- Frequency of breaks: _____

- Pattern: Is there a pattern to your breaks? If so, write down what that pattern is—e.g., you take a break every hour, every two hours, once in the morning, etc.

  _____

- What you do: Use the space below to describe what you do during each break.

  _____

  _____

Look over your answers. If you think you need more breaks, or need to do something different during the ones you currently take, make a wish list that gives you an opportunity to create a plan for improved breaks.

_____

Any further comments about your breaks: _____

_____

Petulance: Attitude Counts

Have you ever noticed that if you're in a bad mood, it doesn't take long to make other people miserable? Conversely, if you're in a joyful frame of mind, and you encounter someone who's a downer, attitude can become contagious. Everyone has a bad day, and many people who are chronically depressed need others to be patient with them as they work through their emotional problems or mental illness. However, I'm not talking about someone who has the occasional bad day or someone who suffers from clinical depression. What I'm addressing here is your typical, garden-variety negative attitude that can waste everyone's time.

In business, it's not phony to be upbeat and positive, even if you're feeling sad. Your job—unless you're in that enviable situation of working with people who truly care about you and are your friends—is usually not the place to be taking up time with an attitude that slows everyone down because of how negative and downbeat you're feeling. Of course, it doesn't help for others to say "Get over it" if you or someone else is dealing with something monumental that has spilled over into the job. But if your attitude is something that you can't change on your own, or it's becoming a problem in your job, it may be time to seek professional help, if you have not done so already.

Having a positive attitude will make others feel more positive and upbeat as well.

LOSE THE ATTITUDE

When's the last time an attitude positively or negatively impacted how you, or someone you know, spent your time? Note that experience below.

_____

_____

_____

_____

_____

When you're in a bad mood, how do you pull yourself out of it? List those techniques now:

_____

_____

_____

_____

_____

That enthusiasm will energize everyone on your team, and when you and others are energized mentally and physically, you will get more done in less time.

Here are some ways to help get over feeling irritable, angry, or in a bad mood:

- Listen to music.

- In person or on the phone, talk to a supportive friend or family member about what's bothering you.

- Play with your pet.

- Write down in a journal what you're feeling and why.

- Read a self-help book or an inspirational article or quote.

- Talk to a therapist.

- Participate in a self-help group that addresses the issue(s) you're dealing with.

- Paint or draw.

- Go window shopping (or, if you don't have a problem with compulsive overspending, go shopping).

- Exercise.

- Watch TV or a movie.

- Volunteer to help others.

- Look over cards you've received or old photos that remind you of positive times and upbeat emotions, reinforcing the idea that your anger or negativity is only temporary.

Other Blocks to Accomplishing Your Goals

Devaluing Your Goal. If you devalue your goal, rather than making it the number-one priority in how you allot your time, it will be harder to attain and take longer to reach. Others may value your goal, but that is not as significant as your placing a premium on it. Whether it's getting to the next level at your company, becoming more efficient, or attending a class to help you master the latest software that you just installed on your computer, you have to value that goal to make it happen.

Overvaluing Your Goal. By contrast, if you place too much value on your goal, it may seem so unattainable that you do not even strive for it. If you have a tendency to overvalue your goal(s), try to minimize what you want to achieve and focus on the actions you have to take, rather than the end result. For example, if you decide that you want to become a surgeon, and you're already a college graduate who is currently working at a brokerage house, focus on taking the courses you need to take so you can apply to medical school, rather than getting caught up in what kind of surgery you will specialize in; focus on the goal of catching up on the missing courses. If you have a report due, focus on writing it well and turning it in on time, rather than on crafting the most amazing report your boss has ever read.

Fear of Failure. If you fear that you'll fail to achieve your goal, you may stall or stop yourself midway toward that goal so that you don't have to face this fear. It's a cliché that you can't know if you're going to fail if you don't try. However, it's a truism that you need to look at, hard and fast, so you don't let your fear of failure sabotage your attempts to achieve your goal.

Fear of Success. The flip side of fear of failure is fear of success. Some people fear success because of all that might accompany that achievement, such as other people expecting them to maintain that success. Others worry about outshining their siblings and other family members, friends, and classmates, and becoming someone who makes people jealous. You rarely hear about the lottery winners who are thrilled with their newfound wealth. It makes for more interesting reading, even if it's the exception rather than the rule, to focus on winnings that lead to disappointment and tragedy. To enable yourself to achieve your goals, you need to rid yourself of all the negative images associated with success and see it for the positive experience that it can be.

Insecurity. Who doesn't suffer from a bout of insecurity now and then? But if it becomes debilitating, or so overwhelming that it stops you from reaching for, or achieving, your goal, you've got to do something about it. Are you insecure about everything, or just certain skills? Look at where you feel strong and secure. Compare that to what makes you insecure. Do you see any patterns to those two disparate situations? Perhaps you have learning deficits that you need to correct, through working with a tutor, taking more classes, hiring a coach, or doing more reading. If your insecurity is based on reality, face that reality and do what you have to do to become more secure. If your insecurity is completely emotional, work on reversing that problem through introspection, self-therapy, or counseling.

Low Self-Esteem. If you don't believe in yourself and in your goals you'll be more likely to put everyone and everything before yourself, diminishing the likelihood that you will make choices about how you spend your time that are in your best interest. If you doubt that your family and friends really care about you, you may automatically say yes to every single demand they make, even if they are unrealistic and unnecessary, fearing that if you explain that you have to take care of something else for yourself that they will stop being there for you. Having a healthy dose of self-esteem will help you make decisions about the best way to spend your time, so you are more likely to achieve your short- and long-term goals.

Colorado-based speaker and author Suzanne Vaughan, who has been conducting time management workshops for more than a decade, agrees that self-esteem is pivotal to improved time management. As she notes in a communication to me: "Self-esteem is a key factor in the success of time management that is rarely addressed. But if we don't care enough about ourselves, or value ourselves and our abilities, there is no way we will manage our time appropriately. It is like a peanut butter and jelly sandwich. You can't leave out one ingredient or it is no longer a peanut butter and jelly sandwich. The same is true in our use of time. We must love ourselves enough to use the discipline necessary to see that we accomplish the things that are expedient for us to accomplish."

Disorganization. Perhaps you're so disorganized that you don't even have a clear idea of what your goals are. Dealing with disorder is discussed in a more comprehensive way in Day 6. For now, just be aware that being disorganized can sabotage your ability to achieve your work, relationship, or leisure goals.

Boredom. If a task seems so boring that it causes you to waste time procrastinating, it's probably a sign that the task should be dele-

gated or subcontracted out, says professional organizer Barbara Hemphill. Or maybe you just need a better system. Hemphill used to dread all the calls she got from people who wanted to find out about organizing as a career. She would spend hours answering the same boring questions over and over again. Finally, she devised an information packet to respond to all those inquiries. Says Hemphill: "That has saved hours of time, is very professional, and gets me out of a lot of boring things."

Failure to Know Thyself. You will become more effective, and you will increase the likelihood that you will achieve your short- and long-term goals, if you have a better idea of who you are. Do you work more effectively in a fishbowl office environment with dozens of other workers, or do you work more efficiently in a room with a door at home, or in an outside office? What about your personality? Your work habits? Are you a morning or an afternoon person? Do you prefer to work at night or on the weekends? I asked Pat Schroeder, CEO and president of the Association of American Publishers, based in Washington, D.C. with a New York City office, what her number one time management strength is and she answered, "I wake up very early and I find that the early bird does get the worm."

Ask anyone who knows Pat and you will probably hear this universal refrain: "She really knows how to manage her time." Part of this achievement is due to Pat's knowing herself and understanding what works best for her. Pat continues: "I try to get to the office by 7:30 and most people don't come in till 9:00. I find during that hour and a half I crank out more stuff. Sometimes I get here by 7:00."

WHAT IS YOUR BIGGEST OBSTACLE AND WHAT'S YOUR MAJOR STRENGTH?

WHAT IS YOUR BIGGEST OBSTACLE?

Ask yourself the question I posed in the CARAVAN® omnibus telephone survey, namely, what is your number one obstacle to managing work efficiently? Is it doing too much at once, procrastination, paperwork, meetings, perfectionism, poor planning, or e-mail?

_____

_____

_____

_____

_____

If it's something other than those seven obstacles, write your biggest obstacle here:

_____

_____

_____

_____

Now you know your primary goal in reading this book: getting help with your biggest obstacle as you defined it above so you can become effective at work.

WHAT IS YOUR MAJOR STRENGTH?

Fill in the blanks in the following statement. My number one time management strength is:

_____

_____

_____

_____

_____

To figure out how you can be more effective and efficient, take the self-quiz titled Your Work Personality, Style, and Values.

YOUR WORK PERSONALITY, STYLE, AND VALUES

1. **I like to work around people:**

a. all the time.

b. some of the time.

c. never.

2. **The word that most closely describes my personality is:**

a. cheerful.

b. moody.

c. negative.

3. **I like to work with the door:**

a. open.

b. slightly ajar.

c. closed.

4. **Sounds:**

a. don't bother me; I tune them out.

b. may or may not be a problem; it depends on the sound.

c. bother me when I'm trying to work.

5. **I prefer working:**

a. in collaboration with others.

b. with or without others; either way is fine.

c. on my own.

6. **I have been told that I am competitive:**

a. rarely.

b. sometimes.

c. all the time.

7. **If I had a deadline to meet I would:**

a. put everything aside to make it.

b. ask for an extension if I couldn't make it.

c. complain a lot about whether or not I was able to make it.

8. **My ideal time to get up and get ready for work would be:**

a. 6 a.m.

b. 7 a.m.

c. whenever I want to.

9. **If someone gives me feedback on my work, especially if it's critical, I would respond by:**

a. saying "thank you."

b. getting angry at first but, upon reflection, being grateful.

c. waiting to consider the feedback until my emotions were more in check.

10. **If someone were to offer me my current job, I would say:**

a. thanks.

b. yes, provided you give me a raise (or change my job responsibilities).

c. no way!

EVALUATING YOUR ANSWERS

If your answers were mostly a's, you're likely to be more of a people person, flexible, goal-oriented, cheerful, driven, and pleased with your current job. If you primarily answered c, this indicates that you are more of a loner with strong emotional reactions to criticism and a tendency toward negativity. You may be highly competitive, a self-starter who prefers to work independently, and you may be dissatisfied with your current job. If you mainly answered b, you are more of a middle-of-the-road worker at this point. You can take or leave situations; you're somewhat flexible and able to adapt to situations. While you enjoy working with people at times, you also derive pleasure from working alone.

With this information, you can decide if your current work situation conflicts with your natural tendencies; if so, you might want to modify your job to match your personality. Or, conversely, you might want to work on some of your traits, like being too negative, that could be holding you back, changing yourself rather than altering your job situation.

The Big Picture

How do you become more productive and efficient so you can earn more money, and accomplish more, but somehow have even more time for yourself, your family, and your friends? You need to look at your job's big picture, as well its myriad details and how you go about doing what you do. You also need to look at the time you spend nurturing relationships with existing clients or customers, coworkers, your boss, subordinates, and service providers. Examine time spent creating or developing new business opportunities, so you are mining for a growing career. How will you find the time to create or develop new business relationships or opportunities while still fulfilling the current demands of your job? The job description exercise is a good place to start.

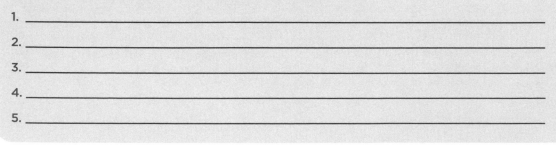

WRITE A JOB DESCRIPTION

By having a clear idea of others' expectations of you (or, if you're self-employed, those you have for yourself), it will be easier to focus on what you need to do to excel in your job. Pretend that you're answering an ad for your current job. How would the job description read? Below, write a job description for your current position (not the one you would like to have—or even the one you thought you were going to have when you were hired).

How is your performance measured? What projects or products are you expected to create, sell, or manage? Deal with the big picture, as well as the details.

_____

_____

_____

_____

This job description will help you to focus on what you need to be concerned with if you are to manage your time efficiently and get better results.

Read over your job description. Now rewrite it, reordering the tasks you need to perform in order of importance. If you did this the first time, fine. Pat yourself on the back for already having a clear idea of your priority concerns. But if you just wrote down a lot of skills, attributes, or job functions without carefully determining which are most important, make this determination now.

REVISED JOB DESCRIPTION, REORGANIZED BY PRIORITIES

1. _____

2. _____

3. _____

4. _____

5. _____

BEAT THE CLOCK

1. Read over the job description that you wrote up in this chapter. What are the skills or tasks that you highlighted as pivotal? Are there any skills for your present job that you are not getting the opportunity to demonstrate? What would you do to rectify this situation? If you have access to a description of your current job from when you were first hired, compare that description to the one you just wrote. Is it the same? If it's different, what are the contrasts? How can you use this information to improve your time management skills, for this job and in general?

2. When was the last time you procrastinated about something? What was it? What were the negative (or even the positive) consequences, if any? Looking back at that incident of procrastination, what could you have done differently to help yourself avoid putting off that task? Could you have tried the reward system to motivate yourself? Or was it

creative procrastination—substituting something else you had to do rather than just goofing off, allowing for delays? Can you think of other solutions, other ways to sidestep your procrastination? Is there anything you are currently procrastinating about? If so, write it down. Create a concrete plan that you will implement to try to get over procrastinating about this situation.

3. The next time you have an idea, think of three reasons why it can't work. Make a list of those reasons, date it, put it aside, and then make your idea work anyway.

4. Think of something that went wrong today. Write down a short summary of the situation. What could you have done differently to have gotten a different outcome? Tomorrow, read over the problem and see if you have any fresh insights into the situation that can help you in the future.

Prioritizing:
Using the ACTION! System for Optimum Productivity

Practically everyone uses the word *prioritizing* in reference to time management. It has become synonymous with productivity: If you're prioritizing and doing what you should do, you are more likely to be moving forward and achieving your short- and long-term goals. Hence, you will be managing your time more effectively. As time management guru Alan Lakein asked in his classic 1973 book *How to Get Control of Your Time and Your Life,* "What is the best use of my time right now?" It's even more necessary to ask this question today than it was in 1973 because of the additional distractions caused by cell phones and 24/7 e-mail/Internet access. By asking, and answering, this question, you will accomplish your current priorities, which will lead to increased effectiveness and better time management.

If you follow the suggestions in the previous chapters on goal setting and getting to know yourself so you can maximize your strengths relating to time, prioritizing will be easier than ever before.

But if you're used to operating in a "busy" mode or relying on others to tell you what's important, rather than figuring it out for yourself, then determining what you need to prioritize may be more of a challenge.

Prioritizing is what Atlanta Life Financial Group President and CEO Ronald D. Brown likes to refer to as the VFP, which stands for valuable final product. Brown believes that "Everybody has all the time that there is," but you need to know what to do with your time. As Brown explained in an interview:

DAY 4

"People get caught in this perpetual spin mode of not ever having enough time to do everything. Well you don't need to do everything! If you're doing everything, you haven't prioritized. Everything doesn't have an impact. There's an ancient proverb: 'Besides the noble art of getting things done, there is the noble art of leaving things undone. The wisdom of life consists in the elimination of nonessentials.' So the biggest job you have is to determine which of those is which. And unfortunately most people at a variety of levels, including the CEO level, don't know the difference between those two things: the things that absolutely need to get done and the things that can be left undone. There has to be an agreement that this is what's important. . . . Unfortunately when people haven't done that upfront [decided on priorities]—you're always second guessing what you don't do and how you spend your time."

Prioritizing Principles: What Should I Be Doing?

I asked Susan, the head of a small business in Connecticut that offers computer solutions to companies, to identify her biggest time management challenge. After initially answering, "There's so many," she then more thoughtfully replied, "Probably keeping myself focused." She, like so many of us, has so much to do that she needs help figuring out what to do first. She has IT (information technology) people who actually do the computer instruction and systems part of the business she runs. She has to keep the business running smoothly. Her answer might be reframed in this way: How do I know what I should prioritize? On what tasks or projects should I focus?

Susan is not alone. Dan, for example, works as the supervisor of a vacation resort with several hundred instructors reporting to him. His failure to prioritize causes him to work far later than he and his wife would like him to do. "If I see something in front of me that is not at the top of my priority list," Dan says, "I feel a need to plunge in and get it done, even if the priority thing is [now] farther away." Dan concludes: "I am personally not good with time management when I have a lot on my plate."

For Susan, Dan, and the rest of us, setting priorities—figuring out what should be on your plate, what should really be on the back burner, and what could be moved onto someone else's plate—is crucial to improving how you manage your time. You can be the most efficient person in the world, but if you're putting too much or even all your time and energy into finishing the wrong task, you can sink your business and your career, as well as hurt the relationships that mean the most to you.

The prioritizing principles that you follow will be different for each job although the overall notion—focusing on what really counts for you to succeed—will be consistent. For example, the commercial real estate salespeople I interviewed, most of whom earn $1 million+ annually from commissions rather than salary, shared with me their golden rule of time management: "Don't do from 9 to 5 what you could be doing from 5 to 9." From 9 to 5, when everyone else is working, they are out in the field, looking at office properties and interviewing prospective clients/customers. They then handle the paperwork and other tasks from 5 till 9 at night, when they can't be out in the field anymore.

WHAT'S YOUR PRIORITY?

How do you know what your priorities should be? It will help to ask yourself these questions every single day:

1. What is the #1 project I have to do today? _____

2. How am I going to do it? _____

   _____

3. How will I know when I'm done? _____

   _____

4. How will I reward myself for doing it? _____

   _____

5. What is the #2 project I have to do today? _____

   _____

6. Can I juggle multiple projects simultaneously, or do I have to complete one task at a time and/or delegate some or all of the work to others?

   _____

But look at how priorities shift if we address the concerns of residential (as opposed to commercial) real estate agents. Since the majority of their customers are usually apartment- or house-hunting in their nonwork hours, they have a much less predictable rule of thumb: They complete their paperwork and phone calls whenever they have a lull in their property showings, which is often during the day, since they are more likely to show apartments or houses to customers from 5 to 9 at night and on weekends.

Think about your job. What hours are you currently working? How much of your day is spent doing your job and how much is spent on related nonpriority tasks? Is there a way to restructure your day and time so that you accomplish more of what you need to and turn to your optional and tangential work in the hours after you've completed your priority tasks? An artist needs to be in her studio painting. But she also needs to budget time for meeting with her gallery director to discuss the next art show. A publicist needs to be familiarizing himself with the person or product he is publicizing or pitching, but he also needs to make time to meet with as many members of the media as possible.

Review the ideal workday that you created in Day 2. Are there tasks you left out of your ideal day that you now realize need to be added? Do you have at least one hour each day dedicated to uninterrupted reading, writing, or thinking? Do you have at least half an hour of free time in case there is a crisis that you have to deal with? Consider this situation: You're working on a report. It's 5:30 p.m. and you're on a roll. After several days of writer's block, you are finally hitting your stride. The report is due in a week and you don't know when or if you'll be able to focus on it again in as concerted a way. The only problem is that you wanted to go to a networking event for an association you belong to. There will be lots of people at this event with whom it would be useful to connect or reconnect. What should you do? What is the best way to spend the next two or three hours? Do you continue working on the report or attend the networking function?

You need to ask and answer some questions to make that decision. For example, who asked you to attend this networking event? A coworker? A client? Your boss? A friend? Are you just responding to an e-mail blast from the association about this event and going because of that blanket invitation, or has someone personally asked you to attend? (It's easier to opt out if it's a general e-mail blast invitation as opposed to a personal request from someone who is expecting you to be there.) If you attended a similar event in the past, how useful was it to you in advancing your priority short- and long-term career goals? If you cancel, how much money will you lose? (However, since time sometimes is money, your answer to this last question may not be the determining factor.)

Use the worksheet titled How Do I Decide What to Do with My Time Right Now? to help you think through this decision. If you prefer, use a different situation from your own recent experiences to fine-tune your prioritizing thought processes.

HOW DO I DECIDE WHAT TO DO WITH MY TIME RIGHT NOW?

- On a scale of 1 to 5, how much of a priority is my current task? _____
- How much of a priority is the alternative task I am considering? _____
- How time-sensitive is the task I'm doing as opposed to the alternative task? _____
- Is either task/event a one-time opportunity, like a wedding, or is it repeated on a regular basis? _____
- Is anyone involved who will not understand, or who will undermine me, if I do not go to one of these events or perform one of these tasks? _____
- Who is involved in each of these concerns (e.g., my boss, coworker, client, subordinate, etc.)? _____

    _____
- If a family member or friend presented these two alternatives to me and asked my opinion, what would I tell that person to do? _____

    _____
- In the short or long run, which task has greater career or personal benefits?

    _____
- Thinking back to a similar situation, what did I do then? What was the outcome? How similar is this scenario to that situation? _____

    _____
- How much money have I invested in attending this event? _____

By answering these questions, we hope the right course of action will become clear. Once you make your decision, observe what happens and learn from your choice, so that you will have a better idea how to proceed the next time you are confronted with a similar situation.

Tools for Prioritizing: How a To-Do List Can Help

Writing down your goals and priorities helps you to concretize them. The common term for writing down what we need to do is the to-do list. Keeping a list of what you need to accomplish, whether you do it on paper, on your computer, or in your electronic organizer, will help you to prioritize these tasks. It will also help you to monitor your progress. There are all kinds of to-do lists. The basic plain piece of paper with whatever it is that you need to do scribbled on it is a simple version. You can create a to-do list template on your computer or you can buy commercially prepared ones at the office supply store.

TO-DO LIST

Here's a very simple to-do list that includes space to write down up to ten tasks.

TODAY'S DATE: _____ **DAY OF THE WEEK:** _____

	TO DO	COMMENTS	DATE COMPLETED
1.	_____	_____	_____
2.	_____	_____	_____
3.	_____	_____	_____
4.	_____	_____	_____
5.	_____	_____	_____
6.	_____	_____	_____
7.	_____	_____	_____
8.	_____	_____	_____
9.	_____	_____	_____
10.	_____	_____	_____
11.	_____	_____	_____

ORGANIZING YOUR LIST

Chronological List

You may want to order your to-do list chronologically—that is, according to time, such as from the beginning of the day until late at night. To do so, divide your list to reflect how you arrange your day: before work, during work, and after work. Within each section, follow a simple chronological system. List what you have to do in the sequence you will do it. For example:

During Work:

1. Call or go online and make airline reservation.
2. Write memo for meeting.

3. Get up-to-date distribution list for the memo.
4. E-mail memo to those who will be attending meeting.

Cross off each item as it is completed.

List by Importance

Alternatively, reorder your to-do list by importance:

1. Write memo for meeting today.
2. Get up-to-date distribution list for the memo.
3. E-mail memo to attendees who will be attending meeting.
4. Call airline or go online and make reservation for trip 2 months ahead.

For certain tasks, especially if you are scheduling appointments around your to-do list priorities, estimating how long a task will take is another piece of information that you might want to add to your list.

Crossing or checking off what you've accomplished is another way of reinforcing that you're moving along in how you monitor the use of your time.

Some find keeping an actual written to-do list is too rigid for them; they prefer to have a mental to-do list. For others, however, having a written to-do list helps clarify priorities. One executive even noted that without the next day's to-do list by her bedside, falling sleep without tossing and turning throughout the night was impossible.

TYPICAL TO-DO LIST PITFALLS TO AVOID

In preparing your to-do list, one pitfall to avoid is failing to estimate how long something will take. Another common mistake is not transferring items you did not complete from your current list to a new list.

To be effective, a to-do list has to work for you. For some, just the act of writing down what they have to do is a reminder, just as a shopping list is a reminder of what's missing in their household that must be bought at the store. By contrast, others need something more elaborate and thoughtful,

like a list ordered by priority or ordered by chronology. What's pivotal is that you have a written record of what you need to do and when you plan to do it, as well as when you have accomplished it. This is a way of clarifying your priorities.

Your goal is not to become a list maker but to use your to-do list as a way of more effectively organizing your time. Certain time-consuming tasks will need to be broken down into smaller projects, with each one having mini-deadlines. For example, you may have at the top of your to-do list, "Write report." If that's going to take a week, you should break down that larger task into smaller ones that you can monitor on your to-do list, for example, "E-mail market research company and find out when data will be available for the report" or "Go to corporate library and research latest articles on competing products."

Improving Motivation

How you spend your time—and how you go about your work—has as much to do with motivation as it does with time management systems and tips. If you're excited by what you're doing and motivated to do well and to be involved in your work, you will value yourself and your time more and you will use your time wisely, rather than wasting it.

GET MOTIVATED

How can you motivate yourself? Think back to other times in your life when you were driven and experiencing the rush of competition. What did it feel like? What were the reasons that you were so motivated? Was it a subject in school that you particularly liked? A teacher or mentor at work who believed in you? Try to re-create those conditions now.

We all have people who need us and people on whom we depend who can affect how we manage our time. They can determine whether or not we can meet or exceed our goals. If you help your coworkers, bosses, subordinates, and even your service providers to feel that they're part of the process that is defining your product or service, you're more likely to have everyone cheering you on. Let others know that you care about them and what they do; they will, in most cases, be much more motivated to see that your priorities are achieved.

Using the ACTION! System

Most of us in the business world today are in a fast-paced, competitive environment that thrives on results as well as speed. In most circles, just being smart, considerate, and competent is not enough. You also have to generate revenue and keep adding products and customers or clients so your business, or the company you work for, thrives. You and your company need to be financially successful; you and your family are depending on you to produce and to be productive.

How can you achieve and maintain that productivity? The ACTION! system may be just what you need as the catalyst to increasing your productivity. It's a way of looking at what you have to do that is results-oriented, as you get the most done in the least amount of time. The emphasis is on speed and quality. Both are important. Neither should or has to be sacrificed for the other if you follow the ACTION! system for optimum productivity. Let's look at what the ACTION! strategy trains you to do consistently:

A = **Assess.** Determine what you should be doing in the first place. As management guru Peter F. Drucker writes in *The Daily Drucker*, an anthology of his key writings, "Are the premises that you base your decision on obsolete? Do you need a new intellectual framework to win in the market, as it exists today?" Once you determine that you are, in fact, working on what you *should* be concerned with *now*, decide what you need to know, or what you need to find out, and do the research, make the phone calls, and ask the questions that will enable you to do your job.

C = **Control.** Take control of what you can influence—your own behavior—and deal with any of the obstacles to working more effectively on a particular task or project that are causing you to slow down or misuse your time, as discussed in Day 3. Practice saying no politely or, if you must agree to competing demands on your time, make sure you return to your own priorities as soon as possible. Apply C (Control) to enhancing productivity by creating a more effective environment to work in (see Day 6), delegating efficiently (see Day 12), as well as through developing clear short- and long-term goals (see Day 2) and dealing with the phone (see Day 8), e-mail, and Internet (see Day 9) so you are in better control of yourself and your time.

T = **Target.** Once you have identified the specific task, project, and/or goal you are going to address today, stay with your target. If you're able to effectively juggle more than one primary target activity or project—multitasking—make sure each one is a priority concern. (See Day 5 for a more in-depth discussion of multitasking.)

I = Innovate. What have you learned about your job, subject matter, or even other projects that you can apply to your own situation, enabling you to accomplish more in less time? Don't be afraid to try new systems or ideas (or go back to the tried-and-true ones that worked for you in the past).

O = Organize. Use organizing strategies that allow you to accomplish your goals better and faster. Group similar tasks together. Organize your files, books, and supplies. Spend the time to keep your database up to date, since this will save you time when you need to find a person, place, or information that is pivotal to the task at hand. (See Day 6 for more organizing tips.) Take special note of some of the more dramatic or radical time management suggestions or organizing tips described in this book for your office or for your home, and experiment with implementing any of those suggestions that might work for you.

N = Now! The key to the ACTION! strategy to help you to become more productive and effective is to address your key priority concern NOW, not tomorrow or after you've done a million other less important things. The N for Now is a reminder that you need to stop procrastinating, making excuses, distracting yourself, and putting everything and everyone before taking—and completing—the ACTION! that will move this project, and your career, along. Doing some-thing NOW will feel oh so terrific when you let yourself focus on an assignment, a project, a key concern that is your #1 goal for today. This usually requires that you immerse yourself in whatever you have to do and not diffuse your energy by tackling multiple less pivotal concerns. Once you apply NOW! to your ACTION! strategy and plan, and complete whatever you have to do, you can go on to the next project as you apply the ACTION! strategy to that time sensitive or crucial project or goal.

WOO: Window of Opportunity

Your WOO—window of opportunity—opens and closes, sometimes quite quickly. You have to know when and how to WOO your career—and the relationships and activities that your career requires—if you are to make sure that your time is always very well spent. Be sensitive to the difference between someone who tells you that he's busy, it's not a good time to discuss new business, and his giving you excuse after excuse because he is really the wrong client for you to be pursuing. This sensitivity will help you to know whether a WOO should be acted upon in a timely manner or evaluated and ignored because it was not an opportunity or relationship in your best interest to pursue after all.

Your WOO detector needs to be on at all

WINDOW OF OPPORTUNITY

Your window of opportunity (WOO) opens and closes, sometimes quite quickly. You have to know when and how to WOO your career . . . if you are to make sure that your time is always very well spent.

times. Sometimes you just don't get a second chance at the opportunities that can make your career. But if you're in control of your time, and you're clear on your priorities, it's more likely that you will assess each WOO more clearly, so you move toward your goals at the fastest pace possible.

RRA: Respond Right Away

How long does it take you to respond to people and requests? In business today, unless you respond right away you can be seen as ineffective and a poor time manager even if, ironically, you are more goal-oriented and hardworking than other members of your team. Understanding the concept of RRA is helpful in improving people's perception of you as a well-organized and effective person, as well as in assessing the reality of how quickly you respond to demands—and whether these time frames are realistic and can be maintained over time.

To help you evaluate your response times, answer the questions in the quiz titled What Is Your Response Time? so you can track how quickly you respond to common office tasks and responsibilities, such as phone calls, e-mails, letters, proposal requests, or offers to speak or to participate in committees.

APPLYING RRA SO YOU'RE PLEASED WITH THE RESULTS

How do you become known as someone who will RRA—Respond Right Away?

- First, agree that it's rude to keeping people waiting.
- Second, realize that you may have different response times, depending on

whom you need to respond to, and that's okay. If you find yourself ignoring or taking too long to respond to a number of people, you probably need a more effective filtering system. Maybe many nonpriority requests sent directly to you could go to others charged with dealing with those inquiries.

- Third, accept that there may be extenuating circumstances, like travel, that may affect whether or not you can RRA. Take those situations into account by either setting up an autoresponder, telling those who contact you that you are away and delays are possible, or programming an outgoing voice message that announces that there are reasons that you may not RRA.

- Fourth, become more sensitive to what are reasonable response times for those you do business with and how that applies to you. Perhaps you are being unrealistic in the standard you have set for yourself, trying to respond to everyone so quickly that you're not accomplishing as much as you would like to, besides answering e-mails or returning phone calls.

- Fifth, see if there are patterns to some of the kinds of written inquiries you receive so that you could have basic information available to send out, such as a brochure, electronic press kit, or letters that you could customize more efficiently than creating all your responses from scratch.

- Sixth, if you're too wordy in your written responses (see Day 9), or too verbose or lengthy in your phone calls (see Day 8), try working on shortening them, without being impolite or cryptic.

WHAT IS YOUR RESPONSE TIME?

1. When I get an e-mail, I usually respond:

a. right away
b. within an hour
c. within 24 hours
d. it depends on who sent it
e. never

2. When I receive a phone message, I usually respond:

a. right away
b. within an hour
c. within 24 hours
d. it depends on who called
e. never

3. When I receive a letter, I usually respond:

a. right away
b. within an hour
c. within 24 hours
d. it depends on who sent it
e. never

4. When I receive a proposal request, I usually respond:

a. right away
b. within an hour
c. within 24 hours
d. within 1 week
e. never

5. When I receive a request to speak at a conference or before a committee, I usually respond:

a. right away
b. within an hour
c. within 24 hours
d. within 1 week
e. never

EVALUATING YOUR ANSWERS

In general, especially if you're in a managerial or supervisory job, if you answered with all d's, you actually have the ideal approach to responding to a message or request: "It depends on who sent it (or who called)." Exercising judgment about each and every demand on your time can help you become more efficient, because you will be more effective. If you responded with all b's, you have excellent response time, since "within an hour" is certainly a reasonable amount of time for most responses. If you had all a's—"right away"—you may be overdoing how quickly you respond at the expense of your priority concerns or projects. If you answered with all c's, you need to decide if always responding within 24 hours is too long a turnaround for some demands. Finally, one or more e responses and you may be jeopardizing your job and career advancement by ignoring pivotal requests. Examine how you might develop a better response time than "never." Perhaps this is an indication that you are getting requests or calls that should not have been directed to you in the first place or that you need to create an autoresponder for some requests—an automatic answer that everyone receives or a standard response that you or an assistant can cut and paste into certain types of inquiries.

Applying the ACTION! System to Your Particular Workday

Each particular type of workday has its own unique time concerns. In following the ACTION! system, you may run into certain obstacles to setting targets and accomplishing your priority tasks. Let's examine some different types of workdays and their related time management challenges—as well as how you can maximize your effectiveness in a given situation.

IF YOU WORK FOR A COMPANY WITH 2 TO 50,000+ EMPLOYEES

The traditional 9 to 5 day is still the norm in a majority of workplaces in the United States, although 9 to 5 may actually mean 8 to 6, or 7 to 5, or 10 to 7, depending on the company and industry standards. Some industries, like financial services, have 7 or 8 a.m. start times, even for executives, with workers leaving at 6, 7, or 8 p.m.

These are the companies that require you to physically be there to be considered "working" (a phenomenon known as *face time*). The advent of the BlackBerry® and other devices that can connect you 24/7 to the workplace and to e-mail and the Internet (as well as cell phones that increase the convenience of receiving work-related phone calls on trains, in cars, on planes, or at home) has not resulted in shorter hours in the office for most people. Instead, these devices have led to a longer (sometimes 24/7) workday, generally without an increase in compensation.

If you work in an office where you're expected to make your presence known during certain hours, be mindful of what those hours are, and make it your business to be on time, every time, and to leave when you're expected to leave, not before. Only stay later if a project or meeting warrants it. Keep in mind what expectations you are setting up in the minds of your employers and employees. Everyone likes a schedule and a routine. If you start on a certain schedule, people may expect you to maintain it. As I advise in the article I wrote about working smart on your first job, published in the *Wall Street Journal's National Business Employment Weekly*, be careful about getting in too early and staying excessively late, just because you're new and you want to impress. When you cut back on those unrealistic and unnecessary hours, you may look as if you're slacking off when you're really just working the more reasonable hours that are expected of you. That advice applies to any new job, not just your first one. In your eagerness to impress, be careful not to overdo it. Not only is it hard to keep up those extreme hours, your coworkers and even your boss might resent you for unwittingly trying to upstage them.

TAKE A BREAK

Whether this is a new job or one you've had for a while, take stock of your company's expectations, including rules about lunch hour. Is there any flexibility here? If you're entitled to a one-hour lunch but you only take thirty minutes, can you leave the office thirty minutes earlier at the end of the day? Or have you just given up thirty minutes of what should be free time? As noted in Day 3, in the section on Poor Pacing, if you fail to take the breaks that are due you, including your lunch break, you may actually be sabotaging your progress, causing yourself to be less, not more, productive. How much will you really get done in that time when you should be taking a break for lunch? What about using that time to take a long walk or to make some personal calls away from your cubicle or office, so you can avoid making personal calls throughout the day?

If there is now an expectation that you will be available 24/7, through electronic devices or a computer that gives you access to company e-mail from home or on the go, you will have to self-regulate just how much unpaid additional company time you are willing to provide. If you do international business, it may be necessary to send and receive e-mails or phone calls at very early or very late hours because of the diverse time zones that you have to deal with. See if those extra hours are taken into account when your time commitment to the company is assessed.

DEALING WITH UNRESPONSIVE COWORKERS

Dealing effectively and efficiently with those you work with or for is as much a part of your job as the work itself. Over the years, in questionnaires, interviews, and in workshops, people consistently complain about having to wait for others to complete their part of a project. This can be frustrating, since you can't go forward without that missing piece, but you also can't force others to make your project their priority. Or can you? Perhaps there are ways to motivate those slow responders to move your project to their front burner. For some suggestions on how to do that, consult Day 12 of this book.

TAKE TIME TO THINK

One of the best ways to increase your productivity in a traditional work environment is to find a way to block out at least one hour of interrupted time to think, read, brainstorm, reflect, plan, or write. Yes, at the workplace, not just on the train, plane, or at home. You are being paid to be at the office; since this uninterrupted hour of "think time" may be the most productive hour you spend each day, you should carve out that hour at work. This may at first seem like an impossible suggestion, especially if, up until now, your workday has consisted of running from one meeting to another, answering and placing calls, and receiving and sending e-mails in a frenzy, only to look up at the clock and find, to your surprise, that it is already six o'clock and you haven't even had your lunch.

SOME TRADITIONAL WORKPLACES ARE CHANGING

At some companies, there have been dramatic changes in how time is structured. As reported in *BusinessWeek*, Chap Achen, a 37-year-old Best Buy Co. employee at the company's Minneapolis headquarters, told his staff at 2 p.m., "See you tomorrow. I'm going to a matinee." This new initiative at the electronic retailer is known as ROWE, "results-only work environment." According to *BusinessWeek*, it's an experiment to change Best Buy's reputation for "killer hours and herd-riding bosses" and the typical corporate philosophy that "equates physical presence with productivity." As *BusinessWeek* reports, Best Buy's goal, one usually associated with freelancers and self-employed individuals, is: "judge performance on output instead of hours."

I asked Victoria Sutherland, who is the Michigan-based founder and publisher of *Foreword* magazine, a trade publication for librarians and others in the book business, how she manages to take a one-month break each year, most recently spending February in Bermuda with her school-age children and her husband, in addition to at least one more annual summer vacation. Sutherland explains the innovative way she runs her company, which has five full-time employees and several dozen subcontractors, most of whom are reviewers:

> When I had a chance to create my own company, a goal was not only to make it very mommy-friendly (since it is essentially women-run) but fun. Everyone is welcome to work from home, from a coffee shop down the street, or in the office as long as the standards of the magazine are upheld. I encourage people to take advantage of vacation time before/after trade shows since their travel expenses to and from have already been taken care of. I feel generous with a three-week vacation package offered immediately; I think it is important for people to get out of their spaces for as long as they can to think outside of the box and find the time to see the "big picture"—not just at their jobs, but in their lives.
>
> I have a great staff. I already travel a lot so they are used to my absences. Yet, they have a lot of flexibility, and in return, I know that I can leave for 30 days and things won't fall to pieces. We set up instant messaging for everyone and, for the five or six hours a day I do work [while out of the office], I can access them immediately, and they me. Everyone knows her position in the company is a critical piece to the whole puzzle, so if she slacks [off] everyone suffers. I have never had a problem. . . . I am able to accomplish more in a half day outside of the office than I can in a day at the office with all the distractions!

Sutherland realizes, however, that taking several months off to run her company from afar would not work. She adds:

> But I do know that a month is the breaking point. There is a certain energy only an owner can bring into the door each morning and if you are absent too long, the work and enthusiasm reflect it. In terms of friends and family reactions, most are good because they witness the quality of our life. Some seem jealous. Others simply shake their heads in disbelief, worried that I would jeopardize our lives so, but I mostly see a tinge of green in their eyes.

FOR PART-TIMERS

The biggest time challenge if you are working part-time, whether you work at home or in an office, is staying in the loop about what goes on when you're not at the office that could affect your particular job as well as the company as a whole. If you depend on other people to do your work, or they depend on you, make sure that you have clear deadlines that work for everyone, so you're not faced with delays or accused of holding up a project.

You also need to make your presence known, especially if you're working part-time. While it may seem more time-efficient to submit work electronically, you may find it useful to set up in-person meetings. For suggestions on how and why to do this, see Day 13.

Be careful of the time trap that many part-timers have reported to me over the years: They somehow find the number of hours actually worked, including work outside the office, creeps up to as many hours as a full-time job, but without the benefits or the status of being a full-time employee. This is not just the social and professional status that accompanies the title of full-time versus part-time employee. I'm also referring to how a company may reward employees on the basis of years worked full-time, in terms of pension contributions or promotions or raises based on seniority—a seniority that is only granted to those working full-time. If you're in doubt about the benefits and consequences of working part-time, discuss your situation with your company's human resources department. If your company does not have an HR department, consider speaking to members of a professional association you may belong to who may have encountered similar situations, or others working in your field whom you trust.

WORKING ALONE: FREELANCERS, ENTREPRENEURS, AND THE SELF-EMPLOYED

If your company consists of just you, your time challenges may be the greatest of all, since delegating tasks to others may not seem to be an option, certainly for those at the beginning of a new venture. How, then, can freelancers, entrepreneurs, and self-employed small business owners maximize their efficiency without being able to say, "I'll ask so-and-so to do it"?

- First and foremost, ask yourself this: What can I do that no one else is capable of doing? What are my particular talents or areas of expertise that no one else or few exhibit? For example, say you're an excellent speaker, but you lack the skills to sell your services to companies. You could find a speakers' bureau that could help get you engagements so you could focus on your speaking skills and leave the selling and contractual work to the experts. If you excel at making outside sales calls, or must work in a concentrated way at your desk without interruption, consider using an outside answering service that specializes in taking messages when you're unavailable.

- Second, if you delegate, delegate tasks, not relationships. (See the further discussion of delegating in Day 12).

- Third, make time for creating new products or providing additional services, while continuing to manage your company, service current clients, and sell your existing merchandise. Budget time for:
  - Testing a new product or service
  - Maintaining current clients
  - Building new relationships or clients
  - Family and friends
  - Yourself

The most successful freelancers, business owners, and entrepreneurs tend to be those who know how to handle, not mishandle, their time. Time management involves value judgments. You can do things more effectively, so you don't have to work 24/7 and fail to take vacation time. It also means that as you juggle multiple projects and clients, you still make each and every person feel that he or she counts, much like a parent who skillfully makes each child feel as if he or she is the favored one. Everything that has to get done, gets done; what is unnecessary is either ignored, delegated, or accomplished after the time-sensitive demands are met.

Time-Saving Tips for Those Who Work Independently

Feeling pulled in too many directions without the support of a traditional employer? Try some of these techniques to get organized and do more in less time:

- Look over the year. Now look ahead to the next year . . . the next 5 years . . . the next 10. What is the pace or rhythm to your particular business? Is it seasonal, with high volume during the December holidays? Are there trade shows you must attend, and are you factoring in prep time for those shows, as well as time spent away from the office while you staff those shows and do the all-important follow-up?

- Do you have a catalog? A website? Flyers? Who's in charge of updating those materials? Having excellent materials that describe your services and that are instantly ready to send out electronically or through the mail can save you lots of time. You also want to make sure you or someone else regularly updates those materials whether it's monthly, quarterly, semi-annually, or annually.

- Make sure you accomplish a priority task or project each and every day. That is why writing down a daily goal or goals helps to maximize your efficiency. You know that you have accomplished something concrete and meaningful because you set a target, and accomplished it. If it's a big project, break it down into smaller goals, assigning a target completion date to each one.

- Avoid leaving things to the last minute as much as possible. Errors are more likely to occur that way. You will probably spend more money at the last minute because you can't shop around for the most competitive price. An exception to this, however, is if you can pick up a bargain if you wait till the last minute because prices are dramatically reduced or find airline seats that cost less if the airline needs to fill up the plane.

Getting Help

Are you working around the clock, as hard as you can, and still not getting everything done (even though you are not procrastinating)? Then you may need to get more help. Hiring staff—part-time or full-time—is one way to get more help, but it might not be the answer for you. Here are some other options:

- Interns (paid or unpaid)

- Commissioned help (no added overhead; they get a percentage of the deals they broker and the income they generate)

- Outsourcing to independent contractors with whom you develop a steady relationship (but who are not employees)

- Freelancers

- Anyone who prefers to work just a few hours a day, such as retirees or mothers with young or school-age children

- Students

- Family members

What you're trying to achieve is an organized life that fits in as many activities and relationships as you need and want, without denying yourself the fulfillment of your own dreams. This, of course, includes time to "do nothing"—thinking, daydreaming, staring into space. A mother with three toddlers, a husband, and a full-time job will probably have to be more organized—and work harder to find extra time—than a retired couple who seem to have nothing but time on their hands. Time is relative, however, and a 76-year-old grandmother without a job or a spouse may feel more rushed and disorganized than her 33-year-old granddaughter with multiple obligations.

ASSIGNMENT/PROJECT SHEET

Set up a system for keeping track of your assignments or projects. You can buy tracking sheets at the office supply store or make your own on the computer. Here's a simple project tracking sheet that you might find useful.

TODAY'S DAY AND DATE: _____

Client Name: _____

Title: _____

Company: _____

Address: _____

_____

Phone: _____

Cell phone: _____

Fax: _____

E-mail: _____

Website: _____

Preferred way to communicate: _____

Referred by: _____

Project: _____

Date assigned: _____

Deadline/due date: _____

Length/type: _____

Fee and/or rate: _____

Budget: _____

Expenses: _____

Letter-agreement and/or contract signed: _____

Project submitted on: _____

Follow-up: _____

Outcome: _____

Notes: _____

_____

_____

Changing circumstances dictate altering how you manage your time. Your primary work role may be that of executive, but your family relations and community activities are other roles that demand your time. You may be an accountant, paid by the hour, with numerous outside obligations, or a self-employed researcher, paid by the project, who is active in sports and cultural activities. Few of us play only one role; how best to perform each one is a recurring theme when planning our time.

TIPS FOR STUDENTS

What are the time management issues that plague most students? Often these issues factor into whether a student does well or poorly in a course, whether a student is on time to class or in submitting term papers, and even what attitude that student has toward the course. I have been teaching at the undergraduate and occasionally the graduate level as well as in continuing education, since my early twenties. Here are some tips for students based on my experiences:

- Find out what is expected of you from each professor and course. The syllabus has always been a pivotal part of every course that I've taught (or taken). It is through the syllabus that your professor will share with you the precise details of what he or she expects of you, the books you are required to read, the due dates for those readings, any reports or term papers that are required, plus the due dates for those written projects, as well as the dates of your midterm and final exams.

- Write down those due dates. Record those key dates from the syllabus in one or more additional places that you will refer to regularly. For example, write them in a daily or weekly appointment book, tack them on the bulletin board in front of your desk at home or at work, or place them in your electronic organizer. Check those dates before you agree to any work, social, or personal commitments that could conflict with your school demands. Plan time before each due date for reading, studying, or researching and writing your term papers.

- Break down each deadline into workable interim deadlines. In addition to those reading, studying, or writing times that you are setting aside, create your own mini due dates that will help you to better monitor your own progress. For example, let's say you have a term paper due by the third week of class. By what date will you pick your term paper topic? How about setting a date for finishing up the research for your paper? What is the date that you are targeting for the first draft of the paper? Make sure you allow enough time to reread your paper, go over the spelling and grammar thoroughly, and then rewrite it so you can turn it in by the due date.

- Remember that *no* usually means no. Occasionally there is some room for negotiation about due dates and what is required of you, but in general if a professor says no, he or she means no.

- Prioritize. The number-one time management technique that serves you as a student well is prioritizing your school work as your primary job during the school year, until you get your degree and graduate (or earn your certificate).

- Back up your work! Make sure you have backed up your work in multiple ways. If you use a computer, back up to an external disk, a CD-ROM, a memory stick, or a second computer. Send yourself or someone else an electronic version of your term paper, so you have another copy in case your hard drive crashes or anything else happens to your original file. If you do not want to rely only on electronic versions of your work, create one or more hard copies of what you're writing. (If you have a hard copy, you can always re-create your electronic version with a scanner.)

You're Too Busy to Procrastinate!

Putting off schoolwork till the last minute might describe the behavior of a lot of students; don't be one of them. Some call that behavior procrastination; I call it self-sabotage. It's self-sabotage because by doing something at the last minute you may not put forth your best effort, since you fail to allow yourself enough time to read or reread the required chapters or to write and rewrite the necessary papers. You may also be decreasing the likelihood that you will get the excellent grades that you know you could and should be achieving if you weren't rushing (or turning projects in after the due date).

If you must procrastinate, do what I refer to as *creative procrastination*. What distinguishes creative procrastination from the garden-variety type of procrastination is that you substitute another priority task for the task you're putting off. Let's say you have to study for a history test and you keep putting it off. Instead of going to the movies—feeling guilty the whole time because you really should be studying history—read over your notes from another class or make a dent in the research on your history term paper. Then go back to studying for the history test. You still get your history test studying done, as well as other necessary schoolwork, just in a different order. If you absolutely can't get into your schoolwork, allow yourself to procrastinate—go to the movie—enjoy it, and get back to your schoolwork upon your return. Give up the debilitating guilt over the delay!

The Rewards Make the Effort Worth It

Making school a priority that you approach with determination, focus, concentration, and professionalism will take you far in getting the most out of your learning experiences. There are, of course, the external rewards for working more effectively in school, as you will find yourself getting better grades and receiving praise from professors. There is also the internal reward of knowing that you are making the most of your time as a student. Instead of drudgery, school is the challenge and eye-opening educational experience it is meant to be.

Most of all, there is a calm that you will begin to feel as you decrease the stress caused by all the demands on you. Keep in mind, as you complete your coursework, that there is an end in sight. Eventually you will finish, graduate, and reap the rewards of all this hard work. By becoming more focused and efficient, you will see the benefits of your increased productivity spill over to other areas of your life, such as your personal time.

ACTION! STRATEGY WORKSHEET

Project or Task: _____

A (Assess): _____
_____
_____

C (Control): _____
_____
_____

T (Target): _____
_____
_____

I (Innovate): _____
_____
_____

O (Organize): _____
_____
_____

N (Now!): _____
_____
_____

DAY 4

1. How many hours in the evening or on weekends do you work in addition to your regular office hours? What is your true weekly total for the number of hours that you work? Did you know that you were working that much (or that little)? Are you compensated for all the hours that you are working? If you are not compensated directly for those additional hours in overtime pay, are you getting other benefits, such as a bigger bonus at the end of the month or the end of the year? Have the additional hours led to increased revenues? If you do not see a definite correlation between the increased hours and greater productivity, make a commitment to yourself that you will implement the suggestions in this book that may enable you to work fewer hours but still achieve just as much.

2. Take a priority task or project that you have to do and apply the ACTION! strategy, described previously in detail in this chapter, to it. Use the worksheet on p. 63 to do just that.

3. What Window of Opportunity (WOO) do you have right now? What are you doing to take advantage of that WOO? What additional WOO possibilities do you plan to go after? How will you do that? Write about a WOO that you are considering or would like to explore.

_____

_____

_____

_____

_____

_____

_____

_____

_____

Multitasking So It Works

I used to caution people, including myself, against doing too many projects or things at once. In theory, it makes sense that doing one thing at a time and focusing all your attention on that one task until you are finished is the most efficient way to spend your time. But some jobs absolutely depend on juggling numerous projects and tasks. A multimillion-dollar real estate broker told me that he has to handle twelve deals simultaneously. He and his family would starve if he were to focus on only one deal. Also, in his job, as in many of our jobs, there are times when you must wait for someone else before you can move forward. For example, the broker may need the manager of the office building to show a potential buyer the piece of property the buyer is considering. You don't just want to wait around idly while that's happening. You want to be doing something else that might be generating revenue as well. Before you know it, you are doing many things at once, or multitasking, as it is called today.

When Does Multitasking Work and When Does It Sabotage You?

There are geniuses who worked on a multiplicity of projects simultaneously; examples are Leonardo da Vinci, Isaac Asimov, and Benjamin Franklin. We can conjecture that such creative thinkers would have been bored working on one thing at a time and felt compelled to multitask. They probably also practiced something known as selective attention: when they worked on one project, that project got their full attention.

Still, research has revealed that switching back and forth between tasks, rather than sticking with one activity, may actually cause you to lose time. Researchers Joshua S. Rubenstein of the Federal Aviation Administration and David E. Meyer and Jeffrey E. Evans, both of the University of Michigan, describe their research into multitasking in the *Journal of Experimental Psychology*. Switching between tasks may result in losing a half-second of time; this may seem insignificant, but if that half-second is lost when switching between driving a car and talking on a cell phone, it could mean the difference between having or avoiding an accident or a collision that results in injury or even death.

Beyond Multitasking

How can you tell if you are creatively and intentionally multitasking—or if you're suffering from something more problematic, such as distractionitis, doing too much at once, or ADHD? Let's take a look at each of these conditions that may masquerade as multitasking.

DISTRACTIONITIS

In certain situations, multitasking can be useful and productive. By contrast, distractionitis is counterproductive. What's the difference? Multitasking is combining two tasks at the same time, either at once or by going back and forth between the two. It is a conscious decision to tackle these two responsibilities at once.

Distractionitis is a knee-jerk response that you can't seem to control. It might be automatically picking up the phone, even though you have voice mail and you promised yourself that you would not take calls for the next hour. Or it might mean going back and forth every hour, every half-hour, even every five minutes to check e-mail, even though you're not expecting anything specific to arrive. This interrupts your concentration and distracts you from the priority task you're supposed to be focusing on. If you suffer from distractionitis, you can't stop yourself from putting aside or leaving a task to do something else, even though you know it's a distraction.

DOING TOO MUCH AT ONCE

Doing too much at once happens when you're taking on more tasks than you can handle, feeling pulled among all these demands. What distinguishes multitasking from doing too much at once is that, ideally, when you multitask you are managing all the tasks well, whether it's one, five, or fifteen projects. It only becomes "doing too much at once" when the workload is no longer manageable. This will obviously differ from person to person and even for the same person from day to day or hour to hour. If you're full of energy, well rested, and the projects you're working on are engrossing, you might be able to handle more projects than if you're exhausted and you've said yes to several commitments that you wish you had turned down.

ADHD

According to an article at an online site maintained by the National Institute of Mental Health (NIMH), "Most substantiated causes [of Attention Deficit/Hyperactivity Disorders (ADHD)] appear to fall in the realm of neurobiology and genetics." Are there environmental causes of ADHD that affect adults as well as children? The NIMH article continues: "This is not to say that environmental factors may not influence the severity of the disorder . . . but that such factors do not seem to give rise to the condition by themselves." As noted in Day 10, in the section on concentration, certain symptoms of ADHD—including restlessness, hyperactivity, distraction, impulsiveness, and difficulty sustaining attention on a task—could lead to going back and forth between different tasks.

Figuring out if your multitasking is due to (1) a conscious decision to undertake two or more tasks at the same time as a way to increase your productivity, (2) distractionitis, or (3) ADHD will help you evaluate whether your behavior is something you want to be doing or something you want to change or treat. Unsure if you have ADHD? For a diagnosis, consult a family physician/internist, a therapist, a neurologist, a psychologist, a psychiatrist, or a social worker.

When Multitasking Reflects Flexibility

Flexibility is important if you are to be an effective time manager. Knowing when to stop what you're doing and switch to something else is an extension of the multitasking concept. Here are some examples of when switching to another task can actually turn

MULTITASKING DO'S AND DON'TS

If you're feeling the strains of managing too many responsibilities at once, try the following handy tips:

1. Whenever possible, work on one thing at a time.

2. If you have to do more than one thing at a time, as you switch back and forth among concerns always give whatever you are doing at that moment your complete attention.

3. Unlike doing too much at once, multitasking means that all the projects you are juggling are priority concerns. If it is not a priority, you should be saying no to a task, or staggering your deadlines so you can attend to the other projects when your key tasks are completed.

4. If you've gotten into the habit of multitasking, it's going to be a challenge to change your behavior. Take it a step at a time and reward yourself for little changes. If you used to do four tasks at once, cut down to three, then from three to two, and finally from two to one. Your increased focus and efficiency may astound you (and others around you).

out to be the best use of your time that moment, that day:

- The muse strikes you with a brilliant idea. If you don't write down that idea at that very moment or talk into a tape recorder and create a permanent record of it, you might lose that thought forever.

- The competing project or assignment is time-sensitive and is an even greater priority than the one you're working on.

- Your boss tells you that something needs to be done now, and you know from previous encounters with your boss that he or she will not wait.

- New information forces you to dramatically shift your focus or extend a deadline. Examples might include a new invention, a timely release by the competition, or someone beating you to market with a similar product.

7 WAYS TO DEAL WITH TOO MANY PULLS ON YOU

If you're not truly multitasking, but rather saying yes to too many tasks, and you would like to free up your time, try some of the following suggestions to clear your plate:

1. Create a to-do list ordered by priority. List the most important thing you need to do first. Make sure you list each and every task that you have to accomplish. (Break up larger tasks into smaller, more manageable actions.)

2. Try to stay on task until you complete one priority project before shifting to another task. Make sure you carry over to the next day's to-do list any items that were not completed the day before.

3. Delegate any nonessential tasks that others can do as well as or better than you can. Spend your time and energy on those items that only you can do (or that you can do far better than others).

4. Learn to say, "No, thank you" or at least, "I'll get back to you" so you give yourself time to evaluate if a new demand on your time is a worthwhile priority or just a pull.

5. Learn your limitations—how much you can comfortably juggle before you feel overwhelmed and out of time. If you think you have too much to do, you're probably right.

6. Get in touch with the calm feeling you experience when you're focused and not pulled in too many directions. Become comfortable being in that state of tranquility as you no longer need, nor are addicted to, the adrenaline rush of the frenzied, hyperactive style of work or leisure activities that you may have gotten used to.

7. You should be able to point to each hour, day, or week and see what you have actually accomplished during that time frame. If you can't, you're probably spinning your wheels and/or trying to do too much at once. Go back to #1 on this list and apply the to-do technique of keeping track of your priorities on an hourly basis, until you are more in control of your time.

Learning to Say No

How can you get a better grip on your work focus? What is a fast way of getting your priorities out in the open for you to see and accomplish? Learning to say no to every-thing that is not a priority is a big step. Not only is it hard for most of us to say and hear "no," it's even harder to say it in a pleasant and inoffensive way.

Certainly it's important for you to know what your priority tasks are and for you to make sure you put in the time to accom-plish those tasks. However, be gracious and tactful about who you state your priorities to and how you express them. It might be more alienating than helpful to state too bluntly to others, when they make a request that you'd like to turn down, "Sorry, that's not my priority right now." Learn to say no in a way that is positive, kind, and gentle. Say no to others in the way you would want it said to you.

IT'S NOTHING PERSONAL

To focus on your priorities, it is helpful to get over seeing no as rejection. The reality is that no one can do everything today. Just because the Internet, e-mail, and cell phones make all of us more accessible to a wider population, it's still important to prioritize what you say yes to in your work and your personal life.

When you do have to say no, make it clear that you are rejecting the request, not the person who is making the demand. The person you say no to today may be the same person you want to say yes to tomorrow. Avoid alienating anyone by being insensitive.

Usually when people ask you for some-thing, they are looking to solve a problem. If you cannot solve their problem, but you know someone who can, referring them to

that person may be appreciated more than a flat turn-down. You may also find it easier to stay on top of your own priorities if, when you do say no to those things that are outside your focus, you say, "No, but maybe at a later date," or "No, but maybe someone else can help you," and the like. This may help you to feel less angst than giving a definitive "no."

HOW TO TURN A NO TO THIS INTO A YES TO THAT

Too many of us are all-or-nothing people. In some instances, that is an incredible time waster. It's okay to be decisive; being deci-sive usually saves you time. But in some cases, saying (or accepting) no without offering an alternative wastes an enormous amount of time. All your initial efforts have now led to a dead end.

When's the last time you called someone and asked for an interview, or an appoint-ment, and you accepted a no rather than trying to turn it into a yes—for another time, another project, or even another person. There is so much effort that goes into an initial connection; every time you take a no and let that be the end of the relationship, you are wasting far more time than you can imagine because you have to start from scratch with someone else.

This is a powerful tool that I am offering to you—very powerful indeed. Try it not just at work but in your personal life and see how much more you accomplish. Here's another variation on the theme: If you have to cancel a meeting or someone has to cancel a lunch or another appointment, try to reschedule another meeting right away. Avoid letting it drift into something vague like, "Let's get back in touch with each other in a month." No, you're both busy and a month will come and go before you know it.

You may forget, he may forget, or you'll both be so busy there's no time left. Mark an alternative "yes" in your appointment books now and see how much time you save.

15 WAYS TO SAY NO GRACIOUSLY

Being able to say no will help you avoid doing too many things at once, as well as doing things you don't really want to do or that are not in your best interest. Here are 15 ways to say no gracefully:

1. "No, thank you."

2. "I'm sorry but I have a deadline and can't do anything until I finish the project I'm working on."

3. "I'm overcommitted right now, so I reluctantly have to say no."

4. "I'm flattered that you asked me, but regrettably I have to say no thank you."

5. "Unfortunately, I already have a conflicting commitment for that date."

6. "Thank you for asking, but I'm not available right now."

7. "I'm unavailable now. Would you get back to me on _____ [fill in time period]?"

8. "I can't accept, but would you like me to suggest someone else for you to contact?"

9. "I'm sorry, but please understand that I have to be firm about this: *No* means no."

10. "No, thank you. My family has asked me to spend more time with them."

11. "I just accepted another assignment that won't allow me to devote the time I would need to your project."

12. "I think so highly of you and your association [organization, company, etc.], but I'm unable to accept your gracious offer."

13. "Sorry, I'm going away on a trip, and I'm trying to finish up everything on my plate right now and not start anything new until I return."

14. "I don't think so, but I could get back to you in a couple of weeks if you can give me more time to decide."

15. "I really want to say yes, but I just have to say no. Please try to understand."

Use the space below to write down your own variations on this theme of saying no graciously so you'll have several ways of expressing yourself that are comfortable for you the next time you're asked to do something that conflicts with your priorities right now.

16. _____

17. _____

SIGNS OF STRESS

Are you overly stressed? Take the following quiz to find out. (*Please note:* This test is not intended as a diagnostic tool or as a substitute for taking a medical stress test administered by a physician, a cardiologist, a technician, or a nurse. It is for general information only.) Answer yes or no to the questions that follow.

1. **I lose my temper at least once a week.**

Yes _____   No _____

2. **I am chronically late by 10 minutes or more.**

Yes _____   No _____

3. **I grab meals on the run.**

Yes _____   No _____   Sometimes _____

4. **I have trouble sleeping through the night.**

Yes _____   No _____   Sometimes _____

5. **I fail to mail letters that I write.**

Yes _____   No _____   Sometimes _____

6. **I fail to return phone calls that I want to return within a reasonable period.**

Yes _____   No _____   Sometimes _____

7. **I do not send thank-you notes, but I want to.**

Yes _____   No _____   Sometimes _____

8. **I forget the birthdays of my closest friends or relatives.**

Yes _____   No _____   Sometimes _____

9. **I forget important appointments or have to reschedule the same appointment multiple times.**

Yes _____   No _____   Sometimes _____

10. **I yell at my children or partner more than usual.**

Yes _____   No _____   Sometimes _____

11. **At least one person has said to me recently, "You seem stressed."**

Yes _____   No _____   Sometimes _____

12. **I feel breathless or frustrated, as if I just don't have enough time.**

Yes _____   No _____   Sometimes _____

13. **To recover from my workweek, I spend the weekend sleeping in, overeating, zoning out in front of the TV, or online, rather than interacting with others.**

Yes _____   No _____   Sometimes _____

14. **I overreact to being ignored, questioned, or criticized.**

Yes _____   No _____   Sometimes _____

15. **Lately I have been overeating, drinking, or taking medications to calm myself down.**

Yes _____   No _____   Sometimes _____

EVALUATING YOUR ANSWERS

Look over your answers. If you answered yes or sometimes to 2 or more questions, you are showing signs of stress. If you marked yes or sometimes to 3 to 5 questions, your stress situation is more severe. If you answered 6 or more questions with a yes or sometimes, you should immediately deal with any factors you can change that will reduce your stress. And if you answered yes to questions 1, 2, 4, 9, 10, 11, 12, 13, or 15, you need to look at how your job is stressing you out, and what you can do about it.

Coping with Work-Related Stress

Taking on too many tasks at once can make you feel overwhelmed or stressed out; work-related stress can cause heart attacks, high blood pressure, sleep deprivation, as well increase the likelihood of getting into a work-related accident. A key theme of *Work Less, Do More* is that we can't control our world, but we can control (or at least try to regulate) ourselves. You may have to work with someone who is difficult to be around or put up with aspects of your job that you dislike, but cutting down on stress by controlling how many tasks you work on simultaneously is one way to manage work-related stress.

Here are some other tips for reducing work-related stress:

- Try to leave the office behind when you finish work, shutting down your computer and turning off your cell phone, or at least trying to screen calls so you only take those that are truly urgent. You need your nonwork time to replenish yourself and reconnect with your family and friends. As noted earlier, making work too much a part of your life in the short and long run can lead to increased stress and burnout, which will waste more time than pacing yourself appropriately—balancing your work and your life—in the first place.

- Build efficiency breaks into your workday to cut down on stress.

- Take lunch, even if it's only thirty minutes. Try to get away from your desk to eat it: Go to the cafeteria or take your lunch to a park near the office. Change your routine of eating hunched over your computer.

- If possible, use part of your lunch hour to exercise. If your company has a health club on site, that's great. If not, see if there's one nearby that you could join or take a class at the local Y. Even a walk around the block can be effective if your job has you sitting all day. Conversely, if your job has you on the go all day—for example, if you're out in the field, a nurse working in the critical care unit, or a teacher standing in front of students all day—use your lunch hour and your efficiency breaks to sit down. Vary what you've been doing all day to help reduce your stress.

- Exercise before or after work, and on weekends (in moderation, of course). As a producer with a high-pressure job put it: "If I didn't head to the Y on a regular basis to just get on the treadmill, I'd be a basket case."

- Squeeze a stress ball.

- Have low-calorie and healthy snacks available that you can eat if you're especially stressed.

- Avoid caffeinated beverages—coffee, tea, soft drinks—when you're very stressed. If you like those beverages, try the decaffeinated versions instead.

- Keep a journal. Write about your feelings, of course being careful not to leave it sitting around on your desk at work. Social scientists have found that even the act of writing in a journal can help you deal with stress.

- Meditate.

- Try yoga.

- If you're dealing with a difficult person or persons, remember that it's not about you, it's about them. Avoid antagonizing this person further, but don't take his or her demanding personality as a reflection on you.

- Talk to the person who is stressing you out and let him or her know how you are feeling. Make some suggestions about how you two can interact so it's less stressful for you. (Proceed with caution, of course, if the person stressing you out is your boss or if you have any fears that this person is emotionally disturbed or potentially violent. Also assess if the person you're asking to change is someone who welcomes feedback or who will take it badly and retaliate by giving you a bad evaluation, passing over you for plum projects, or even labeling you as someone who can't handle stress well.)

BEAT THE CLOCK

1. Consider the jobs you do that you could easily combine together, multitasking efficiently. Make a list here but make sure you don't list anything that could compromise your safety or the quality of your work.

   While I _____

   I could _____.

   While I _____

   I could _____.

2. Is your workplace or job stressful? What can you do to lower the stress level? See if your coworkers, subordinates, boss, clients, or customers will work with you to reduce stress at work. Consider creating a suggestion box that you leave on a table in the lunchroom or near the coffeemaker, and label it Stressbusters or something similar.

   Review the suggestions regularly, alone or at the beginning or end of the meeting of a team, department, or of the whole company. (For more stress-reducing suggestions, see the sections on technostress at the end of Day 8.)

3. When is the last time you said no to something that you really wanted to do but knew it was not the best use of your time? How did it feel? Did you feel guilty afterwards or proud of yourself? If you haven't said no to a nonpriority task lately, are you finding yourself overcommitted? Think about everything you have to do tomorrow. Is there anything you agreed to that you should have turned down? If there is, what can you do about it now? Is there a graceful way to get out of it without offending anyone or hurting your reputation? Start keeping track of all the times you say yes when you should have said no.

DAY
6

Getting Organized

What are the consequences of disorganization or using outdated information? The costs may be embarrassing or even life-threatening. For example, it's embarrassing if you miss a business dinner because you misplaced the invitation or forgot to write the date in your appointment book. But it's life-threatening if a laboratory's disorganization causes an administrator to send out the wrong lab result to a patient, who fails to get early treatment for a curable disease since the patient does not learn in a timely fashion that she has the illness. It is critical if disorganization causes a military operation to use an outdated map for a bombing mission that results in hitting the wrong target, killing innocent civilians, and creating a diplomatic storm of protest.

Disorder can cause increased stress and, as we have seen, stress is both the cause and the consequence of poor time management. It may not be that easy to deal with some causes of stress, such as the challenge of coping with a tough work situation, economic hardships, a recent promotion that includes unfamiliar job duties, or problems with which your family or friends are struggling that you feel helpless to assist with. Fortunately, disorder is one cause of stress that does have some clear and relatively easy solutions. Take the quiz titled Signs of Disorder to see if you have disorder issues that you need to deal with.

SIGNS OF DISORDER

See how many of the following typical signs of disorder you can relate to. Answer the following questions with yes or no; keep track of your answers.

1. I misplace a file at least once a week.

Yes _____ No _____

2. I misplace my car keys, house keys, or eyeglasses more than once in a great while.

Yes _____ No _____

3. I regularly misplace a phone number or the name of someone I need or want to contact.

Yes _____ No _____

4. I find myself going to a meeting without a key file because I could not find it in time.

Yes _____ No _____

5. I wonder, "What should I be doing now?"

Yes _____ No _____

6. I find out that someone I want to impress is visiting my office, and it takes more than 20 minutes to clean my desk.

Yes _____ No _____

7. I can't remember the last time I saw the top of my desk.

Yes _____ No _____

8. I would send out a mailing to my key clients or customers, but since I have not been maintaining my database on a regular basis, I first have to find and/or update that information.

Yes _____ No _____

9. I can't find the file stored in my computer that is the most recent version of a document I have been writing.

Yes _____ No _____

10. I burst out, on a regular basis, "Why can't I find anything that I need?" or similar words.

Yes _____ No _____

11. I pay late fees on credit cards because I get my payment in too late more than once a year.

Yes _____ No _____

12. I discover that I've made two appointments for the same time.

Yes _____ No _____

EVALUATING YOUR ANSWERS

If you answered yes to 2 or more questions, you have disorder that is slowing you down and decreasing the joy in your life, as well as potentially sabotaging your ability to do things effectively and efficiently. If you had 3 to 5 positive responses, you are in such a state of disorder that it's probably increasing your stress level. If you had 6 or more yes answers, you are so chronically disorganized that it may be jeopardizing your job as well as seriously impacting how you handle your time as you spend more and more minutes, hours, and even days searching for missing files or rewriting letters or reports that you already finished but cannot locate.

How to Combat Disorder

Here are some effective ways to organize yourself and your materials:

- Organize by a principle: by date (chronologically), by category, by file color, or alphabetically.

- Rearrange your materials so that files or books related to current, active projects are close at hand, as well as supplies you use every day.

- Group similar tasks together. (See the Repetitive Tasks Organizer box.)

- Eliminate clutter: Discard, give away, pass along, recycle, or sell unnecessary items.

- Make a commitment to getting and staying organized as part of your job, not something you will do when you get around to it.

- Have a master appointment book or calendar where you record all your upcoming meetings. See Figure 6-1 for an example of an efficient organizer.

- Whether you use an electronic or a paper organizer, use this central place to store phone numbers and reminders and to schedule projects and appointments, both business and personal, since each will probably impact on the other.

- If you use an electronic appointment book or organizer, back up your data.

Fig. 6-1. *An ideal appointment book allows you to see your week at a glance.*

TIME	MONDAY	TUESDAY	WEDNESDAY	THURSDAY	FRIDAY
5 a.m.					
6 a.m.					
7 a.m.					
8 a.m.					
9 a.m.					
10 a.m.					
11 a.m.					
12 p.m.					
1 p.m.					
2 p.m.					
3 p.m.					
4 p.m.					
5 p.m.					
6 p.m.					
7 p.m.					
8 p.m.					
9 p.m.					
10 p.m.					
11 p.m.					
12 a.m.					
SATURDAY:					
SUNDAY:					
NOTES:					

REPETITIVE TASKS ORGANIZER

Do you perform tasks regularly that you could be organizing more efficiently, rather than reinventing the wheel each time you do them? For example, do you have a master list of upcoming meetings or dates that you can incorporate into your planning calendar going forward, so you can budget your time accordingly? Are there supplies that you or your assistant have to reorder regularly? If so, do you have those specifics noted so that you don't need to keep looking up preferred brand names and order information? Do you have a system for regular updating, backing up, scanning, or purging paper or electronic files? Make a master list of tasks for yourself like the one below.

Tasks done daily:

_____

_____

_____

Tasks done weekly:

_____

_____

_____

Tasks done monthly:

_____

_____

_____

Tasks done semi-annually:

_____

_____

_____

Tasks done yearly:

_____

_____

_____

Organizing Your Office

Having a space where you can function well is key to maximizing what you accomplish when you're in that space. Of course, not everyone has total control over his or her workspace. If you have a home-based office, or if you're the owner of the company that you work for outside your home, you'll probably have a lot more say about furniture, equipment, and even what you can hang on the walls than if you're a typical employee. But everyone has *some* control over his or her office space, even if it's just what's kept on the desk, whether or not there are piles of papers on it, or how the desk is positioned within your office, if you're lucky enough to have an office. How to create and maintain an effective office filing system will be discussed in Day 7. At this point, let's address key considerations for organizing your office.

I first learned about the value of using a chair or desk designed with ergonomics in mind when researching my book *Making Your Office Work for You* in the late 1980s. At that time, ergonomically designed office furniture—designed to boost productivity by improving users' comfort—was very expensive and not as widely appreciated as it is today. Today, you can get a chair for less than $100 that is designed according to ergonomic standards, so you are less likely to get a backache. To help yourself work more efficiently, look at your office chair. Is it ergonomically designed? Some indications include padded sections and movable parts that adjust to your back or arms. In general, if your chair is in one piece—if it looks more like the kind of chair you would find at a kitchen or a dining room table than at a desk in an office—it's probably not an ergonomically designed chair. If the chair is not ergonomically designed, consider replacing it with one that is, since most office jobs require you to be at a desk for some or most of the day.

In addition to organizing your office so the furniture meets ergonomic standards, you might want to consider the impact that color has on your productivity. Everyone reacts differently to color. What colors promote *your* concentration and focus? What about lighting? There are entire books on the topic of organizing your office, but, for starters, look at the space where you work. Use the worksheet titled What Is Your Office Like Now? to consider the different components of your office space. Check the correct choice for your situation.

When's the last time you looked at your office space and organized it for effectiveness and efficiency? Who originally set up your office, and when? Was there a master plan?

Consider all your answers on the worksheet opposite about how your office is currently organized. Now consider what you would prefer to do with your office—add shelves, take away shelves, add another desk, or a sofa instead of two chairs? You want your office to be efficient for your particular kind of job, but you also want it to be comfortable and inviting. You will, after all, be spending hundreds of hours in it—as many as 160 to 200 hours a month if you work 8 to 10 hours a day or 40 to 50 hours a week when you're not in the field or at home.

WHAT IS YOUR OFFICE LIKE NOW?

MY OFFICE SPACE IS A:

_____ Separate outside (non–home-based) office space with a door

_____ Separate outside office cubicle

_____ Bullpen (open office)

_____ Home-based office

    _____ Separate room

    _____ Corner of a room (kitchen, family room, bedroom, etc.)

_____ Other _____

WINDOWS:

How many? _____

Do you face the window? _____

What can you see out of the window? _____

WALLS:

Color: _____

How many? _____

What are you allowed to put on the walls? _____

FLOOR:

Color: _____

Type of floor (carpet, wood, area rug, other) _____

NOISE:

What sounds do you hear? _____

From other offices? _____

From outside? _____

FURNITURE:

What kind of desk do you use? _____

Chair? _____

File cabinets? _____

Bookcases? _____

Storage containers for supplies _____

Here are some basic organizing principles to keep in mind for your office space:

- If your office is filled with clutter, consider putting your papers away in drawers or storage units, rather than allowing piles to rise on your desk.

- Schedule regular clean-up times, preferably daily but at least weekly, so you maintain an organized workspace.

- Shift to a completely or partially paperless office, implementing the suggestions offered in Day 7 for dealing with paperwork, including correspondence (but be careful to back up your electronic files in multiple ways).

- Have files or supplies that you use regularly nearby and accessible.

- Where will your visitors sit? Make sure you provide a comfortable chair for one or more visitors.

- Consider having two office spaces: a public office space where you receive visitors, which you keep completely organized and clutter-free; and a second space where you actually do your work, away from prying eyes. One office I visited accomplished this by having a large folding screen that stood at the back of the one-room office, closing off the desk where this professional did her writing, reading, and busywork.

Organizing Your House or Apartment

Even if you have little control over the setup of your office, you certainly have a lot more say in how your house or apartment is organized. If you're reading this book in your home right now, stop for a moment and look around. What do you see? Is it clutter-free and well-organized, or are there piles of papers, coats, shoes, and other items covering the floor, furniture, and tabletops?

ORGANIZING YOUR WARDROBE

Have every household member go through his or her wardrobe. (You probably will have to help the children in the household to do this.) Have everyone prune their wardrobe by giving away or discarding any item that does not fit, is not a favorite piece of clothing, is in poor condition, or will never be worn again. Donate or sell anything that you or your family members don't absolutely love to wear. The fewer items in your wardrobe, the faster you can look through what you have and the less time it will take you to decide what to wear.

You can organize your wardrobe by category—pants in one place, blouses next, followed by suits and dresses—sorted by color as well as by season. You may find that you possess items with nostalgia value, with which you don't want to part, even though it's unlikely you'll ever wear them again. Examples may include your wedding dress, the first holiday gift your spouse gave you, period pieces of clothing that you may not want to currently wear but you want to keep for posterity, or two or three outfits your children wore when they were infants or toddlers. Store these items in another part of your house or apartment to which you do not need ready access.

ORGANIZING YOUR SPACE

Tackle one room at a time, beginning with the room you use the most. Start with your kitchen, or family room, or even your bedroom, if that's where you spend the most time. Consider this room. What are the activities that take place there? I'll list some possibilities; add to the list if any activities are missing.

- Watching TV or movies
- Playing video games
- Entertaining
- Reading
- Eating
- Cooking
- Playing games or cards
- Listening to music
- Exercising
- Using the computer
- Sleeping
- _____
- _____

Do any of these activities require materials such as books, DVDs, CDs, or a music system? If so, how do you display the equipment or store the supplies? How did you organize this room initially? Did you hire a decorator or do it yourself? When was the last time you considered how this room is set up and how it functions? How old were you? How old were your family members? Have you done any rearranging or reorganizing as your children have matured? Does the room reflect your current tastes and hobbies?

If you're not completely satisfied with how this room is organized, consider creating a new master plan for the space. (If you're satisfied with how this room is organized, move on to the next candidate for reorganization, such as your kitchen, basement, bedroom, or garage.) Sketch the basic shape of the room on a piece of paper, or use the drawing tools on your computer. Make sure to include any windows, doors, doorways, or other openings.

If you like your existing furniture, draw those items on your home reorganizing sheet. However, unless you're completely satisfied with the current location of each piece, let your imagination go and consider new possibilities. Do you want to move your sofa to an opposite wall? Would you like to replace the love seat with two comfortable chairs? What about trading your three-person sofa for a sectional that would seat four to six? If you have another room where you could temporarily store your furniture while you imagine these possibilities, you might want to do so to free up the space. After all, if you have been living with a certain arrangement for 5, 10, or 20 years (or even longer), you might find it difficult to envision any other way of organizing the space. It might be easier to imagine other options if the space is as empty as it was when you first moved in.

Once you've dealt with your furniture, start to position your storage units, or consider purchasing new ones. What will you store in each unit? Are items currently in view, giving the room a cluttered look? Could you instead relocate those items to a closet so the room is more clutter-free? What are you storing in the closets now? What might be stored?

Continue going through your house or apartment, organizing one room at a time. Or, tackle one specific area at a time such as closets; shelves, including the pantry; storage units; drawers; wall hangings; and knickknacks.

Remember these tips when reorganizing your home:

- Always consider function as well as aesthetics. Yes, that DVD/CD holder is attractive, but if it's a real dust catcher you might want to select a different storage unit.

- Work with organizational or decorating experts, if possible, even if you just go for a consultation and implement the suggestions yourself.

- When selecting new furniture, storage units, or decorations, consider how it will stand up to factors specific to your home or apartment, such as pets (who may shed hair, and chew or scratch leather upholstery if they have claws), and children or teenagers. Keep in mind that certain fabrics and colors are more durable and practical than others.

- Eliminate clutter by going through everything in the room, especially those items that are visible, and giving away, recycling, throwing away, or moving to storage anything that is unnecessary, outdated, or useless.

- Establish a rule that everything should have a specific place where it is kept and, if it's removed from that location, it should be returned there (and not piled up or misplaced).

1. Look at your desk. Don't rearrange a thing; just look at it. Is it messy or is it organized and neat? If it's messy, take out your appointment book and see when you can block out at least one hour to turn your attention to cleaning up your desk. Make an appointment with yourself to tackle your desk, a commitment to yourself as definite as an upcoming priority business meeting.

2. Select a place, such as the top of your desk, and reorganize it alphabetically, chronologically, or by priority, file color, category, or number. For example, let's say there are lots of files on the top of your desk, as well as yesterday's mail and a stack of papers you were planning to file. In the midst of all these papers is the proposal that you're working on that's due at the end of the day. That's your priority project, which you want nearby. Move the other papers to another place, perhaps the top of a file cabinet across from your desk. If you have time to file away the nonpriority papers, you could do that as well.

3. What are the organizing principles for each of your major storage areas at work? If you lack satisfactory organizing principles, create them now: Organize items chronologically, by file color, alphabetically, by category, by assigned number, or by urgency.

4. Write down where you keep each item: pens, last year's daily calendar, the dictionary, medical records, a scissors, different-size batteries, and contact information for 50 key business contacts. By writing down where you keep pivotal items or the information necessary to run your office, you will be that much closer to developing an organizational system, or at least a list that you could systematically organize. You may want to create or purchase a database that manages your business contact information. Until you do, having a list of 50 key business contacts that you update regularly will cut down on the frustration and time spent searching for someone's name, e-mail, or phone number on a slip of paper or trying to locate that person's business card from months or years ago.

5. Start clipping out of magazines and newspapers (or finding online) examples of organized houses or apartments that you would like to emulate. What about those spaces is commendable? Are there any clear organizing principles that you could adapt to your space? Are there local organizers, closet experts, or decorators who could help you reorganize your home space if you think you need additional help?

6. Pick one closet in your house. Look inside it. What do you see? Is it organized according to any principles? For example, are frequently used items located near the front or are items organized by color, function, or age? Analyze what should be stored in this closet and why. Is there any other way to reorganize the closet that would be efficient and effective? Could some of the items stored in this closet be relocated to a less accessible area if those items are rarely used?

DAY

7

Simplifying and Mastering Paperwork

Do you have piles of important papers mixed in with junk mail that you wish you could efficiently file and retrieve, as needed? Have you dreamt of moving toward a paperless office but seem to have more paper to sort through than you did when you used a typewriter? In this chapter, on this day, you will learn some basic techniques for achieving the goal of properly managing paper. Whether you mainly file electronically on your hard drive or to an external electronic source or you still get some or all of your information as hard copy—catalogs, journals, magazines, newspaper clippings, hard copies of e-mails, books, or reports—this chapter will help you to determine what really needs to be kept and to quickly and easily retrieve this paperwork.

An Ounce of Prevention: Getting a Grip before You're Drowning in a Sea of Paper

How can you deal more effectively with all this paperwork? Here are some suggestions:

- Don't bring it into your office in the first place. When you pick up your mail, try to read it or open it with a garbage can or recycling bin nearby, tearing up and discarding or recycling materials that you want to deal with quickly.

- Become ruthless and firm about what you do with paper in your office. Rather than putting it in a pile:
    - Throw it out.
    - Shred it and then throw it out.
    - Recycle it.
    - Pass it along to someone else.
    - Scan it and save it electronically.
    - File it.

- Set aside a regular time to sort through your paperwork.

- Get off mailing lists or cancel publications (or switch to the electronic version).

TYPES OF PAPERWORK

What paperwork are you dealing with? It will help for you to clarify just what you need to be concerned with on a daily, regular, or occasional basis. Check off every type of paperwork that you need to store and/or retrieve in your office:

_____ Catalogs

_____ Magazines

_____ Journals

_____ Newspapers

_____ Specific newspaper articles

_____ Legal documents

_____ Reports

_____ Tax returns

_____ Receipts

_____ Cards (greeting, employee, or customer recognition, holiday)

_____ Memos

_____ E-mails (hard copy)

_____ Contact information

_____ Books

_____ Booklets

_____ Instructional manuals

_____ Warranties

_____ Employee evaluations

_____ Report cards (for students)

_____ Bank statements

_____ Phone plan document

_____ Record of mailing

_____ Record of gift giving

_____ Daily planner

_____ Weekly schedule

_____ Other

_____

_____

_____

_____

_____

_____

USEFUL EQUIPMENT FOR MANAGING PAPER

To help you simplify and master your paperwork, have the following equipment available to you:

FOR FILING

- Filing cabinets (vertical and horizontal)
- File folders (manila and hanging)
- File labels
- Bulletin board
- Bookcases
- Shelves
- Storage cabinets
- Container with small compartments for supplies
- Scanner
- Shredder
- Garbage can and/or recycle bin

FOR STORING ELECTRONIC FILES

- A second or third computer
- External hard drive
- Memory or travel stick (flash drive)
- DVDs
- CDs
- An outside, reliable, confidential service to back up data

FOR ORGANIZING PAPERWORK ON THE DESK

- Metal, wood, leather, or plastic organizers, in graduated steps for easy visibility of files
- A vertical or horizontal system with slots, available in a range of heights and widths
- Plastic or metal boxes, single or stackable
- Wicker baskets of varying sizes

FOR LABELING

- Label machine with a keyboard
- Software that enables you to create and print labels with your regular printer
- Labels available in various sizes for printing out or handwriting

FOR CUTTING DOWN ON PAPERWORK

- Scanner
- Paper shredder and/or a shredding service that regularly visits your office and shreds and disposes of papers for you.

The Importance of a Filing System

Filing is one of the necessary aspects of office work, especially for those in the information management and retrieval businesses like publishing, writing, research, teaching, advertising, publicity or for service providers like doctors, dentists, optometrists, psychologists, coaches, consultants, accountants, real estate agents, safety inspectors, and a host of other jobs or occupations. Filing is pivotal for those who have clients, patients, or customers and who have to create, maintain, and keep track of key information about those individuals or accounts, such as, in addition to those listed above, attorneys, therapists, speakers, meeting planners, manufacturers, website designers, computer consultants . . . the list goes on and on.

In today's competitive business world, whether it's an executive filing copies of correspondence, an arbitrator organizing her caseload, or a screenwriter keeping track of the registration of his original work and the submission history of his screenplays, the ability to file—and to effectively maintain files and retrieve filed papers and other materials—has short- and long-term consequences.

I often hear this refrain: "I'd like to have a better filing system. I'll definitely get to it when I have time." When I ask what that person's job is, I'll hear a description of this or that specific task, but filing is rarely included as part of that job. Yet, having a dependable filing system is a crucial part of each person's job, even if it means just knowing to whom you delegate filing and making sure he or she has a reliable system that others are able to access. Just ask a patient whose physician has misplaced her file detailing ten years of office visits—as well as vital information about her weight, medications, and the results of key blood tests—whether faulty filing interferes with doing the "real" work.

Leaner Files in Less Time

You, your personal assistant, or the administrative assistant for the entire office has to do something with each and every piece of paper that enters your office. Those choices include:

- Filing the original.
- Making a copy of it and filing the original and the duplicate separately.
- Throwing out the original without keeping a copy—either whole, torn up, or shredded.

- Passing along the original to someone else to deal with.
- Scanning the original, maintaining the material electronically, and tossing out the original paper copy.
- Placing it in the recycle bin.
- Putting it in a "dump drawer" or leaving it on your desk, in a pile, until you decide what to do with it.

The last possibility is one of the least desirable, since pieces of paper have a way of accumulating quickly. Piles can become cumbersome, disorganized, and, if left on the floor, even dangerous. However, especially for those who do their own filing, unless there is an urgent reason to retrieve one of the accumulated pieces of paper, this may be the "filing" system that is most frequently employed. To avoid this option, ask yourself the following questions when dealing with each piece of paper:

DAY 7

1. Can someone else besides me readily find this piece of paper if I'm away or reassigned to another office?

2. Is there a filing system with a logical order to it that systematically places this piece of paper into a specific location?

3. Is there a master plan or instruction sheet accompanying the filing system that explains where or why this item is filed?

4. Are there other clear visual cues, such as labels on the file cabinet or clearly marked notebooks on a shelf, that advise me or the office staff that specific types of information will be found in this filing system?

As noted in the last chapter, there are several key ways to get organized. You can organize:

- Chronologically, by date (most recent or oldest first)
- By file color
- By importance, from more to less important, or vice versa
- Alphabetically, by last name, first name (for individuals), or by company or product names
- By category (creating master categories and subcategories within those master categories, also organized by an overriding principle, such as chronologically, alphabetically, or by file color)

Simple File Systems

You can put a basic filing system in place, or rearrange your current one, with the simplest of supplies: beige or color-coded manila file folders that you label by hand, using labels (single color or color-coded) that you print out on your computer or your typewriter or that you create and print out electronically. If you prefer a binder system to filing in a cabinet, you can use two- or three-ring binders of varying widths, from 1/2" to 4", organized by file tabs you can buy that are sized to the binder. Alternatively, you can make your own dividers by using tabs that you can add to any type of paper.

In the binders, you can store papers related to one type of material, such as "Human Resources documents" or "Rewards programs," or specific to a topic, such as "Surveys 1 to 100" or "Trade Show Exhibition and Attendance."

The advantage of using loose-leaf binders over files stored in a filing cabinet is that the notebooks are on a shelf and are therefore more visible. (Some people put files on shelves, color-coded, so the files are more visible. That's a compromise solution.)

Aside from tabs, if you choose to use the binder filing system, you'll want to purchase plastic holders or pockets that are open on one side so you can slip in items like photographs, booklets, or even DVDs.

On the spine of the notebook, use a labeler or a marker to indicate, in clear letters, what it contains. You may also find that a three-hole punch is useful, so you can adapt papers to fit into the notebooks.

Filing in Plain Sight

We've all heard the expression "out of sight, out of mind." This filing system is based on doing just the opposite: Theoretically, by "filing" important papers right on a bulletin board that you can easily see, you won't ignore them. You might post invitations for upcoming events on the bulletin board as well as schedules for projects with due dates, to-do lists, or other pieces of paper that can be grabbed at a moment's notice. The downside of using a bulletin board as a visual filing cabinet, or using the walls of your office or cubicle in the same way, is that this could contribute to clutter in your environment. If clutter makes it hard for you to concentrate, and contributes to distractionitis, having blank walls may be more effective for you. Take down all those slips of paper from your wall—or maybe just leave one or two—and see if you're more focused and productive as a result. If the bulletin board system works for you, then keep it. If it's slowing you down, reconsider it or maybe just rearrange what's on the bulletin board.

Overcoming Obstacles to Leaner Files

The more papers you have to go through to find what you need, the more likely it is that you'll be disorganized. There are lots of reasons that someone keeps excess paperwork or other clutter. There is the nostalgic type who holds on to clutter because there is something in that pile that he or she treasures from the past, whether it's an object or a piece of paper. Even a clipping from a newspaper can evoke a wave of memories for the nostalgic type. Other reasons people refuse to part with paperwork include:

- A fear of tossing out
- Indecisiveness about what you actually need
- A need to amass material (even if it's readily available through other sources)
- Procrastination

Let's explore some solutions to each of these obstacles that will help you have leaner files in no time.

FEAR OF TOSSING OUT

Insecurity about whether something is important can cause you to hold on to paperwork that is outdated or unnecessary. For each piece of paperwork, ask: "If I got rid of this item would I be able to easily replace it?" If the answer is yes, it should be easier to toss out that paperwork than if your answer is no. If it's something meaningful from your childhood or from your research or your career, and there is no other copy of it anywhere, consider keeping it. But if it's an article or item that you can easily retrieve from the archives of a publication or through a library database, keeping the physical material is not as crucial.

However, tax experts, like attorney Julian Block, emphasize that some caution when it comes to throwing things out is advisable. To have more confidence about what you should be throwing out and when, ask your accountant or read any of the books or free online publications from the IRS that specify how long to keep certain records and which ones to save. Block advises his clients to "err on the side of caution in deciding which files to save and which ones to toss out."

INDECISIVENESS ABOUT WHAT YOU ACTUALLY NEED

It may be the bigger picture that you need to address, not the paper clips or the file folders but what, exactly, are you dealing with at work? What are the projects you deem essential to your career? What are the plans you need to make and execute to help you manage your time more effectively? If you have a clear understanding of your job functions and what is important to you in the short and long term to do your job well, you will be more decisive about what to keep and what to heave. If necessary, review the job description you created on Day 3.

DAY 7

A NEED TO AMASS MATERIAL

For some, having lots of papers around provides comfort. They feel that they have the answer they're looking for somewhere in those piles, if they only could take the time to look. By having so much that needs to be sorted through, they can always imagine that the solutions are there—somewhere. If things were more streamlined, they might have to face the deficiencies in what they really have.

I have observed that there is a tendency to re-create externally the chaos that someone feels internally. So if you have a lot of clutter around and you're disorganized, you may have to dig deep inside yourself to see what is causing that disorder. Are you worried about something? Are you clear about the project you're supposed to be doing and confident in your ability to do it competently? Are you feeling overwhelmed and pressured?

PROCRASTINATION

This is the Rhett Butler excuse from Margaret Mitchell's epic Civil War novel, *Gone with the Wind:* "Frankly, my dear, I don't give a damn." If you are to make filing a priority, you need to care; you need to see it as fundamental to your efficiency, not something you put off again and again. If you're procrastinating about dealing with paperwork and other clutter, review the solutions for dealing with procrastination in Day 3.

GETTING RID OF CLUTTER

Allowing paperwork to pile up, rather than filing it, is a stopgap solution rather than one with a long-term positive outcome. Here are some tips for dealing with paperwork and other clutter:

- Help yourself by cutting down on accumulating new clutter. If your clutter is mainly paperwork, assess where the paper is coming from. Are you printing out every e-mail and then wondering where to file it? If so, consider alternatives, such as electronically backing up your e-mails so you don't accumulate lots of paper. Do you get a lot of magazines or newsletters that contribute to your clutter? Try to cut down on those subscriptions so you have less clutter to cope with. If there's an electronic version of some of the paper publications that you receive, switch to those versions.

- Are there legal or tax considerations relating to how long you need to keep papers that justify your clutter? If so, make sure you are up on the current requirements; you may be holding on to materials long past the time that is necessary, because you're basing what you're doing on outdated information.

- Try turning yours into a paperless office. This can save you both space and time spent filing. (We'll delve into the specifics of how to accomplish this later in this chapter.)

- Consider hiring someone to help you sort through the clutter—a professional organizer, for example. You could ask a coworker or friend to help you sort through your clutter—or at least be there when you're dealing with it—so you don't keep putting it off. Getting someone else involved will make you accountable to that person, and you'll be more likely to follow through on your commitment to get organized.

- Declare an Organization Day to get yourself and your office (or home) to the clutter-free state that you know you need to function more efficiently. Make the time to organize yourself from top to bottom. Do you need a new filing cabinet or should you just clean out the old one? Do you have enough file folders? How about a labeling machine to keep track of what's in each and every drawer? Would a color-coding system work for the kind of files you need to keep? Is there someone in your office who's in charge of such matters, or do you have to do it all?

BACKING UP, REVISITED

I can't stress this enough: Back up your electronic data often and, preferably, in multiple ways. The way you do so is not as important as backing up your data regularly and making sure the backup system is reliable. (For more on this topic, see Day 8.)

Help for the Chronically Disorganized

For some, getting rid of clutter is just a question of creating better systems that will catch the clutter before it proliferates. For others, the situation may be more dire.

The National Study Group on Chronic Disorganization (NSGCD) defines chronic disorganization as "having a past history of disorganization in which self-help efforts to change have failed, an undermining of current quality of life due to disorganization, and the expectation of future disorganization."

If you're in that category, your disorganization, which probably includes a clutter problem, is a chronic challenge. This means that as soon as the clutter is cleared, if it can be cleared at all, the volume quickly accumulates again, resulting in as much or more clutter than before.

For those who are chronically disorganized, clutter is as much an emotional issue as it is a time management concern. If clutter is something that you truly feel so attached to that giving it up feels as if you're giving up part of yourself, you may need to discuss this with a trained therapist or an organizer or coach who has an understanding of the depth of your challenges and the help you may need.

What's important to know is that there is help for the chronically disorganized. There are books for those with this kind of a severe clutter problem, such as Judith Kolberg's *Conquering Chronic Disorganization,* as well as organizers who specialize in the chronically disorganized, who are available for in-person or phone coaching. Referrals are provided by the National Study Group on Chronic Disorganization or the National Association for Professional Organizers, listed in the back of this book.

DAY 7

Taking Steps to Make Yours a Paperless Office

In order to move to a paperless office, you need reliable backup systems for your electronic files. If you're used to having one or more hard copies of every single electronic file that you write, including e-mails, then you're going to have a more difficult transition to a paperless office than will someone who is just fine with everything existing only within the computer. A scanner is one way to make the transition from paper to paperless, allowing you to turn paper into electronic files. Backing up the scanned files will also help allay fears of deleting scanned electronic versions of discarded original paperwork.

Developing and Maintaining an Up-to-Date Database of Key Contacts

For some professionals, such as publicists, meeting planners, fundraisers, financial consultants, commercial real estate brokers, and sales managers, their jobs are only as good as the databases they develop and maintain. The quality of a database is judged by the following criteria:

- How it's initially created (is it bought or is it customized?)
- Whether it's kept up-to-date
- How easily accessible any one piece of information is
- How extensive the information is (in addition to cell phone numbers and e-mail addresses, does the database contain useful personal or business data, such as date of birth, hobbies, and a history of phone, written, or in-person communications?)
- Whether it's backed up in one or more ways in case something happens to the original database

Scrambling for a piece of paper with a name and a phone number on it is a primary source of wasted time at work; by contrast, having a well-maintained database can be a real time saver. It can also lead to real money. I remember the anecdote that Texas-based speaker Ed Peters shared at a presentation that I attended in Manhattan a while back. Peters had been hired by a thoroughbred racetrack to help them sell more tickets. Peters soon discovered that the racetrack had been collecting information on every single attendee at the racetrack for years. What did they do with the information? They had not done anything with the slips of paper with the contact information; it was just kept in big boxes. As Peters explained to me when I asked him about that anecdote:

> I suggested that they hire me, and they did. My firm, the 4Profit Institute, entered all the information into a database and we ended up with 50,000 people who had visited the track. I designed a program where we sent a betting slip to everyone, guaranteeing the slip would be worth at least $2 and one would be worth $10,000. Result: 38% of the mailing—19,000 [people]—showed up to the track on the designated day. It was the largest non-special event crowd in the track's history.

What kind of database do you want to use? There are countless possibilities, starting with creating your own customized database, using the database option that your word processor offers, or purchasing a database program, such as Microsoft Excel, Microsoft Access, or ACT!. You might also use the address book included in your online service, such as aol.com, where you may include basic contact information as well as the person's web address, notes about his or her interests or job, or a record of your e-mail, phone call, or letter exchanges. There are also industry-specific, commercial databases you can purchase for a wide range of prices. One example is a database for publicists who need to contact the media, available for an annual fee from Cision (previously known as Bacon's), which charges to use its database on an annual basis. (Alternatively, users may buy a print version of the database organized by type of media or location, for example, and updated annually for a couple of hundred dollars.) If you use a handheld device such as a Palm Pilot or Treo, among other brands, you can use the information you store for placing phone calls as a database as well.

The first step in creating your own database is to put someone's contact information into some electronic format as soon as you get it, whether it's gotten through a phone call or a business card that you are handed at a trade show or at the end of a meeting. Do not let this information sit around. Do not talk to someone on the phone without getting all of his or her contact information, spelled correctly, and then entering it into a database of some kind. Why? Because tomorrow, next week or, even more likely, in six months, when you want to remember who that person was who you spoke to about x, y, or z, it will be difficult to find him or her if you don't have the information in a database with some kind of association to that person. Create a broad category association or, if possible, as specialized a category as possible to reinforce your memory. For example, within the broad category of "TV producers," you could organize your contacts alphabetically or geographically, by city. Or you could create a more specialized category, such as "TV producers of morning national talk shows" or "TV segment producers of national or syndicated shows." In addition, when you meet people, record their names and phone numbers, and the context in which you met them, in your daily diary. This way you may be able to track someone down by the day or month when you met him or her.

Your database can be more than just a place for contacts; it can become a record of various types of business interactions that you initiate or that are requested of you. It helps avoid that most frustrating time waster of all: "I know I spoke to someone about just this project a couple of months ago, but she said to give her a call after the first of the year and I can't remember her name or what company she was with."

In addition to, or in lieu of, a customized database, you may wish to purchase a commercial one, in electronic or print form. You may choose to edit information or add notes to any commercial database that you purchase. Be careful to periodically purchase a new print or electronic database, transferring your own notes and information to that commercial one. The years have a way of slipping by and if you're still customizing a commercial database that you purchased three, five, or more years ago, your basic data may be very out of date.

YOUR DATABASE

Your database can be more than just a place for contacts; it can become a record of various types of business interactions that you initiate or ones that are requested of you.

BEAT THE CLOCK

1. In order for databases to be time savers, some simple principles have to be followed, whether the database is created from scratch or purchased commercially for hundreds or thousands of dollars:

   - Keep it up-to-date. For customized databases, input any changes in someone's key contact information. For commercial databases, see whether you are provided with an update component free of charge, or if you have to purchase that option, regularly or once a year.

   - Back up the database at least two additional ways, especially if you're creating it from scratch. It will be time-consuming and, if you lose information that is not easily duplicated, virtually impossible to re-create the database if you lose your data.

   - Consider why you have contact information, as well as how you will group people together. Being able to quickly find someone is a time saver, but being able to find the right people (who will be pleased to hear from you and will respond quickly) is even more important.

   - Prune your database so you have a manageable number of entries. When I interviewed the late Muppets creator Jim Henson about his office, he shared with me that he tried to keep the holiday card list for his company to no more than one thousand.

2. What filing system do you use right now? Write down a description of how it works, as if you were going away for several weeks or even months and someone else had to maintain the files for you. How would you direct him or her to find or retrieve a specific item in the files?

3. Do you have any obstacles to having leaner files? If you do, what are those obstacles? What are you going to do to overcome those obstacles?

4. What system do you have for backing up your electronic data? How frequently do you back up? If you do not have a backup system, create one now, including a commitment to backing up at regular intervals.

More Effective Ways to Use the Phone and Other Equipment

While central to most jobs, the phone can be a huge time waster if you're not in control of it. In this chapter we'll discuss uses and misuses of the phone, so your phone use can become more effective. We'll also discuss other equipment and technology that may improve your efficiency, such as your computer and printer. We'll touch on PDAs, such as the BlackBerry®, but you'll find a more extensive discussion of these devices in the next chapter, Day 9. We'll conclude with a discussion of what's been called *technostress*—stress related to the use, or overuse, of technology, including spending too many hours each day staring at a computer screen.

What are the most common ways that the phone is misused during business hours?

- Taking too long to get to the reason for a call.
- Staying on the phone too long. (Keep a clock or egg timer next to your phone. Keep track of how long you talk.)
- Too much personal chitchat.
- Not enough "conversation" to facilitate a useful telephone exchange.
- Failing to return a phone call within a reasonable period.
- Being too abrupt or communicating negative feelings and thoughts that create distance with the caller and might even sabotage the business relationship.
- Failing to end the call by having an action plan for the next call or step (setting up a meeting, sending an e-mail or written communication, or following up in another specific way).

Reasons for Telephone Abuse

Why does someone misuse the phone, staying on too long for a business call, going into too much personal chitchat, straying from the point of the call, or talking on his or her cell phone in every conceivable situation, from walking up and down the office building corridor to riding in the elevator or the train (even in the "quiet" car)? Here are some common reasons.

Longwinded or Verbose Phone Abusers

There are some people who just don't know how to keep it short. For most of them, it's a lifelong habit that's going to be hard to break. The roots and cures are complex; if you fall into this category, you might want to get outside help for this tendency. Being longwinded can definitely hurt you in business, as you get a reputation for being a time-gobbler, about whom people say: "You'd

better have an hour or more if you're going to call so-and-so." This may lead to the gabber being left out of the loop in business or getting passed over for promotions, as well as failing to close sales or attain other results-oriented accomplishments that a specific job requires.

Poor Habits

Talking too long on the phone may just have become a bad habit. However, if it is not that ingrained it might be possible for someone to change, once the behavior is pointed out and the negative consequences of it are noted.

Problem with Endings or Closure

It's not that this person is longwinded or has gotten into the bad habit of staying on the phone too long; if someone has a problem with endings or closure, it's going to be tough to terminate a call. Such a problem may be a deep-seated challenge, dating back to the formative years when having to stop an activity or say good-bye without tears and tantrums was an issue that never got resolved over time. Practicing sample endings that you have scripted and placed at your fingertips may help you to break free of a conversation once its usefulness is over (discussed later in this chapter).

Lonely on the Line

The person you are calling may have a very full life, but perhaps he or she works alone and talking on the phone, even during business hours, breaks through that isolation. For some cell phone users, the phone enables them to feel connected to someone when they are alone and on their own—on trains, walking in the street, or in between appointments, for example. BCP (before cell phones) individuals like these would deal with their feelings of loneliness in other ways—some productive, such as structuring their workday so they worked in teams; some not so healthy, such as overeating, overspending, or avoiding the situation that was causing the feelings of isolation, like having to travel alone for business. The cell phone is an easy way to try to assuage feelings of loneliness, but if the cell phone is overused or misused, it has time consequences; worse, you can get labeled as someone who wastes others' time, if you are the one dialing for company. By misusing the

cell phone during business hours to avoid feelings of isolation, that cell phone caller is depriving himself or herself of the benefits of using that free time to plan, strategize, think, or even relax in between appointments or business calls.

Phone Log Review

Are you finding that the telephone moves your career along or is it soaking up time and interrupting you when you could be addressing higher-priority tasks? The first step is to analyze the phone logs that you made during Day 1 for your incoming and outgoing calls—for both your landline and your cell phone, if you use that for workday calls. (If you previously tracked a workday, you might also want to use the blank phone logs in the Appendix to monitor your use of the phone on a leisure day.) If you use your BlackBerry or PDA for phone calls, as well as for sending and receiving e-mail, include a log for that device as well.

Look over your phone logs. Do you see any patterns? Look at the times when calls come in as well as who is calling you. Are you the right person for those calls, or do a lot of those calls need to be redirected to someone else? Figuring out how to head off such misdirected calls at the pass will

PHONE MISUSE

Fill in any other reasons for misuse of the phone that you have encountered, or of which you have been guilty:

_____

_____

_____

definitely free up a lot of time (and eliminate distractions).

Now look at how long you're on the phone for each call. Is it more or less time than you expected? Look at whom each call was to (or from). What did you accomplish during that phone call, if anything?

Now that you have a clearer idea of how much time you are spending on your regular or cell phone, as well as who is calling you (and vice versa), look at the suggestions throughout this chapter to help you make more effective use of your phone.

Using Your Phone(s) More Efficiently

First of all, you need to decide if the phone is the most efficient way for you (and the person you're trying to reach) to communicate. Whenever possible, whether directly or indirectly, find out how each person you deal with at work and in your business prefers to communicate. (Note that the Assignment Sheet that I shared with you in Day 4 had a place to record each client's preferred way to communicate.) Use the Preferred Ways to Be Contacted survey in your initial conversation with someone, or at an appropriate time later on, to enhance your communications.

PREFERRED WAYS TO BE CONTACTED

Ask the person you're contacting the following: Please list, in order of preference, how you prefer to be contacted. Mark your top choice as #1, your second choice as #2, and so forth. If there are any extenuating circumstances that might change these answers, please indicate that as well.

_____ By phone

_____ Regular office phone

_____ Cell phone

_____ By e-mail

      _____ Regular e-mail address

      _____ Special work e-mail address

      _____ Personal e-mail address

_____ By instant messaging

_____ By BlackBerry or similar device

_____ By fax

_____ By letter

_____ By typewritten or handwritten memo sent through the mail

_____ In person

      _____ By appointment

      _____ By drop-in visit

      _____ Other (please list)

If there are extenuating circumstances that would change the recommended order of contacting you, such as emergencies, time-sensitive matters, breaking news, please indicate below:

_____

_____

_____

"I'M NOT A PHONE PERSON"

Knowing the way that someone you deal with in business prefers to be contacted not only saves you time, but can also move your business relationship along in a positive way. For example, some of us are just not phone people. You've heard them confess this: "I don't like to talk on the phone!" That's the kind of person you might communicate with much better by e-mail or even by fax. For some, it's a personality issue. For others, it's the nature of their work. Chuck Scott, who heads a technology company in Connecticut called The Avanti Group, Inc., explains why the phone does not work for him and his business: "The phone is a very inefficient means of communication. Yes, it is necessary and critical but best to keep it to an absolute minimum. Coding on servers takes tremendous concentration and complete focus and if distracted, even by a 10-minute call, it can take a half hour or more to get back into [the] rhythm, let alone [deal with] introduced mistakes."

If you're like Chuck Scott, you may want to minimize the phone in your business and to pay closer attention to dealing more effectively with e-mail (see Day 9). But even if you prefer to avoid using the phone, if you have to deal with others who do use it, the rest of this chapter may still be useful to you. You may also fall into an ever-growing category of professionals: those who stopped using the phone in favor of the seemingly more convenient use of e-mail or instant messaging, only to realize that their business was actually suffering from that lack of phone contact. Even though the phone can be potentially annoying and a time waster, especially if you find yourself in a time-consuming telephone tag situation, when you do actually talk to someone on the phone, hearing each other's voices, laughs, sighs, and even the sounds in the background, can be a bonding experience and a time saver in the long run. (You will find advice for cutting down on telephone tag later in this chapter.)

WHEN TIME IS MONEY

Maximizing your phone efficiency can yield a big payoff in terms of minutes a day, hours a week. This was dramatically illustrated in the movie version of the best-seller *The Pursuit of Happyness,* the autobiography of Chris Gardner, a high school dropout who went on to get an unpaid internship at a brokerage house, which led to a multimillion-dollar career. During his internship, Gardner had to place calls to prospective clients. The more calls he could make from his lead sheet, the greater the likelihood that he would land some viable leads. He figured out that if he didn't hang up the handset between calls, he could save eight minutes a day (or almost an hour a week). This competitive edge is part of what helped him to get hired out of a pool of 20 interns.

When's the last time you were so motivated to drum up business that you figured out where you could save, or find, an extra eight minutes each day? Consider your phone systems and how you could make improvements. You could purchase a phone that announces who's calling, saving you countless minutes by allowing you to prescreen callers. (This is different than having an answering machine that allows you to hear callers as they leave messages.) Caller ID lets you know who's on the line before the answering machine (or voice mail) picks up.

REACH OUT AND PHONE OTHERS

If your business depends on relationships, it may be a real time saver—if you've gotten out of the habit of calling clients, customers, or service providers—to just pick up the phone and make that call. Yes, in-person visits are even better, but it may not be possible to fly around the country or internationally if your clients, customers, or service providers are spread out over a huge distance. In most cases, the phone is still a good second choice (after in-person visits), followed by writing either e-mails or letters. The good news is that a little bit of phone calling goes a long way. Since communication is only 7% verbal and the rest is nonverbal, the phone provides more nonverbal cues than just e-mail or letters, such as the tone of your voice and the pauses between sentences. (See Figure 8-1.)

The phone also provides a back-and-forth to the conversation. Yes, instant messaging provides that same kind of back-and-forth, but you miss the nonverbal cues in an instant message and it's even harder to politely tell someone in an IM that it's not a good time to "talk" when you're "talking" electronically. (Instant messaging during one's leisure time or with one's family members or close friends is very different than when it is used in a business or work setting.)

Fortunately, there are low flat-fee services for calling long distance throughout the United States and even to other countries. There are also prepaid phone cards that may be purchased if you're fearful of running up too much of a phone bill on long-distance calls. Alternative services that use the Internet for the call may cost even less or, like Skype™, nothing at all. You don't have to stay on the phone for very long; you can just say "Hi," hear each other's voice, connect, and follow up with an e-mail, a handwritten or typed note, a card, or a letter. But get back into the phone habit. To save time, figure out when each person you're calling is more likely to be in his or her office so you will avoid voice mail or telephone tag. If you know someone is more likely to be available at 8:00 in the morning, call at that time. If he or she stays later than the rest of the company and you have the direct line so you can call even if the switchboard has closed down for the day (if applicable), call later in the day. But call, once a month, once a year, whatever it takes to keep that relationship going. If you see each other at trade shows or conferences, that's fine and dandy, of course, but call before or afterwards to say how nice it will be to see each other, or to review what you discussed at the show.

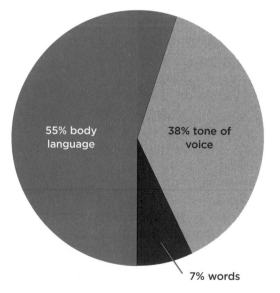

Fig. 8-1. How do we communicate? *Words represent only 7% of how we communicate. We express ourselves primarily through body language, including facial expressions (55%), and volume and tone of voice (38%). This figure is based on the research and writings of Albert Mehrabian, Ph.D.*

Phone Equipment Checkup

Recently, I was part of a five-way conference call. One of the callers was on speakerphone. She might have thought she was saving herself time, freeing her hands to do other things while still being part of the conference call, but every other word she said was obscured by her faulty speakerphone equipment. Someone finally said something to her about it: "Are you on speakerphone?" She agreed that she had been, she took herself off speakerphone, and the rest of the call went smoothly, and clearly, for everyone.

That experience was a good reminder of how important it is to make sure that the phone equipment you are using is in optimum condition. If you use a headset to make hands-free phone calls, make sure you can be heard clearly. If your cell phone has intermittent service in your office or when you're traveling, be careful to avoid starting calls in those situations, since you'll just frustrate yourself and whoever you're trying to talk to with unclear conversations or continual time-consuming hang-ups and redials.

Developing More Effective Telephone Skills

Fortunately, more effective telephone skills can be learned. Here are some suggestions:

1. Prepare a script or at least make notes before you make a call. Make sure to do the following:
   - Include an effective opening line(s).
   - Introduce yourself.
   - State why you're calling this particular person. Name-drop, use a referral, and/or mention an advertisement that he or she answered. Such referrals must be true, since you're establishing your credibility in this first phone call. Any exaggerations or lies will eliminate the chance of having a trusting working relationship now or in the future.
   - Say the person's name. (Everyone likes to hear his or her name spoken.)
   - Succinctly describe yourself, your product, and the reason for your call.
   - Clearly state what you want this person to do. Give you an appointment? Answer questions? Tell you who the right person is for you to contact? Have a specific goal for the call.
   - Establish a rapport with the person without getting excessively chatty.
   - Have a memorable and pertinent closing line.
   - Be careful about spending five, ten, or more minutes socializing on the phone. Those minutes add up and take away from time you could be making more phone calls or doing other pertinent work.

2. Take notes on your phone call.
3. Keep track of how long you stay on the phone.
4. Have an action plan for the next step.
5. Consider using a telephone headset or portable phone to allow you to tend to other tasks and improve your productivity.

5 WAYS TO START A PHONE CONVERSATION WITH SOMEONE YOU DON'T KNOW AND INCREASE THE LIKELIHOOD THAT YOUR CALL WILL GO THROUGH

What works best for starting a phone conversation? As often as possible, have your reputation precede you, so whenever you call someone he or she (or his or her assistant) knows who you are. Even if he or she is not expecting your call, if there is enough familiarity with you, or if you have been given a green light by someone, you will avoid that embarrassing exchange where you try to talk someone into wanting to speak with you in the first place.

If you're calling someone who will know your name, and he or she has a secretary or administrative assistant you first have to go through (also known as a *gatekeeper*), make your initial call short, simple, and to the point.

1. "Hello. This is _____.
   May I please speak to _____
   _____? He's expecting my
   call." (Of course, only say this if it's
   true.)

If you're calling someone who probably has an assistant and it's a cold call, you'll need a more detailed description of who you are and why you're calling as well as a compelling reason why this person should put your call through. Having what I call a POR—point of reference—is one of the best ways to expedite a cold call to a total stranger (in the world of sales, having a referral turns a cold call into a "warm call"):

2. "Hello. My name is _____
   and I'm _____
   [brief description of who you are].
   _____ [referring
   person] told me to call
   _____ [person you
   want to speak to] because she is
   an expert in an area that I'm
   researching for a report. I'll just need
   a few minutes on the phone at her
   convenience.

Alternatively:

3. "Hello. To whom am I speaking?"
   (Once you know this information,
   you can insert the person's name so
   the exchange seems more personal-
   ized.)

Alternatively:

4. "Hi. My name is _____.
   Do you have a moment to talk?"
   (This is good if you're contacting
   someone directly. By asking if it's a
   good time to talk, the person you're
   calling may not feel as pressured and
   may be less likely to try to rush off
   the phone without talking to you
   at all.)

5. If you're calling a main number:
   "Good morning. May I speak to
   _____?" If the person you're
   calling answers and says his or her
   name, immediately shift to who you
   are and why you're calling: "I'm
   _____ and I'm calling because
   I _____."

5 WAYS TO END A CONVERSATION WITHOUT ALIENATING YOUR CALLER

How you end a call can be just as important as how you begin it. Practice using these polite and effective closing lines:

1. "I'm so very sorry that I have to cut this short, but I have to go right now."

2. "I'd really like to continue discussing this but, unfortunately, due to a previous commitment, I can't talk much longer. Would you like to call me back later today or set a time to continue our discussion tomorrow morning?"

3. "I have a staff meeting starting in a minute, so we have to wrap this up."

4. "I can't talk right now. I have a roomful of people."

5. "What's a good time to get back to you? I was just on my way out the door."

HAPPY ENDINGS

Write down any closing lines you have successfully used to end a phone call.

_____

_____

_____

_____

_____

_____

_____

_____

Tips for Avoiding Telephone Tag

Telephone tag, or leaving back-and-forth voice mail messages without reaching your contact, can be a big time waster. Here are some ideas for sidestepping this problem:

1. Decide if you even want to leave a voice message. By leaving the message, you are giving power to the other person to return your call or ignore you. Some top salespeople will keep calling back numerous times until they finally get the person, rather than leave a message.

2. If you decide it's best to leave a message, state your name and phone number slowly and clearly. Repeat your phone number.

3. Explain the reason for your call and what you want from them when you call back. If you just leave your name without the reason for your call, you may be necessitating two return calls instead of one (one call to find out what you wanted, and a second call to provide the information you need.)

4. Decide how many times you are willing to play telephone tag and when you will say "enough." Note that different rules apply to social versus business calls. For example, if it's social and you're just calling to say hello, be patient about a call back. If there is something specific that you need or want, say so. However, if it's a business call, responding immediately—especially to a boss, coworker, client, or customer—may make the difference between getting, keeping, or losing business.

5. Specify a time when someone is most likely to get you in.

6. You may want to include your cell number as an option for returning your call. If you only want those with urgent matters to call you on your cell phone, say so.

7. Consider giving out your fax number and/or your e-mail address as a way of increasing the likelihood of communicating without telephone tag.

8. Keep your voice mail as brief as possible, while still providing essential information. Everyone's busy today. The key is to get someone to call you back, not substitute talking to the machine for the interaction.

Take a Technology and Equipment Inventory

We've all had that frustrating experience of buying a new computer, or a cutting-edge piece of technology, only to find out that an updated model is released almost immediately after our purchase, or certainly within a few months, which makes us feel that our old equipment is obsolete. You might think that upgrading to the newer technology is the most efficient course of action. Sometimes it is, but even if you or your company had the funds to continually buy new equipment, the learning curve involved in mastering how to work something new may offset the increased speed or additional features. In some cases, such as with cell phones, the bells and whistles found on newer models may not actually be necessary for the simpler tasks that you use your tech-

nology for, and may even prove to be time wasters.

At the other extreme from the person who continually upgrades his or her technology is the person who sticks with the old devices because "everything is still working." Yes, you could replace your dot matrix printer, but since it's still printing, why bother? Your computer never fails you, even if it still takes floppy disks, is very slow, and cannot run newer software because your old operating system cannot support these programs.

Get out your appointment book or your electronic organizer. Look over your schedule for the rest of the week or over the next month. What day could you commit to having a technology upgrade day? Write it in your book and use that day to research new office equipment that you could use, such as a computer with more memory or a cell phone with more features. You could also use that day to get training in how to use new technologies or take better advantage of your existing hardware or software. Keep that appointment—it's an important business meeting on your road to enhanced productivity.

I won't tell you what technology to buy—technology changes too often to make those recommendations pertinent—but I will help you to revise the way you think about technology so it works as the time saver it's supposed to be. We'll also explore when, or if, to upgrade or replace your hardware, software, or other office equipment. What needs to be upgraded? Updated? Donated? Replaced? Call Support Services for help, read those user manuals you've ignored, or do some research and register for an e-learning or in-person course to improve your technology skills and efficiency.

YOUR TECHNOLOGY INVENTORY

YOUR PRINTER

WPM (your printer's words per minute, i.e., printing rate). Check what the WPM is for your current printer. Compare that to the WPM for a new printer. You might just find that the time you save in faster printing offsets the cost of a new printer.

_____

Ink Cartridge. How quickly do the ink cartridges in your printer need replacing? How much time do you spend purchasing, and installing, new cartridges?

_____

Printer Functions. If space is a concern in your office, how many functions does your printer perform? Today there are cost-effective and fast printers that combine the functions of printing, scanning, copying, and sending a fax.

_____

YOUR COMPUTER

Hard Drive Memory. This refers to the amount of space on your hard drive available to you to add software programs, including word processing, database, or graphics programs, before your computer is "full" and unable to efficiently store and retrieve data. The amount of memory is measured in megabytes, although today memory may be as big as 1 or even 100 gigabytes.

_____

RAM or DRAM. How much RAM or DRAM do you have? These terms refer to the computer memory available to you for loading or running programs and for the temporary storage and manipulation of data. (RAM stands for random access memory; DRAM refers to dynamic random access memory.)

_____

REASSESSING YOUR COMPUTER

If you do writing, research, or office work, unless you're still using a typewriter or writing in longhand, a computer has become necessary to your work and is likely a huge time saver. In addition to the ability to cut and paste electronically, saving the effort of typing, you can perform complicated procedures on a computer today, including editing videos with software that allows you to edit for a couple of hundred dollars what used to cost tens of thousands or hundreds of thousands of dollars.

But computers become obsolete quickly. Also, if you're accustomed to using a desktop computer, which confines you to one place in the office, consider a laptop. You may find changing to a laptop computer, which allows for mobility, very liberating. Years ago, laptops had very little memory and were much heavier, so you had to worry about hurting your back if you carried a laptop around for too long. Today, laptops have an enormous amount of memory and can weigh as little as two pounds, with the typical laptop weighing between four and five pounds.

Having time-saving equipment, such as the latest computer with lots of memory and portability, however, means that only certain aspects of a job may go faster. Other functions may go as slowly as before.

How much memory does your computer have? This will determine how much you can store in your computer as well as how quickly you can access and perform certain programs. If you lack sufficient memory, your computer could be operating very slowly. Weigh the cost of purchasing a new computer with increased memory against the expense of adding more memory to the computer you have now. RAM (Random Access Memory) is important for speed as well. Now that you know how much RAM or DRAM (Dynamic Random Access Memory) your computer has, is it enough? This will impact how quickly your computer can perform multiple tasks simultaneously, another key time management consideration.

To increase your efficiency by using technology to your best advantage, it would be helpful if you have an IT (information technology) expert that you trust to help you with computer issues and related issues. (See "Do You Have a Technology Coach?" later in this chapter.) Some of the computer concerns that you need to be addressing right now include understanding what's new in hardware and software; protecting yourself against viruses that could wipe out your hard drive; keeping spam on your computer to a minimum; avoiding spyware that can attach to your system, gaining access to your files and company information; upgrading your video e-mail transmission capability; and gaining the ability to send, or participate in, audio or video seminars conducted entirely online. Few of us can envision what additional concerns the future may hold.

There are some key questions to ask yourself in deciding if an upgrade is worth the time, money, and effort involved. After all, just upgrading to a new version of your existing software can take time and money and in some instances can even cause some of your existing programs to operate differently or shut those programs down completely.

CREATING A RELIABLE BACKUP SYSTEM FOR YOUR FILES

Just ask anyone who has had his or her hard drive crash, losing thousands of original files, and they will tell you that backing up your files, even in multiple ways, especially when it comes to original, creative writing, is an essential task if you are to have a time-efficient office. Yes, unless you have an automatic backup system, it may take some time to back up regularly, but the amount of time—and worry—that you will save in the long run, knowing that you have a duplicate of key files, is worth it. Of course if you do have a hard drive crash, the time you will have saved because you haven't lost your data—some of it irreplaceable—is hard to calculate but it could be hours, days, or even months of saved time.

SHOULD I UPGRADE?

What am I considering upgrading?

Hardware? _____

Software? _____

What is the cost? _____

How long will it take me to learn how to use this upgrade?

_____

Can I teach myself how to use it, or will I have to hire a consultant, take an online or in-person course, or read a manual? _____

What is the estimated financial commitment for learning how to use this upgrade?

_____

What could I do with the upgrade that I can't do now?

1. _____
2. _____
3. _____
4. _____

Which, if any, of these improvements will affect the quality or the speed with which I can do my work?

_____

How often does this computer manufacturer upgrade this particular product?

_____

If I don't upgrade now, when will there be a new version to upgrade to again?

_____

Do I know anyone who has upgraded recently and/or to this specific product?

Yes ____ No ____

If yes, provide contact information: _____

Notes (on this potential upgrade, on discussions with those who have upgraded, etc.)

_____

_____

Bottom line: Will any potential learning curve or hardware or software malfunctions be offset by the increased productivity or improved quality of work that this upgrade will provide? Will the cost of this upgrade be justified? When would I most likely have to upgrade again if I go through with this upgrade now?

_____

_____

WAYS TO BACK UP YOUR COMPUTER FILES

Here are some ways to back up your files.

- Hard copy (print out and carefully file key documents so you have a physical copy in addition to the electronic one)
- DVDs
- CDs
- Zip disks
- Memory sticks or flash drives
- iPod
- External Internet-based backup systems that you pay to access

- External hard drive
- Another computer
- Other

_____

_____

_____

_____

_____

_____

DO YOU HAVE A TECHNOLOGY COACH?

If you have a problem with your car, do you work on it yourself or do you take it to an auto mechanic at a gas station or the dealership? Do you have an accountant who files your annual tax return, or do you do it yourself? Who do you turn to when you have a problem with your computer? Do you go back to the retail store where you bought the equipment or access the manufacturer's online or phone technology troubleshooting service for a fee or, if it's still under warranty, for free?

Consider finding a technology coach or an IT company, preferably one that's nearby so their reps can make house/office calls or you can stop by the company's office for on-site training or service. The company may charge by the hour or by the project. They may offer online courses in how to more effectively use a certain type of word processor or specialized software, or they may give courses at their company during the day, at night, on weekends, or through the local school system or college.

Understanding and Dealing with Technostress

For some, technology has made a positive difference in how they go about their work, saving time that used to be spent typing and retyping or performing other manual functions. For others, technology provides amazing work opportunities that were much more difficult—or impossible—to attain before. Shirley Cheng, for example, a motivational speaker and the author of six books, is a blind woman in her early twenties who lost her eyesight at the age of seventeen. Her life has changed for the better because of technology. She explains: "In short, a screen reader has enabled me, a blind writer, to become an author." In an e-mail communication to me about her screen reader, Cheng writes:

> The screen reader I'm using is called JAWS and it is made by Freedom Scientific, Inc. JAWS is computer software that reads what's on the screen and tells you which keys you type. It comes with

great functionality that enables its user to use many computer programs and the Internet. . . . Without the screen reader, I doubt that I would have become an author. . . . I cannot use Braille because of my severe juvenile rheumatoid arthritis so that is not an option for me.

Others have rejected these changes in how they go about their work. For example, there are authors who still compose on a typewriter because they fear changing to a computer may stunt their creativity. For some people, technology has caused physical or mental problems. Here are some examples:

- Jack, a communications executive, decided that he could put in extra hours on his laptop computer when he's home in bed, watching TV. However, now he's developed chronic back pain and he's wondering if being hunched over his laptop for several hours a night might be the cause.

- Linda, a medical secretary, works for a hospital that switched to a new dictation system. The new system, unlike the old audiocassette method, is centrally controlled and stored. Now, if she hits the wrong key, she loses everything that she's been working on. Within a few months, Linda's little finger started feeling numb, and she developed a severe case of nerves.

- After Dale, a paralegal, switched from a typewriter to a computer, she developed blurred vision, seeing pink when she looks away from the video display terminal, as well as pain in her shoulders, her neck, her lower back, and her arm.

- Geraldine, a recent college graduate, has to limit the number of hours she works at

her computer keyboard because of a wrist problem that her doctor has diagnosed as carpal tunnel syndrome.

These are just four illustrations of a type of stress that some are calling technostress—stress related to the introduction, or use, of technology. I first became aware of this term while reading psychotherapist Craig Brod's 1984 book, *Technostress: The Human Cost of the Computer Revolution.* Technostress is different from work-related stress, which is caused by other factors, such as too much work, extreme deadline pressures, role ambiguity, or dealing with difficult or overly demanding workers, clients, or customers. It's important to understand and deal with technostress because stress of any kind, including stress caused by technology, has been linked to such health problems as heart disease, hypertension, ulcers, backaches, and migraine headaches.

Common sources of technostress include computer phobia, old or misused technology, high performance pressure, and computer monitoring, whereby a company keeps track automatically of how long someone takes to complete a specific task, such as answering or completing a phone call (if you're in customer service). Computer monitoring is applied to work groups as varied as bank tellers, phone operators, truck drivers, college professors offering online courses, paralegals, managers, and even executives.

Some symptoms of technostress include bodily strains, muscle tension, a short temper, absenteeism, a higher-than-usual error rate, demanding quicker responses from human beings, and an inability to deal with ambiguity. Neck, shoulder, and lower back pain may be the central nervous system's way of saying, "Enough."

Sociologist Anne Statham, along with Ellen Bravo, national director of 9 to 5, an advocacy organization for working women, did a study of how 75 workers in three settings responded to the introduction of technology. At the financial institution they studied, managers who were trying to meet an unrealistic deadline to get a new computer system up and running missed their vacations and some had to be hospitalized with stress-related problems. (Mid-level managers had estimated it would take two years to make the new technology fully operational. Top management demanded that it be done in one year. After all the stress-related problems, it still took the original two-year estimate.) The major technostress symptoms reported by their sample among three workplaces included eye strain, headaches, muscle strain, exhaustion, "nerves," feelings of instability and anger, and depression.

What were some of the practices Dale, the paralegal mentioned earlier, encountered at work that may have caused technostress? Dale says:

> They didn't know about proper lighting. They were unwilling to put money into enlarging the secretarial spaces to accommodate the computers. There were no proper [ergonomic] chairs. They did not order the correct finish [on the computer screen] to reduce glare. They took no account of the people facing large windows. There was no proper advanced training. We're expected to produce more, and faster, and the machine cuts my sociability. All those factors created, and still create, stress.

By contrast, some companies introduce technology in a way that alleviates technostress. They do a workstation analysis and they also interview workers and supervisors to see what needs to be modified in the workstation because of the new technology.

HOW TO BATTLE TECHNOSTRESS AT YOUR OFFICE

What steps are you taking to avoid technostress at your office? Try the following:

- Emphasize the people aspect of your business, even if it's technology-driven. For example, a public utility corporation based in Massachusetts has quarterly meetings for the entire technology staff of 100. Free pizza is served and there is a "state of the division" presentation, as well as an internal or outside speaker providing an educational component, and then an opportunity for the employees to network. One of the topics for the quarterly meeting: using time management to improve workplace relationships. Another example: The manager of a courier service has created a familylike atmosphere at her company by having employees socialize on many Fridays as part of the weekly routine.

- Make sure the standards you set for yourself and your staff are high, but not so unrealistic that unnecessary performance pressure is created. The computer enables generating "letter perfect" documents, but does your task require it? Should interoffice memos be letter perfect? Does that in-house report need to be done on a laser printer with the look of published material? Decide the standards for yourself and your staff based on what each task demands, rather than letting technology take over.

- Create a work environment that is pleasant, comfortable, and ergonomically designed, which means the equipment and furniture are designed with consideration for the body's frame.

- It helps to exercise and take frequent breaks, according to California therapist and *Technostress* author Craig Brod. Brod suggests keeping a clock near your computer or word processor since, as you lose yourself in advanced technology, you may be unaware of just how long you have been working. Let the clock ring every hour, reminding you to take a break.

- Purposely put some necessary office supplies in another part of your office, instead of nearby on your desk, so you are forced to get up and walk around, rather than always staying at your computer, uninterrupted, for hours on end. By having additional filing cabinets in other rooms and placing books throughout your office space you will motivate yourself to take walks so you can consult those books or directories.

- Spend your nonwork time interacting with people, away from your computer (as well as your handheld electronic business devices).

In his article "Overloaded Circuits: Why Smart People Underperform," psychiatrist Edward M. Hallowell recommends contact with people on a regular basis as a way to head off what he calls ADT or Attention Deficit Trait (as distinctive from ADHD). "Have a friendly, face-to-face talk with a person you like every four to six hours," Hallowell recommends. This is easier if you work in a traditional office environment, surrounded by others, especially if you work with people you appreciate and who like you. If you work alone and there's no one around, you could call someone on the phone and chat. Alternatively, take a short break and drive or walk to a nearby coffee shop to meet a colleague or friend for a chat while sipping a cup of coffee or tea, or take a walk together.

DAY
8

TAKE FREQUENT BREAKS

It helps to take frequent breaks, according to California therapist Craig Brod, author of *Technostress: The Human Cost of the Computer Revolution*. Brod suggests keeping a clock near your computer or word processor. Let the clock ring every hour, to remind you to take a break.

BEAT THE CLOCK

1. Look over your phone logs for regular and cell phone calls from Day 1, Getting Started. Do you see any patterns? Are there calls that are going to you that you immediately redirect to others? Are you using your phone to your best advantage? Do you answer each and every call when it comes in, or do you try to have a set time each day when you're available to callers? Look over the calls you're placing. Are there names missing from those lists? Are you relying too heavily on written or face-to-face communication when you could be using your phone more effectively?

2. When did you last update your cell phone? Is there a newer model with features that would help you save time? Visit your cell phone service provider's online or brick and mortar store, and see if there are any time-saving innovations that you should consider purchasing. Is it time to consider switching over to a phone that also allows you to retrieve and send e-mails, such as a BlackBerry, Treo™, or IPhone®? What are the cost and time considerations for such a switch, including any time spent in a learning curve to become proficient with your new device?

3. How long is your average phone conversation? Do you take notes during your calls? Do you plan in advance what you're going to say so you get maximum benefits from your business calls?

4. If applicable, make sure you have phone call follow-up materials—flyers, brochures, catalogs, samples of your work, and client or customer testimonials, a DVD or online demo—accessible and ready to send out (by regular mail, electronically, or even accessible by providing a link to a website where the materials are located). If not, work on preparing those materials before you make your next calls.

5. Take an office inventory. What equipment or products do you need to more effectively handle the paperwork and e-mails that you deal with at work? Make a list and a budget for those items. Shop for the items you need immediately to take better control of your paperwork and e-mail communications. Poll those people whose efficiency and effectiveness you admire. Ask what computer they're using right now. Get as specific as possible: How much hard drive memory do they have? What company manufactures their computer, and what do they like about it? Are there any new and innovative pieces of office technology that others have discovered that might boost your productivity?

E-Mail and Communicating Electronically

For some, e-mail can be the most productive aspect of their job and the greatest technological advance besides the computer. For others, checking e-mail too often throughout the day has become a major distraction and productivity drain. Whether you check e-mail on a desktop or laptop computer, or on a PDA (personal digital assistant) such as a BlackBerry, it's imperative that you take control of this technology, rather than letting it take control of you. You'll explore how to do just that as you move further into this second week of your productivity makeover. In this chapter we'll explore e-mail use and compare it to telephone use, and we'll deal with the question of Internet addiction.

Coping with Ever-Expanding E-Mail Demands

How can you deal more effectively with e-mail so it increases your productivity? First of all, decide when you will check your e-mails. If you have priority tasks to accomplish, work on those items before you check your e-mail. Or, if you decide to check your e-mail, put off responding to any nonpriority inquiries until the priority tasks are done. The rule of addressing your priority task first thing in the morning, before you do anything else, applies to e-mail, just as it does to dealing with nonpriority phone calls.

Try to establish a set time when you read and send e-mails, rather than doing it throughout the day. You could adapt a version of the autoresponder that an organizer sent out, which announced that she only reads e-mails once a day, at 4 p.m.; if people send e-mail earlier in the day, they will just have to wait for a response from her. Not only was the message clear, but it demonstrated that she controls her e-mails, rather than the other way around. However, for your business, which might include receiving time-sensitive inquiries from the media, from your boss, from others in your department, or from clients or customers, it could actually hurt your career if you ignore all e-mails until a certain time each day. Getting back to someone immediately could, in some cases, mean the difference between acting on or losing a major career opportunity. Here's a potential compromise if you deal with time-sensitive e-mails: To avoid or minimize distractionitis, selectively respond to e-mail based on whether or not the e-mail is a priority, as indicated by either the name of the sender (for example, your boss, a top client or customer, a coworker you're working with on a key project, and the like) as well as by the information provided in the subject line of the e-mail. Read e-mails when you're taking a natural break from your work, rather than interrupting the flow of your work to check your inbox. Consider implementing a modified version of that organizer's once a day e-mail checking policy with a more regular checking schedule of once in the morning, once at noon, again at 3 o'clock, and one more time before you leave your office for the day, whether your office is at home or outside of your home.

Some find that PDAs, such as the BlackBerry, have helped them to take more control of their e-mail. California-based press representative Jane Covner of JAG Entertainment has nothing but praise for her BlackBerry. She shared those thoughts with me:

> My BlackBerry has changed my life for the better. No longer do I have to call my office to check e-mails or messages. Recently [my husband and I] took a three-week trip to Europe and I could check my workload daily by e-mail. I know I was supposed to be on vacation, but it was a relief to monitor the daily goings on because, when I returned, it didn't take me a week to plow through all the e-mails to catch up. I came back ready to go and completely up to speed on everything.

Here are some additional tips for managing your daily e-mail onslaught:

- The most important line in an e-mail is the subject line. Make it specific and clear. This is your chance to get your recipient's attention and in some cases to even have your e-mail read. If possible, include a time element in your subject line to help move it to the top of the dozens, even hundreds, of e-mails received that day. For example, "Re: 12 noon tomorrow deadline from Chicago Tribune reporter " is much stronger than "Re: Reporter media request."

- If possible, have multiple e-mail addresses. Direct certain individuals or types of accounts or inquiries to one address as opposed to another. (Having a business and a personal e-mail account is another option. Some alumni associations are creating e-mail accounts for their graduates that will redirect e-mails to their graduates' company or personal accounts.)

- Keep up with your e-mail by cleaning out your inbox on a regular basis.

- Have a spam filter that will prevent you from getting oodles and oodles of unsolicited junk e-mail. Spam can slow you down and make you vulnerable to computer viruses or spyware.

- Beware of signing up for too many e-mail newsletters; unsubscribe to those that you don't need—or read—anymore.

- Use your e-mail service's autorespond function if you're going to be away or unavailable.

- Pace how quickly you respond to someone. You may decide that a rapid exchange of e-mails is too disruptive to your other work and may purposely delay answering an e-mail for hours, or even a day, rather than right away. (Also, if someone sends you multiple e-mails in quick succession, you may decide to answer them all in one message, rather than returning each one separately.) If you prefer to compose a response right away without sending it, put it on a delay, if your e-mail service allows you to do

that (AOL® for example, offers such an e-mail delay). Alternatively, save the text of your e-mail to your word processing program, date it, and cut and paste it into an e-mail later in the day or sometime down the road. You can also save your e-mail as a draft in your e-mail program and send it when you're ready to do so.

- Failing to respond at all to an e-mail (excluding those that are just announcements or mass mailings) is an answer—but probably a rude one. If someone makes a request and you're not the right person to comply with it, have your assistant let the writer know that the inquiry is being directed to a more appropriate person. If you do not have an assistant, try crafting a response you can automatically or manually direct back to the writer, advising him or her of the appropriate party to handle the request. If you need more time to respond, let the writer know that as well: "Thanks for your e-mail. I look forward to getting back to you as soon as time permits."

- Keep your e-mails brief. The rule of thumb is this: the shorter, the better. (But not so short that you seem curt and you offend the recipient!)

- Keep it simple. As organizer Barbara Hemphill suggests: Include only one subject per e-mail message. Not only will this method simplify e-mail filing and retrieval, but it eliminates the possibility of someone reacting to the first issue you bring up and missing the second.

How quickly you answer your e-mails may vary, based on whether or not you're in your office or on the road. Before you get upset when you don't hear back from people, find out if they're out of town and if their e-mail is working properly. Similarly, if you know you are going to be traveling, try to have an autoresponder alert those who contact you that there will be a delay in your response.

Internet Addiction: Who's in Control?

Still can't get a grip on when and how often you look at your incoming e-mails? Still surfing the Net, even though you have a report due in two hours? Maybe you're addicted to the Internet. Like any other addiction, Internet addiction becomes a habit that controls you, rather than something that you're in control of. The first step is recognizing that you have this habit. The next step is to understand what might be the underlying cause. Finally, you need to wean yourself away from the addiction—which does not necessarily mean giving up e-mail and the Internet forever, but instead using these tools in service to your job and your personal time.

Dealing with an Internet addiction is like dealing with any other addiction: You need to look at its root causes and then decide what you will do to overcome it. Will you try to change the habit on your own, or will you seek out an individual or a group therapist? There are social workers, counselors, psychologists, psychiatrists, and business coaches who may be able to help. Each one has a particular type of training and some may have more or less direct experience working with those who suffer from Internet addiction.

Here are some of the possible underlying causes of Internet or e-mail addiction, and some possible remedies. (These are not offered as a substitute for therapy or psychiatric help, if that is what's needed, but just as general information.)

CAUSE: Fear of having e-mails pile up

SOLUTION: Look at each message's sender and subject line and determine what, if anything needs to be answered right away. Everything else you can put aside until you can get to it. It is not the number of e-mails piled up in your inbox that determines whether or not you're a good time manager; rather, it's who sent those e-mails. You can also send a quick e-mail that says, "Deadline pressure. Back to you _____" so you don't feel as guilty about ignoring someone.

CAUSE: Failure to have a system

SOLUTION: Create a system for managing your e-mail that dictates how quickly you respond, so you don't have to make decisions over each and every e-mail. For example, anything related to a current project will get your prompt response, but e-mails that relate to past or future commitments are responded to within 24 hours, rather than right away. Your system may also specify that certain individuals—for example, your boss, your spouse, or your children—always receive your prompt attention, but even they will wait until you take a break in your work or until the end of the day, when you catch up on nonpriority electronic communications. Organize your e-mails by category, such as priority work, nonpriority work, association or professional memberships, research, top 50 business contacts, and the like. Then create subcategories that make sense for your particular work needs, such as business travel, media inquiries, human resources, alumni-school. Also, consider having an autoresponder that redirects people or suggests alternative ways to communicate if an inquiry could be handled more effectively in a way other than e-mail.

ARE YOU ADDICTED TO THE INTERNET AND E-MAIL?

Answer the questions that follow as honestly as possible:

1. When you try not to look at your e-mail for a certain period, do you get fearful, anxious, or fixated on it?

Yes ___ No ___ Sometimes ___

2. Has spending time reading or sending e-mails caused you to miss an important appointment or to be late to a meeting at least once in the last week?

Yes ___ No ___ Sometimes ___

3. Are you sending e-mails to those in nearby cubicles or offices, or even to family members in the same apartment or house, rather than talking in person or over the phone?

Yes ___ No ___ Sometimes ___

4. Do you enjoy reading e-mail, or surfing the Internet, more than eating, exercising, socializing, experiencing physical intimacy, or reading?

Yes ___ No ___ Sometimes ___

5. When you go on vacation, do you feel compelled to read and respond to e-mail, no matter how remote a location you may be in?

Yes ___ No ___ Sometimes ___

6. Has one or more friend or family member said to you, even jokingly, "You're addicted to the Internet" or "You're addicted to e-mail"?

Yes ___ No ___ Sometimes ___

7. Do you wake up in the middle of the night to check your e-mail?

Yes ___ No ___ Sometimes ___

8. Do you have to check your e-mail when you wake up each morning, or when you first get to the office, even if you have other priority tasks that should be addressed first?

Yes ___ No ___ Sometimes ___

9. Do you feel depressed or disappointed if you don't get a certain number of e-mails each day?

Yes ___ No ___ Sometimes ___

10. Are e-mail and the Internet taking up more and more time during your day, evening, and weekends—as much as three or four hours a day?

Yes ___ No ___ Sometimes ___

EVALUATING YOUR ANSWERS

If you answered yes to one or more of these questions—especially to questions 1, 6, or 10—you may be addicted to the Internet. If you answered "sometimes" to one or more of these questions, you may want to look at your Internet habits before they become even more extreme.

DAY 9

CAUSE: Constant interruptions because your computer is set up to alert you visually and verbally when you have a new message, which may automatically trigger your instinct to check your inbox

SOLUTION: Reset your e-mail program so it doesn't do this, or keep your e-mail program closed until you're ready to check it.

CAUSE: A need to be loved or a need for attention

SOLUTION: Don't judge how loved or popular you are by how many e-mails you receive each day. Find love and attention in other ways that won't eat up so much of your work time, attention, or focus.

CAUSE: Failure to delegate properly

SOLUTION: Cut down on the amount of e-mail you get by directing messages to others who should be dealing with those inquiries.

CAUSE: Boredom

SOLUTION: Yes, checking e-mail can help you if you're bored with what you're doing, but it's also a leading cause of distractionitis. It takes your focus off the job at hand, possibly impacting the quality of your work and your ability to meet your deadline. Find other ways to deal with your boredom that are positive, such as taking an exercise or people break, rather than just checking or sending e-mails.

CAUSE: Distractionitis

SOLUTION: As noted before, distractionitis has become a major obstacle to more effective management of your time, since it takes away from the focus and concentration that enables you to work efficiently and swiftly. Like all habits, once you surrender to distractionitis, it is a challenge to break this pattern. Start by checking and sending e-mail less and less frequently; if you are at the point of checking every few minutes, cut back to half-hour or hour, then cut back to every two hours, then every three hours. If your job requires you to check e-mail hourly, that should be part of your plan, but checking hourly is still not checking every five or ten minutes to see if you have any new exciting e-mails!

CAUSE: Curiosity

SOLUTION: Find other ways to satisfy your curiosity over who's thinking about you—or what new possibilities await you in your inbox—that won't kill your productivity and sabotage your goal of being more effective and efficient. Ask yourself, "When was the last time I got an e-mail that was so important and amazing that it was worth constantly interrupting my concentrated work?" Remind yourself that e-mail is a terrific time saver, when used appropriately for the work that you do, but it's an obstacle to greater efficiently when it's misused for curiosity or other nonwork reasons.

Using the Telephone versus Sending E-mail

Let's explore the pros and cons of using the phone (landline or cell/mobile) versus sending e-mail. This may be especially helpful if you have fallen into the habit of relying on one type of communication over the other.

ADVANTAGES OF E-MAIL

- You can e-mail any time—day, night, or weekends.

- You are in control of when and where you send (or reply to) messages.

- You can rewrite a message until you're pleased with it.

- Those who write well can excel at e-mail.

- You can communicate complex information in short sound bites.

- If you use instant messaging (IM), this medium is interactive, just like the phone. But, unlike the phone, IM is silent so the interaction can be more private and confidential, especially if you work in a busy office setting where phone conversations can be easily overheard or are distracting to others who may be trying to concentrate.

- If you use audio or video versions of e-mail, these include more than just text.

- With e-mail, you have a record that you answered an inquiry or delivered information, and you can go back and reread a communication at any time if you've forgotten something or are unclear as to what transpired.

- If you're upset, you can wait to write back until you've calmed down. In this way, you may avoid damaging your reputation by calling and screaming at someone, especially a superior.

- _____
  _____
  _____
  _____
  _____

(Add other advantages)

DISADVANTAGES OF E-MAIL

- As so many people now receive 100 or more e-mails a day, your message may be ignored or delegated to someone else to answer.

- In the case of computer malfunction or a faulty server, your e-mail may not be sent or received.

- Your message may be mislabeled as spam, without your knowledge that it was not received.

- Since e-mail has become so easy to send, it may not be as valued as a phone call.

- E-mails are one-way and not interactive (unless you use instant messaging).

- Text lacks the nuances and pauses of human speech (unless you use audio or video versions of e-mail).

- An e-mail may be sent to the wrong person by mistake.

- E-mail may be saved and used for various purposes other than those for which it was originally sent.

- If you're writing about issues that could have legal or human resource implications, you may not want a written record of your communications.

- Some people are better able to express emotions, especially powerful ones like joy, grief, or disappointment, through e-mails (compared to saying such things face-to-face).

- _____
  _____
  _____
  _____
  _____

(Add other disadvantages).

DAY 9

ADVANTAGES OF TELEPHONES (LANDLINE OR CELL/MOBILE PHONES)

- Phone conversations are two-way and interactive.

- The phone permits you to hear each other's tone of voice, instead of relying solely on words.

- By building on the conversation, you may be able to find out things that you might not have otherwise known to ask.

- The phone is more social and less isolating.

- Since it takes more effort and is becoming less common, the phone call is seen as something special.

- Depending on their writing skills, some people may be more comfortable expressing themselves by phone than e-mail. Although it's more common for people to declare, "I'm not a phone person," meaning they don't like to talk on the phone, there are those who are not "e-mail people," meaning they do better communicating by phone or in person.

- Cell phones make it easier to reach those who are constantly on the go.

- _____
_____
_____
_____

(Add other advantages).

DISADVANTAGES OF TELEPHONES

- What could have been a quick question can turn into a 20-minute discussion.

- You can easily get caught in telephone tag.

- It's hard to know when someone is there to take the call.

- If you call at an inconvenient time and a conversation ensues, there can be resentment toward the caller.

- You might blurt out the wrong things.

- Phone calls, especially international ones, cost more (unless you use a free service or a plan with a flat-rate or low-cost fee).

- You have to take into account differences in time zones and work schedules, within the United States and internationally.

- Talking on the phone while driving, even with a handheld device, may not be as safe as avoiding cell phone use while driving altogether.

- _____
_____
_____
_____
_____

(Add other disadvantages).

BEAT THE CLOCK

1. Look over your Internet Time Log from Day 1. What do you see about how you spend your time online? Is the Internet increasing or decreasing your productivity? Do you see a pattern to your Internet usage that you want to change? Perhaps you want to check or send e-mail only once or twice a day. Do you want to set up a second or third e-mail account, delegating responsibility for those messages to others and cutting down on the number of e-mails that find their way into your inbox?

2. Find the last e-mail that you sent. How long is it? Try to shorten it without changing its tone. What about the subject line? Is it clear and succinct or could it be stronger?

3. Consider the most important business relationships that you need to cultivate and maintain to be successful at your job—for example, those with your boss, your key clients, your customers, your coworkers, your colleagues, your employees, or your service providers. Make a list of the top ten individuals in all those categories. Consider how, when, why, and how often you communicate via e-mail with each one. When was the last time you spoke on the phone or met in person? If you determine that you're now overrelying on e-mail, try to allocate the time to call or meet with these key business contacts, in addition to communicating by e-mail.

Handling Change and Interruptions

How does change occur? What happens to our brains when we have to shift gears? And who is ultimately responsible for change? In his brilliant and inspirational book, *How People Change,* therapist Allen Wheelis concludes that it's up to the individual to change. According to Wheelis, even psychotherapists are only the *catalysts* for change; *you* are responsible for making change happen.

How do you accomplish change? Psychologists debate whether you first need to change how you think before your actions will change or whether you need to change your actions first, and your thinking will then follow suit.

In my experience, both ways work. At different points in your life, you may find that you bring about change by changing your actions; only in time does your thinking also come around. By contrast, you may find that you are unable to take a particular course of action without *first* changing your thinking.

In this chapter you will learn how easily you cope with change, as well as ways to more effectively deal with interruptions. This is a fundamental time management skill because learning to adapt to a variety of situations is an essential part of dealing effectively with new experiences, challenges, and relationships. You or those you work or live with may be going through changes: Perhaps you have to move to another part of the country, you are starting a new job, or you just got engaged. Even when you stay put, little surprises crop up every day: Your boss unexpectedly asks you to stay late at work to finish up a report that has to be turned in the next day (even though you have plans for the evening) or you get a call from your child's school nurse that your child doesn't feel well enough to stay for the rest of the school day.

No matter how conscientiously you create to-do lists and make plans for your day, unexpected changes and interruptions sometimes force you to change course. In this chapter, we'll explore how you can better regain your focus when confronted with new situations or interruptions that may otherwise lead to distractionitis, feeling overwhelmed, or juggling so many tasks at once that nothing gets finished and what you *do* work on doesn't receive your best effort.

DAY
10

How Adaptable Are You?

Do you handle change well or does it throw you? Knowing how you respond to change will help you to determine if you're the type of person who is able to handle lots of interruptions and distractions or if you do better in situations where there's consistency and minimal change. Take the quiz titled How Well Do You Handle Change? on pages 124 to 126 to find out.

HOW WELL DO YOU HANDLE CHANGE?

Do you approach new work situations with confidence and common sense, or does change stress you out, throwing you into a tizzy of fear and anxiety? To test your adaptability, answer the following questions as honestly as possible.

1. **You're moving away to take advantage of a challenging new job. You feel:**

a. Sad to be leaving your friends and home.

b. Excited but a little bit nervous, too.

c. Thrilled. Here's your chance for a new life.

2. **It's Monday, and your boss suddenly announces that a project you assumed was due the following Monday must be completed before this Wednesday's office meeting. You're:**

a. Unhappy, but resigned to the unpredictable nature of bosses.

b. Panic-stricken.

c. Eager to get to a phone and cancel all your social plans between now and Wednesday.

3. **It's your first day on the job. How do you feel?**

a. Worried about whether you'll be capable.

b. Glad your boss is a close colleague of your uncle's.

c. Enthusiastic and up to the challenge.

4. **You've just been told that you're getting an unexpected promotion. You're:**

a. Happy, but you wonder if there's a catch.

b. Pleased and eager to tell the boss how things could be run better.

c. Exhilarated. You can't wait to celebrate with friends.

5. **You just got notice of a rent increase that you can't afford. What do you do about it?**

a. Look for a cheaper apartment or find a source of extra income.

b. Move back in with your sister.

c. Ask your family to help you out financially.

6. **One of your top customers is moving across the country. You:**

a. Pledge to still provide service from afar.

b. Plan to keep in touch occasionally.

c. Become more concerned with your other customers and gradually forget about this one.

7. **You have a business dinner tonight. As you leave for the restaurant you're thinking:**

a. "If we hit it off, maybe I'll get the account."

b. "I wonder whether we'll want to do business together."

c. "Why did I ever agree to this business dinner?"

8. **Your boss has a new assistant and suddenly she has little time for you. What do you do?**

a. Ignore her, too.

b. Pretend not to care, but tell everyone how hurt you feel.

c. Talk to her about it and try to keep up the boss-employee relationship you've forged, even if it takes more effort on your part.

9. **You're looking forward to going on vacation with your family; then your boss asks you to go on a business trip at the very same time. You:**

a. Accept and try to figure out what excuse you'll give your family.

b. Explain why you can't make it and tell your boss that you'll go on the trip another time.

c. Try to do both.

10. **Your coworker mentions some things about you that bother him. What do you do?**

a. Tell him if he doesn't like you as you are, he can get lost.

b Feel hurt and depressed.

c. Consider his comments carefully and try not to let them harm your relationship.

11. **You've been at this new job for two months, and you really like it. Suddenly, you're told that there are some problems with the way you're doing your job. You:**

a. Ask what's wrong and take the feedback into account.

b. Quit.

c. Immediately start looking for a new job.

12. **After nearly a year on the job, you realize that you no longer like what you're doing. You:**

a. Tell your boss and ask what you should do.

b. Get your resume in shape and get it out to headhunters, employment agencies, or send it to online job search sites.

c. Continue working there anyway because you're used to it.

13. **You're taking a continuing education course at the local college. Which books do you read for it?**

a. Whatever sounds most interesting.

b. Only required and recommended books.

c. Both required books and whatever suits your fancy.

14. **If your boss were asked to rate your attitude toward change, he or she would probably say you're:**

a. Eager to try new things.

b. Very nervous when confronted with a new or unexpected situation but open to the challenge.

c. Fearful, especially if a new situation seems difficult.

15. **Write down two changes that you've considered making recently.**

_____

_____

SCORING

For questions 1 through 14, find the point value below for each of your answers. Then add up your total score:

1.	a. 1	b. 3	c. 2
2.	a. 3	b. 1	c. 2
3.	a. 1	b. 2.	c. 3
4.	a. 1	b. 2	c. 3
5.	a. 3	b. 1	c. 2
6.	a. 3	b. 2	c. 1
7.	a. 2	b. 3	c. 1
8.	a. 1	b. 2	c. 3
9.	a. 2	b. 1	c. 3
10.	a. 2	b. 1	c. 3
11.	a. 3	b. 1	c. 2
12.	a. 2	b. 3	c. 1
13.	a. 1	b. 2	c. 3
14.	a. 3	b. 2	c. 1

For question 15, if you wrote down one or two changes, give yourself 1 point. If you're in the process of making one of those changes, give yourself 3 points. If you left this answer blank, deduct 2 points.

DAY

10

EVALUATING YOUR SCORE

Handling change well means weighing your options and choosing the course of action that will work best in the long run. Don't be discouraged if your score isn't as high as you'd like it to be. You can improve your ability to adapt. In fact, just by becoming more conscious of your weaknesses, you've taken the first step.

Under 25 points: New situations frighten you so much that you either freeze up or automatically do what you think is expected of you. Change threatens rather than challenges you, perhaps because you underestimate your own ingenuity and strength. But by always playing it safe, you're narrowing your horizons and lessening your chances for getting what you really want. For example, if you hold onto a job that you no longer enjoy, you'll have security—but you may lose out on the chance to be truly satisfied and fulfilled by your career.

To improve your adaptability, you have to learn to have faith in yourself and believe in your own strength. You also have to learn to deal with situations and people as they are now, not as they used to be or as you wish they would be.

25 to 40 points: You recognize when change is inevitable, and you're generally strong enough to face it. But sometimes an unexpected turn of events flusters you, and you lose your sense of perspective. You may overreact, for example, by quitting a job because you're told that you need to work on some aspects of your performance.

Adapting to a new situation doesn't always mean taking some new and drastic course of action. Remember the adage, "Don't burn your bridges." Usually you don't have to make an all-or-nothing decision. For example, when your boss asks you to go on a business trip but you already have vacation plans with your family, you need to be confident enough to try to find a way to appease everyone. Can you change your family vacation plans to another week and still go on the trip that is necessary for your job? If you can't, or if you prefer not to, rearrange your family vacation, how about asking an associate to go on the business trip this time?

Next time you're confronted with a new situation, try to think through your options more carefully, considering the consequences of each. If you can keep a cool head, your better judgment will prevail, and you'll have an easier time voicing your decision with confidence to others.

Over 40 points: Your excellent adaptability is demonstrated by your realistic assessment of change as something exciting and challenging that also requires advance planning. You're not likely to plunge into the unknown without careful forethought, and you're levelheaded enough to see that while a major change—such as moving away to start a new job—will be a growing experience, there may also be painful or difficult aspects to the move.

When you feel that taking a risk is necessary, you'll summon the courage to do it. For example, you'll leave a job that no longer excites or satisfies you. On the other hand, you aren't likely to overreact to a new turn of events: You won't call it quits with a boss you still want to work for although he gives you negative feedback. You're self-assured without being blasé and are likely to do well in whatever situations or relationships that you find yourself.

Now take the self-test What Has Changed Since You Started Your Job? so you can focus in on the changes in your workplace and see what other changes might help you there.

WHAT HAS CHANGED SINCE YOU STARTED YOUR JOB?

There may be changes in what you need to do or should be doing since you started your job. Have you stayed abreast of those changes so you adjust how you handle your time accordingly? Consider when you began your job. Make a list of what it was like at that time.

Priority tasks when the job began: _____

The way the industry was: _____

What was going on in your personal life at that time? _____

What was your salary? _____

How many people were reporting to you (if any)? _____

Now look at yourself and your job today. What's changed? For example, suppose you are an acountant who used to get into the office at the crack of dawn and work till 8 or 9 p.m. You're now married with an infant at home and attempting to work 9 to 5. How do you accomplish more during your reduced work hours (compared to your pre-baby schedule)?

Priority tasks today: _____

Changes in the industry that are impacting how you prioritize your work/perform your job today: _____

What is going on in your personal life now that is impacting how you spend your time at work? _____

What is your salary or income? _____

How many people are reporting to you (if any)? _____

What relationship or technological changes do you need to take into account now?

_____

Are there any changes that you would like to make that could help you increase your productivity as well as the quality of your work? If so, list those recommended changes:

_____

Make a commitment to implementing each of those changes, including a date and/or a plan for each one. Write down those dates and plans now, and take those goals into account as you budget your time.

6 Ways to Cope Better with Change

Coping better with change will help you to manage your time more successfully because you'll respond to change, which is inevitable, more easily and with less debilitating stress. Here are some suggestions for helping you deal with change more effectively:

1. See change as inevitable and challenging, rather than something to be dreaded.

2. Instead of being thrown by change, think of it as a way to learn new skills and as a means of altering the boring routine you've fallen into.

3. As human beings, we're able to adapt to different situations. Use that adaptability to your advantage.

4. Don't view change as a loss of the old ways but as a gain of fresh and better ways to achieve growth and improvement.

5. Our lives are continual works in progress. We're always changing and evolving, as are our work habits, workstyles, technology, relationships, and knowledge. Try to become more comfortable with the continual change that occurs in your life, rather than expecting everything to reach a point where things are always consistent. The next time something happens that's new and unexpected, try to be flexible and calm as you face the change, rather than seeing it as a trauma that should have been avoided.

6. Technology forces us to change the way we work periodically—as frequently as every six months. (Consider the floppy disks of varying sizes you might have that are now obsolete.) Even if your technological tools are in good working order, consider replacing one or more items with more efficient and up-to-date equipment that will serve you better. Look at your technology and decide if the reason you're hanging on to it is your fear of change. If that's what's holding you back, embrace new, improved technology and allow ample time to learn how to master the changes.

COPING BETTER HELPS YOU MANAGE TIME

Coping better with change will help you to manage your time more successfully, because you'll respond to change, which is inevitable, more easily and with less debilitating stress.

Why Interruptions and Distractionitis Are the Leading Causes of Inefficiency Today

Whether it's getting a promotion that requires you to master new tasks, or a coworker being replaced by someone else on a temporary or permanent basis, change is inevitable in our work and personal lives. In addition, the direction in which things evolve is often unpredictable.

Interruptions can be viewed as mini changes. Some interruptions are necessary; for example, the research department is shutting down its systems for a day to upgrade, so you have to work with them today rather than tomorrow to get the data that you need.

By contrast, as I've mentioned, in my time management research I have observed an amazing (and disturbing) increase in what I call distractionitis. (If you recall, distractionitis is the bombardment of competing priorities and information input from a variety of sources—especially from e-mails, the Internet, phones calls, and drop-in visitors—causing workers to lose sight of their key projects and shift back and forth between pulls.) Distractionitis is strong, pervasive, and—if not addressed or dealt with—can be responsible for a substantial decrease in your productivity at work and even in your leisure time, as well as an increase in related stress and anxiety.

Causes of this increase in distractionitis include new technologies and the time demands those technologies are making on everyone. (Have you ever gone out to dinner with people who are so addicted to their PDAs that they check those devices every few minutes for work-related messages—in between the salad, the main course, and dessert—instead of engaging in conversation?) Other causes are age-old but still important to address. For example, a newsletter editor, who works in an office, cited socializing as the number one cause of distractionitis at her job: "It happens to me at work sometimes when a coworker who sits nearby gets in a chatty mood and starts talking about movies, gardening, the weather, etc. It is difficult for me to turn away to get back to work without feeling rude." She welcomes finding more effective ways to deal with this situation—and, fortunately, there are better ways, as noted in the pages that follow—since this type of distractionitis not only cuts down on her productivity but also causes her to work more hours and even to miss her lunch!

The good news is that there are ways to dramatically and clearly combat distractionitis—whether it's caused by people or technology. For example, find a quiet place removed from the interruptions of others, even if it has to be at six o'clock in the morning before everyone else in the office arrives. (Of course, be careful not to put yourself in a vulnerable position whereby you're the only one in a deserted building.) Or, put in time at your home office before you even go to work. Wake up early, telling everyone not to disturb you unless it's an emergency. If your distractionitis is caused by Internet addiction, time yourself so that you stay off the Internet for a certain number of minutes or even hours during the day.

In my second book on time management, *Creative Time Management for the New Millennium,* I emphasized that distractions *usually* come from within. But I have had to modify that insight. In the last couple of years, the bombardment of interruptions from cell phones that ring 24 hours a day—your own, a coworker's, or a stranger's on the train, bus, or even in the elevator—as well as from e-mail that may be announced with a sound as it is delivered to your in-box, and the increase in work setups that are cubicles or offices without walls, have resulted in externally driven distractionitis. For some, technological advances have become the primary way that they communicate, not just with business associates in other parts of the world but even with coworkers, bosses, or employees working on the same floor or in the same office building. Surfing the Internet for information to help answer questions for one's job can be a real time saver, but surfing the Internet in unrelated ways, including following up on breaking news stories online that have nothing to do with your priority project that day, are real obstacles to improved productivity.

Today, there are real and strong distractions from the workplace, and you need to see this as the battle that you have to face and win if you are to triumph over the decreased productivity that is plaguing so many. There has been an increase in "busyness" and a decrease in genuine output and measurable productivity. Betty Lin-Fisher, writing in the *Akron Beacon Journal,* noted that a recent study by Basex, a research firm, found that office distractions were taking up 2.1 hours each day for the typical worker.

WAYS TO DEAL WITH INTERRUPTIONS AND DISTRACTIONITIS

Here are some suggestions that will help you to perform at your optimum level, as well as decrease the likelihood of mistakes or injuries on the job.

1. **If possible, relocate where you work to minimize distractions.** Reposition the location of your desk or even your office so you decrease the distractions eroding your all-important concentration. If your office is next to the coffee machine, where fellow employees congregate throughout the day, try to move the coffee machine to another part of the floor. If you can't physically relocate, try making other changes that might improve the situation, such as closing your office door, if you have one. If you don't have a door, try turning away from the noise and distractions so you're able to focus better. Also consider making the workplace less distracting by removing the clutter in your office, such as the twenty or thirty family photos you keep on your desk (leaving just one or two). Look over what's on your desk. What do you need close by? What could you move to a shelf or file away in a cabinet so the top of your desk is less cluttered and you are less distracted?

2. **Create a to-do list.** If you didn't create a to-do list before, start doing it now. If you're used to creating to-

do lists, become more vigilant about being clear in your priorities and your goals. Order your to-do list by urgency and importance. Check off each task that you complete and move on to the next item. Rewrite your to-do list as many times as necessary to help you focus on your priorities. Reward yourself for moving forward in accomplishing pivotal goals.

3. **Show others that you are committed to eliminating interruptions.** Let the world know that you are serious about gaining the much-needed concentration that will help you succeed at your job. Put a sign on the door at work, if necessary, announcing that you are not to be disturbed for the next hour (or two or three) unless it's absolutely urgent. Let your voice mail pick up your calls so you're not interrupted. If your phone lacks caller ID, look into getting this feature so you don't have to worry about missing important calls. Some phones even have a Send All Calls (SAC) feature that automatically directs all incoming calls to voice mail. (There are also phones that offer a voice component to caller ID; you can hear who's calling, and decide if you're going to pick up the phone or not, which may be less distracting than having to locate the handset and read the name and/or phone number on the caller ID display. For some, however, voice caller ID may be even more distracting, since the name and phone number will be announced automatically whenever there's an incoming call. Since this feature lets everyone within earshot hear who's calling you, voice caller ID might be better in a home office or solo practitioner work environment than a traditional outside office environment with numerous coworkers or employees.

4. **Become more familiar with what it feels like to be in the zone.** The next time you are in the zone of concentration, free from distractions, focus on and remember what that state of mind feels like. Compare it to the frenzy you experience when you respond to every impulse to go online and check your e-mail, or when you allow yourself to be interrupted by drop-in visitors or other outside pulls. Become comfortable with that in the zone feeling; begin to see that sensation as normal and feeling frenetic and distracted as the state to avoid. (Sadly, many of us have grown so used to being frenzied and pulled in a million directions that we have started to define that as normal.)

5. **Create appropriate and definitive boundaries so you no longer work 24/7.** Avoid interruptions in your personal life by turning off the PDA, laptop computer, or cell phone when you're home or on vacation. Start enjoying life, rather than working 24/7 and feeling guilty as you try to sandwich some fun or family time in between.

6. Other ways to avoid distractionitis.
Are there ways to reduce or even eliminate distractionitis that you have considered, or are currently employing, which are not listed above? Write them down.

_____

_____

_____

In the next section, we will examine concentration, one of the best weapons in combating interruptions. How does this work? Apply the suggestions that follow on improving your concentration and you'll notice, if someone tries to interrupt you, how much easier it is to say, "Sorry. I'm in the midst of something and I can't stop right now. I'll call you as soon as I'm able to put this aside and we'll deal with your issue." If you're really concentrating, you will also be less likely to interrupt yourself.

Improving Your Concentration

Enhancing your concentration is fundamental to time management. You can't control equipment breaking down or a traffic jam that causes you to get to work 45 minutes late. However, you can take steps to improve your focus so that, even if you do arrive late, once you're there you're able to accomplish more so that you make up for the time you lost because of lateness.

It's not enough to set up the optimal conditions for concentration. The motivation has to come from within. I know this first-hand from attending an ashram in India. Visitors to the ashram (from diverse locations and occupations) were all on the ground. The leader told us to close our eyes and meditate. How wonderful it would have been if I could have followed those directions. Instead, I can still see myself lying there, with one eye open, watching everyone else as they concentrated, rather than concentrating myself.

By contrast, as I sit here working on this book, I am concentrating so intently that I have lost track of time. I look up and see that the clock says 9:05 a.m. The last time I looked it was 7:10 a.m. I have been writing and thinking for more than 2 hours I don't have the radio turned on; I am not distracting myself by compulsively checking e-mails; I am fully in the zone. This is the state of mind we all want to aspire to when we are tackling key tasks. Know that this moment is all you have. If you lose your concentration, you may lose this moment and, along with it, a chance to do the best work you can do right now. (But, as we have seen, it is also important to take an occasional break for efficiency. I have accomplished enough for now so that I take a short break, standing up, stretching, and walking to another part of my home office to get a cup of decaf coffee.)

7 WAYS TO ENHANCE YOUR CONCENTRATION

Here are some simple tips for improving your focus:

1. Tackle your most challenging tasks during the time of day when you're most alert. If you're a morning person, you might want to schedule a breakfast brainstorming meeting rather than a session at four in the afternoon, when you're starting to fade. If you're unable to adjust your tasks accordingly, work around the natural tendencies of your body. For instance, if you're a morning person,

avoid eating a heavy lunch, laden with carbohydrates, that might slow you down in the afternoon.

2. Plan out your week for optimum productivity. According to a survey conducted by the temporary staffing firm Accountemps, 48% of executives polled found Tuesday to be the most productive day of the week. (Tuesday also won out in two similar polls conducted four and five years before this one.) The results make sense: Concentration should be higher on Tuesday than on Monday, when most workers are still recovering from the distractions of the weekend.

3. Block out or minimize external distractions that can impair your concentration. For example, shut a window to block out unwelcome noises from the street. Adjust the temperature in the room, since working in an environment that is either too hot or too cold can affect your concentration. Or, if the glare from the fluorescent bulb in your office is driving you crazy, consider buying a more user-friendly lamp.

TIMING IS EVERYTHING

Want to plan a meeting or event around the most productive day of the week? Then pick a Tuesday. A study of 150 executives working at the 1,000 largest companies in the United States, conducted by temporary staffing agency Accountemps, revealed that Tuesday was considered the most productive day of the week by the majority (48%), followed by Monday (26%), with Wednesday (9%) and Thursday (5%) in very distant third and fourth places. Friday was in last place (1%). (11% of executives didn't respond or didn't choose a day.)

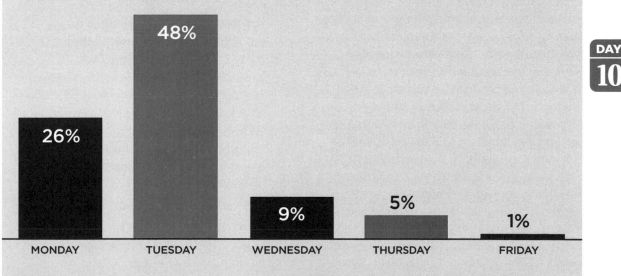

Fig. 10-1 *Which day of the week are employees most productive? Source: "Thank Goodness It's . . . Tuesday?" Press release issued on January 10, 2002 by Accountemps from the company's Menlo Park, California headquarters.*

4. Scientists suggest that concentration peaks between the ages of 12 and 40. If you're over 40, work harder at minimizing the distractions that you can control.

5. Have a no cell phone rule during meetings or presentations.

6. Keep your work area uncluttered and the shelves and walls around where you write or think suited to your style of concentration (for example, you may not be distracted by artwork and lots of papers, but others might find that these items impede their concentration).

7. Say no to nonpriority tasks or demands, freeing up your mind and your focus as much as possible.

WHEN LACK OF FOCUS BECOMES A MEDICAL CONCERN

As discussed in Day 5, certain symptoms of distraction may indicate that you have an adult version of ADHD (Attention Deficit Hyperactivity Disorder). Among them: You're restless; easily bored; fidgety; a workaholic; have an excessively low tolerance for frustration; become extremely upset by anything requiring the slightest bit of time; or are incapacitated by procrastination (beyond a tendency to occasionally put something off). Although it has been widely known that children may suffer from this disorder, society has only recently become aware that ADHD can also affect adults, whose condition often goes undiagnosed. Estimates are that 2% to 4% of the adult population—8 million or more Americans—may have ADHD. If you suspect that you have ADHD, see a doctor for proper evaluation and diagnosis. There are approved drugs that you can take, under medical supervision, to boost your concentration if it's affected by adult ADHD. See a qualified physician with expertise in this area for help.

How to Perk Up Your Memory

No matter what steps you take to prevent them, interruptions and distractions are bound to happen—once or twice a day, hourly, or even every couple of minutes. With a perked-up memory, when you do return to work after such an event, you'll be more likely to remember just where you left off. In that way you'll be able to pick right up and go back to what you were doing more quickly and effectively.

In their excellent book, *Brain Workout,* coauthors Arthur Winter, M.D., a neurosurgeon, and Ruth Winter, M.S., a science writer, share these suggestions for developing your memory:

1. Practice mnemonics, which is the technique of associating something unknown with something familiar.

2. Try to organize tasks by priority, but if you have a tedious job to do, try to tackle that one first. "You'll be less likely to forget projects that are more interesting," the Winters write.

3. To exercise your brain, add, multiply, or subtract without the use of a calculator as much as possible.

4. Memorize something each day.

5. Find out if any medications you might be taking for ulcers, high blood pressure, or anxiety are affecting your memory.

6. Take a break after 15 to 45 minutes of working on a task, since concentration is known to decline after that amount of time.

7. Say something out loud that you're trying to remember, as an aid in retaining the information.

8. Repeat out loud spoken or written instructions or directions.

9. Categories are easier to remember than random information, so group related information together.

10. Practice visualization, since creating a mental image aids memory. The Winters suggest sketching the furniture in a room without looking up. "You don't have to be an artist," they note.

Keys to Faster Reading

If your job involves a lot of reading, you may find it nearly impossible to block out enough uninterrupted time to get through it all. While the tips in this chapter should help you to minimize interruptions, you may find that another option is to try to read more in less time. Luckily, there are speed-reading techniques that can help.

Do you still read a word at a time? If you do, you could gain more time by learning to read faster. "I used to hate to read," says Abby Marks Beale, who has been conducting reading workshops for 20 years. "When I learned the strategies that I teach now, it was incredibly eye-opening how easy and simple it was to find good information, quickly."

What's the key to reading faster? Beale and others call it *pre-viewing*. She explains

that pre-viewing works best for reading published materials, rather than communications that have not gone through a professional editing process, such as e-mails. But for anything published, whether it's a magazine article, a newspaper article, or a nonfiction book, pre-viewing can save you minutes, even hours, of reading time. As Beale explains:

> Pre-viewing is based on the understanding that every piece of published nonfiction is written from an outline which includes an introduction, body of the material, and the conclusion. By reading the first paragraph—basically the introduction—and only the first sentences of the paragraphs, you will find the "meat" or main ideas of what the author intended without spending time on the "potatoes" or details. Once you get the main idea, you can decide whether or not you need to read more and, if you do, you can go back and read the sections in which you are interested in more detail. It's a weeding out process that helps you get what you need quickly without wasting time. It can also serve as an introduction for unfamiliar material like textbook chapters or procedure manuals.

Beale's technique can help you speed through books or articles, picking out the key material that you need to know. However, be careful that you don't ignore examples and details that may be integral to your learning and may reinforce key concepts. For example, while I recommend that you read this entire book, Beale's technique could be helpful when you're initially pre-viewing each chapter and then revisiting (rereading) specific chapters or ideas, reading or rereading what is important to you in each chapter and even in the entire book.

DAY 10

BEAT THE CLOCK

1. What's the last major change you made in your work situation? How did you handle it? How can you apply that change to your current circumstances or to future changes you are contemplating?

2. Do you have a problem with interruptions or distractionitis? Put a clock on your desk and start working on a priority task. Keep working, uninterrupted, until you are stopped by an external factor—such as a phone call, a drop-in visitor, or an incoming fax—that shifts your focus away from this priority activity. How long were you able to concentrate on your task before the first interruption occurred?

   _____

   Now repeat the exercise above, but this time ignore *all* interruptions. Don't answer the phone. If you have a door, close it to discourage drop-in visitors. How long were you able to focus before succumbing to a distraction, such as checking e-mail unnecessarily?

   _____

   Repeat this exercise in a few hours; see if you can increase the amount of interrupted time, as well as how long you go without distracting yourself. Stretch your uninterrupted time from minutes to an hour or even longer.

3. Look around your office. Are there photographs or objects unrelated to work that may be distracting you? Pick your favorite one or two pictures and put the others away. Remove some or all of the knickknacks from your desk if they are sources of distraction.

4. When's the last time you were truly engrossed in what you were doing, or in a conversation or a project? What did it feel like to really listen to the person with whom you were engaging? How did it feel to be completely immersed in something you were reading or thinking, or completely absorbed by what you were writing? Was it a comfortable or uncomfortable feeling? How productive were you when you were totally immersed? Apply this same level of intense concentration to the next meeting you attend at your company. Instead of letting your thoughts drift away from what the speaker is saying, or focusing on the question you want to ask, force yourself to be focused in the moment, in the now.

5. Consider your workspace. Is there any place you might relocate to, even temporarily, to help cut down on interruptions or distractionitis? If you work from home, could you retreat to another part of your apartment or house, away from family members or loud noises? Is there outside space that you could rent that would allow you to work in a quieter environment? If you work in a cubicle or an office, perhaps there's a corporate library where you could go to with your laptop computer or notepad. Sometimes just shifting to a new environment, even temporarily, can cause a dramatic improvement in your productivity.

Winning Deadline Strategies

How many times have you been given a deadline only to find yourself dreading, resenting, or fearing that deadline? Ironically, if you shift the way you look at a deadline, you can see it as a useful date to help you pace yourself so you can complete everything you need to get done on time. Deadlines actually help you by bestowing active status on a project and assigning it a tangible date to which you are committed, rather than allowing the task to fall into an open-ended morass, where it may be less likely to get finished. In this chapter, you'll learn how to deal with deadlines so that you optimize your efficiency. We'll explore why deadlines are helpful, as well as how to set a realistic deadline that you are likely to achieve, rather than one that is unrealistic and unattainable and likely to sabotage your efforts. We'll also discuss why setting mini deadlines along the way to a final due date may prove useful, even if you have to establish those deadlines yourself.

The Value of Deadlines

The key to a deadline that's not overwhelming is to create mini-deadlines along the way. Whether it's a speech that you have to deliver in two months, a report that you must research and write in two weeks, or a business function you're organizing on a certain date, the final deadline—or date when an event is set to occur—is just one date. It's a key date, of course, because meeting that deadline—or having everything well-prepared and completed by the date of an event—will separate those who are perceived as organized and efficient from those who are seen as disorganized and poor time managers. Barring catastrophic, unforeseen circumstances, you want to make that final deadline or shine at that event. You don't want to be dismissed as ill-prepared or even lacking certain materials or documents.

But you also need to work your way back from that final deadline. If you don't create benchmarks along the way, how will you pace yourself to arrive at that one major date?

Creating mini-deadlines is part of the time management system of breaking big, potentially overwhelming tasks into more manageable mini-tasks. You're not writing a book, you're writing one page a day so you'll have 365 pages in one year. Or, if you're writing an article for the company magazine, you're spending 1 day on background research, 1 day on interviews, 2 days writing the first draft, and 2 days rewriting the article after you get feedback from your boss and from the legal department.

If you're writing a term paper, there are predictable steps you have to follow, and you'll want to create a mini-deadline for each step, not just one final deadline. For example, you're picking your topic, conducting the research, and writing the first draft. Creating mini-deadlines assigns a clear time frame to those interim tasks so you've made a commitment to actually do something by a certain date; there is no ambiguity or confusion. You can even add specific parameters to those mini-deadlines. For example, you're writing one page a day but you're doing it between the hours of 8 a.m. and 1 p.m. You block out those hours for writing. You're writing a chapter a week, but you establish a plan for each day, whether it's writing x number of pages or writing for x number of hours. You're working on the report between the hours of 2 and 4 p.m., in between your other appointments and commitments.

For making marketing calls for your job or business, you've set a deadline of Friday to have five face-to-face meetings with new clients lined up, and you spend from 10 a.m. till noon every day placing calls, sending e-mails, or writing letters. For that business event that you're responsible for, you develop mini-deadlines for calling the caterer, ordering the extra chairs, hiring the event manager, gathering materials for the giveaways, or writing and editing any written materials including handouts.

How Do You Create Realistic Deadlines?

How long should something take? Creating a deadline that you can actually meet is part science, part art, and part stubbornness. The science part involves considering how long it has taken you in the past to complete similar tasks and using that time frame to guesstimate how long it will take you this time. However, not all tasks are equal or similar. Certain factors cause some projects to go faster and others to go more slowly than you predict. If you're a dentist, you'll probably spend around the same amount of time on each filling, but if you're writing a speech for your boss to deliver at the annual meeting—depending on the topic, how much research you have to do, and whether what you write is what you had hoped to write in the first draft or if you need multiple rewrites—it's probably going to be harder to estimate how long that will take. Determining how much time to budget for a project that is not quite like anything you've done before is the art part of the equation.

Sometimes a project moves along far more quickly than you thought it would. If you've properly prepared for a project, it may go faster than you anticipated. If you're in the zone, and not allowing yourself to get distracted (as discussed briefly in the Introduction and in greater detail in Day 10), you may find yourself progressing at a much faster pace, able to make or even beat your deadline.

How does stubbornness factor in? This last element comes into play when you're faced with an unrealistic deadline that is arbitrarily thrust upon you. You know it's impracticable, and you also know that if you agree to it you're setting yourself up for failure, an ulcer, or both. Here's what Dave, a 55-year-old technical writer in Wyoming, did when faced with just such a deadline challenge:

> When a project manager I worked with [gave] me a new deadline, I told her that it just wasn't possible. She looked at me with resolve and said, "Well, it has to be," and I replied, "Nope, it's not possible. I don't care how much you want it to happen and think it needs to happen, there's just no way it can be done."
>
> After going back and forth a few times, it finally sank in, and she realized that arbitrarily establishing a deadline didn't make it possible to achieve.

Dave explained to me that the project finally was completed successfully, but his contract was not renewed, even though his work was considered excellent. He still wonders if part of the reason might have been that he had the deadline changed to a later date. What happened to Dave points out a caveat about pushing for a realistic deadline: Whenever possible, get the other person to understand why the deadline needs to be changed and have that person—especially if it's your boss—be the one to change the deadline. You want to have him or her actually thank you for helping to make the target date more realistic. No one wants to look bad to his or her superiors; having a powerful justification for changing a deadline could help avoid any backlash over pushing it back (or, in some cases, moving it closer, if the deadline is too far in the distance). However, if the deadline absolutely cannot be changed or you risk potentially losing your job or not being called on for additional freelance work in the future, have some contingency plans in place, e.g., working late into the night, over the weekends, outsourcing certain tasks, temporarily postponing social distractions, etc. Be careful, however, to avoid skimping on your sleep, since that could put you and your coworkers at risk. Lack of sleep is associated with increased workplace accidents and errors, as well as car accidents, injuries, or fatalities related to sleep deprivation.

TIMING VARIES, SO KNOW THE RULES FOR YOUR INDUSTRY, BUSINESS, OR CUSTOMERS/CLIENTS

Every industry—and every company—has its own standards of what grace period it will allow for meeting or missing a deadline. Some companies might find it to be a greater problem if a product is delivered early or if a project is completed in advance of a deadline, as the resources necessary for the next phase of the job may not yet be available. Having something sit around an office or having a file languish in a computer may lead to more complications or misplaced materials than if it were delivered on time.

Concerns over deadlines, however, usually revolve around missing target dates, not around getting something in too early. Think of all the scrambling that occurs between Thanksgiving and Christmas when there's a hot new holiday toy or product with too few units to meet the huge demand. Timing of the delivery of goods can make or break some companies or, for entrepreneurs or freelancers, make or break your reputation as reliable. You also have to take into deadline consideration holidays or summer vacations that are observed by other people. This includes those who are waiting for you to provide them with a product and those you are waiting for to get data or materials to you. For example, some companies close down between December 18th and January 2nd. If you need to get a project into production, if you fail to return materials in advance of the 18th there may be a two-week or more delay because of the vacation slowdown. Similarly, summer breaks from work may last as long as two months in some countries. That may differ by geographic region. For example, the summer break in Australia actually occurs during December, which is the wintertime in North America and, for some, a holiday break.

YOU CAN'T PLEASE EVERYONE

Sometimes you do know what's realistic as a deadline but the person in charge—the person with the power and the money—is dogmatic about what he or she wants. So

you find yourself agreeing to meet an impossible deadline, because to push for more time might kill the project before it ever gets off the ground. But at what point do you let someone know that the deadline is looking unrealistic? How much advance notice should you give so a contingency plan can be formulated or orders canceled or placed on hold, without incurring business, legal, or ethical consequences? The answer to that question will be different for every industry, every company, and every project. But if you cannot meet a deadline—even if you work around the clock, take on additional staff, or find every way imaginable to speed up the production time—it's crucial to communicate the change in the deadline to those who need to know about it.

Linda Marsa, a successful, seasoned West Coast based magazine writer, deals with this issue all the time. She's usually working on multiple assignments for a variety of national magazines, and each editor wants her to be sure to make the agreed-upon deadline. Here's how she handles this situation so she is more likely to meet each and every deadline and to get additional assignments:

> What I do try and do is put the ball in their court. Something along the lines of "Let's talk about what this project entails so I'll have enough time to do a good job for you"—rather than saying this is [an] unrealistic [deadline]. People get very defensive. I find it's better to involve them in the process [as early as possible], i.e., "Let's think of a plan that works well for all of us."

Deadlines should be realistic. Delivery dates that are unrealistic or artificially trumped up because the person issuing them believes he can use time pressure to force people to bend to his will, may have consequences—and not always ones of a positive nature.

For example, if you ask someone to submit an assignment during a holiday period and she discovers that the deadline was more arbitrary than real, you may generate bad feelings and distrust; furthermore, the next time a deadline is imposed, this person may doubt that the date is real or that it needs to be honored.

Jared Sandberg addressed this practice in his *Wall Street Journal* column, "Rise of False Deadline Means Truly Urgent Often Gets Done Late." Sandberg begins: "In many offices, setting false deadlines has become as chronic as breaking them." Later on he continues, "But like false fire alarms, high-priority e-mails (!) and 'Urgent' voice mails, false deadlines can dilute a sense of urgency, making everything seem like a top priority so nothing really is."

Every job has its own deadline realities that you need to be aware of, both in your field and at your company. When freelance writer Linda Marsa worked at the *Los Angeles Times,* deadlines were quick, frequent, and inflexible. She states that it was, "impossible to re-negotiate deadlines." Once she switched to writing for magazines, she had seven years of being in the habit of working up against tight deadlines. Linda continues, "I don't usually re-negotiate deadlines." She emphasizes that she almost never asks for an extension: "It's rare that I'm working on a magazine story that's not scheduled [for a specific issue] so the best I'm able to negotiate is an extra day."

Tips for Meeting Your Deadlines, Every Time

Here are some pointers to help you make your deadlines, each and every time:

- Use judgment and foresight when you agree to a deadline in the first place.

Figure out how long you think something will take and then, if possible, increase that amount by 50%. For example, if you think a project will take two days to complete, budget three days for it in your schedule. Of course, if it's a time-sensitive project or situation, you might not have this flexibility. You need to know which category—time-sensitive or more open-ended—each deadline fits into.

- When budgeting your time, factor in personal obligations as well as commitments to others who matter to you—such as your spouse or partner, your children, your extended family, and your friends. If your best friend's wedding is in two weeks and you've got lots of parties and last-minute details to deal with, you might just need a few more days to research that report. (To increase your likelihood of considering personal as well as professional obligations that could impact your deadline, record all your commitments in one central place—whether that's a daily or weekly appointment book, or an electronic scheduler that you keep in your PDA or computer.)

- Look back at a task that is similar to the one you need to complete now. How did you go about completing that task? How long did it take you? Are there any strategies that you learned that could help you speed up how you work on this new project without sacrificing quality, creativity, or originality?

- Remember to practice saying no to any new demands on your time that will interfere with meeting your deadline.

- Create mini-deadlines that will enable you to pace yourself. Rather than just having that one final due date, set interim goals that you mark in your appointment book along the way. Each of those dates should serve to keep you on track, so you make your final deadline.

- When initially estimating how long a project like a report will take, factor in time for possible rewrites or to rework your approach. You want to leave enough time to do quality work. You don't want anyone to comment that your work looks rushed.

- Have a contingency plan in case the unexpected happens—your computer crashes, you (or your children) get sick, or some other emergency occurs.

- Set a date to send the project to someone else for review. By making a commitment to a peer or a friend, you will be more likely to make your final deadline.

- Increase your motivation by establishing a reward for yourself for meeting the deadline. If possible, pick a time-sensitive reward, such as tickets to a concert or a show, dinner with an old friend, or, if having something unplanned is a motivation for you, commit to a weekend getaway but leave the destination as a spur-of-the-moment decision. In that way you'll reward yourself for meeting your target, further reinforcing the benefits of getting this project done on or before the deadline, even if some of the details of your reward are being left open-ended.

- If you happen to beat your deadline, use the time to review your work—unless you think turning it in early is in everyone's best interest. Ironically, if you turn something in too far ahead of your due date, others may actually resent you because it may throw off their own schedules or it may show them up if they are still struggling to make, left alone beat, their deadline.

Dealing with Lateness

There are some people who are always on time. Steve Cone, chief marketing officer of Epsilon, a strategic database marketing company, is one such person. As Cone says, "I have been on time since I was born, including being born on time." He admits to finding lateness an annoyance. "I don't like it when people are late," which he defines as more than five minutes past the agreed-upon time.

Are you like Cone—always on time—or do you have a problem with lateness? Whether it's you or someone you work with who is the guilty party, the first step to recovery is to understand what it feels like to be kept waiting. How late do you tend to be? Fifteen minutes? Half an hour? Get to an appointment early and wait the number of minutes that you are usually late; see what it feels like to be sitting there, waiting for someone else. At what point do you become annoyed, fidgety, even worried that someone has forgotten your appointment or that something has gone awry? At what point do you go from being annoyed to being angry? Five minutes? Ten minutes? Longer? Get in touch with those feelings, and remind yourself that this is how you make others feel about you when you're late.

OTD (Out the Door)

Whatever the industry, a product's failure to get OTD—out the door—usually hurts a company, directly in terms of revenue and indirectly in terms of its image. Reports fail to get written, edited, and mailed out in time. Business function invitations, mailed out much too late, arrive after the event (causing embarrassment and frustration, plus untold overspending for food and services for guests who failed to materialize).

Unrealistic deadlines, as discussed above, as well as trying to do too much, can sabotage efforts to get projects, e-mails, assignments, letters, and proposals OTD. If something gets out the door, but it arrives late, you'll have to deal with the consequences. To avoid these repercussions of failing to get something OTD, whether it's a project or yourself for a meeting or appointment, try the following tips:

- Track exactly how long it takes you to get from point A to point B or to go from task #1 to task #2. For example, you may drive from your home to the train station every day, but have you measured that commute precisely under a variety of conditions, such as rain or snow, heavy traffic, and at different times of day? A similar philosophy applies to getting ready in the morning or leaving your office to meet someone for lunch. Having a clear sense of how much time you need for each task will help you to plan better so you're not late.

- Reward yourself for being on time. Complete this statement: "If I'm on time for _____ I'll reward myself with _____." Treat yourself to some luxury you've wanted, make a phone call to a friend or relative you always put off because you didn't have the time, purchase tickets to a cultural event, and so forth.

- Free-associate on paper about why you think you're late as well as when you're typically late. Look for patterns in those answers. Are you always late in the morning? Afternoon? Evening? Is it only going to certain events, or even meeting with certain individuals? Keep a lateness diary for information that can help you address the problem.

- Try to understand what might be behind your lateness. Is the cause a mechanical problem, such as an alarm clock that doesn't work? Or is your lateness the result of an emotional issue, such as the need for the negative attention that lateness causes (the feeling of being noticed, even if it's being noticed in an uncomplimentary way). For some, being late is better than being ignored. Think of a quiet conference room, where you can hear a pin drop, with someone presenting at the front of the room. The audience is hanging on the presenter's every word when all of a sudden the side door opens and in walks a latecomer, making noise, tripping over feet to get to that one empty chair all the way at the end of the room. All eyes are temporarily turned to that (annoying) latecomer.

- If you've gotten into the bad habit of consistently being late, begin by adjusting your self-concept. You need to shift your paradigm from seeing yourself as someone who's always late to someone who's occasionally late to someone who's on time. Each shift requires a corresponding modification in actual behavior to reinforce your new self-perception. For example, start by getting to work on time at least once this week, then at least three days out of five the following week, and then every day.

- Consider cultural views of lateness. In Latin America and Spain, for example, running 15 minutes behind schedule may not be considered late. In the United States, however, arriving even 10 minutes late for a meeting may have you dubbed late. Understand and adapt to the culture in which you find yourself.

DAY 11

- Have something important happen at the precise time you're supposed to meet someone; this helps reinforce the benefits of being on time. For example, throw your boss or coworker a surprise lunch and have everyone gather at a certain time, with the guest of honor arriving 15 minutes later. Have everyone call out "Surprise!" at a precise time, so if someone's late, the excitement of the event is gone and cannot be re-created.

- If possible, avoid answering the phone on your way out the door. This is a typical cause of lateness in getting to appointments. Let the call go to voice mail or have your voice mail direct urgent calls to your cell phone. Do activate caller ID, however, so you're careful not to ignore a call from the person you're supposed to meet, who might be calling to alert you that he or she is running late or even has to cancel.

- If your projects are not getting OTD in a timely fashion, consider what is causing this. Are you afraid of reactions to your projects, postponing the completion of those works so you also avoid any criticism of your efforts? If that is the reason, shift your imaging from seeing yourself getting negative feedback to your completed projects to an image of yourself receiving positive praise. Internalize and fixate on those positive images to help you get your projects OTD.

5 TIPS TO BEING ON TIME, EVERY TIME

1. Increase the consequences of being late so that you reinforce the positive behavior of being on time.

2. Keep at the front of your consciousness what it feels like to be kept waiting or to make someone wait. Remember that being on time is a sign of respect for yourself and others. Being late does not make you look powerful; rather, it makes you look disorganized and thoughtless.

3. Have a clear understanding of everything you need to do to get somewhere or accomplish something, and how long each step takes. Use those specific and clear time frames to guide your behavior.

4. Wear a watch and check it so you can keep yourself moving along (or check the time on your cell phone if you don't wear a watch).

5. Never agree to a time range. For instance, you don't want to say, "Let's meet between 12:00 and 12:15," because one person may arrive at 12:00 on the dot and the other at 12:15. You're both technically on time, but one person is perceived as late. Always pick a specific time to meet or complete a task. "Let's meet at noon." Or "The press release is due on the first of next month."

BEAT THE CLOCK

1. Write down how many times you were late today, or in the last week. What were the reasons for your tardiness? How could you have handled each situation differently, so you could have arrived on time? (If you weren't late even once, apply this question to someone you know who was late and who inconvenienced you. Was there a way you could have avoided being the victim of this behavior? What did you do while you were waiting for this person? Did you use the time productively or were you consumed with anger or frustration?)

2. What do you want to get OTD (out the door) today, this week, or this month? How are you going to make sure that you achieve that goal? Do you have a specific deadline that someone has given you? If not, have you set one for yourself? Remember to choose a reward for meeting that deadline.

3. Think over the various tasks you have to perform for your job. Do you know exactly how long each one takes? Make a list below of your key responsibilities and the estimated average time it takes to complete each of those tasks. This list should help you when you're next asked to set or agree to a deadline.

TASK	DESCRIPTION	AVERAGE TIME FOR COMPLETION

DAY 11

DAY 12

Delegating with Success

Trying to do it all is a variation on the theme of doing too much at once. When you try to do everything yourself, rather than appropriately delegating tasks that others can do (sometimes even better than you can do them), you slow yourself and your company down, as well as potentially sacrificing the quality of your services or product.

For some, delegating comes easily. For others—perhaps the entrepreneur who has grown her business from a one-person to a ten-person firm—letting go is next to impossible. You've heard this type of person referred to, in hushed voices, as a control freak or a micromanager. Still others keep theirs as a one-person company, and their refusal to hire help causes them and their business problems. Failure to delegate may even make someone go out of business, leading this person to have to get a job working for someone else. For those who are not self-employed, the inability to delegate may lead to time and project management problems. In this chapter we'll examine what delegating means to you; how, when, and to whom to delegate; and how to deal with those you work for, with, or above, so that productivity for each individual—as well for as your department, division, or company—is optimal.

What Does Delegating Mean to You?

For some, the word *delegating* conjures up an image of a full-time assistant or even something grander, such as a workforce of thousands, making you basically just your company's administrator, far removed from the creative role you might have played initially. For others, delegating is not a big deal; you either report to someone or someone reports to you. In any company with more than one person, it's just a question of who gives orders to whom.

The reality is that delegating can be one of the fastest ways to gain time and to free yourself up from tasks that you hate doing and may not even be good at—if it's done the right way. What is the right way to delegate? We'll delve into specific methods in a moment. But it's important to note that there is no one way that delegating has to look. For example, you do not have to hire someone on a full-time basis. You can take on additional freelance or part-time help, directly or through an agency; establish a paid or for-credit internship program; or hire students or working parents to assist you on a seasonal basis. Assigning work to telecommuters located off-site, and even around the world, is still delegating, and still a potential time saver. But whether the person is in the cubicle next door or on another continent, you have to have some system in place for managing those to whom you delegate.

Before we move on to methods of delegating, let's assess just how effectively you handle this challenge right now. To find out, take the quiz Are You Delegating Effectively?

Learning What, When, and How to Delegate

Based on research and observations, here are the seven steps that you could take to effective delegation:

1. **Choose what tasks you are willing to delegate.** What defines you and sets you apart from everyone else? That's what you should be doing with your time. Pick as many nonpriority tasks that others could do as well as you, and delegate those efforts. Focus on your priority task and delegate any tasks or jobs that prevent you from concentrating on it. Delegate what you can't do yourself because you don't have the requisite skills or expertise. Delegate what you won't do yourself because the task doesn't interest you or is not the best use of your time.

2. **Pick the best person to delegate to**. Learn the traits, values, and characteristics of those who will perform well when you delegate to them. Pay attention to whether someone asks questions at the time a task is assigned. Listen and observe. As a North Carolina sales director notes,

DAY
12

"You find out pretty quickly about people who are willing to take on responsibility if they're already taking it on their own." A health care director realized that delegating a key phone call to someone who was new to the job and was overwhelmed by covering for another worker (who was away for several days at a training session) put her patient's care at risk when the new person failed to make the call.

3. **Trust those to whom you delegate.** Along with trust, you also have to give the people to whom you delegate the chance to do a job their way. There is more than one acceptable way to do most tasks, but you do have the right to require that whatever you delegate is done accurately and well. Bob Danzig, former CEO of Hearst newspapers, emphasizes how key trust is to effective delegation:

ARE YOU DELEGATING EFFECTIVELY?

To find out if you need help divvying up your workload, ask yourself the following questions.

1. Are you working much longer hours than everyone around you, especially your subordinates or your boss?

2. Are you spending an inordinate amount of time each day on tasks that could be easily delegated to an on-site employee or even a virtual assistant, such as routine correspondence or nonpriority phone calls, leading to the gnawing feeling that you are spreading yourself too thin?

3. Have you had an ulcer since taking your current job, or do you feel much more stressed—tense, jittery, nervous, pressured—than you ever have before?

4. Do you doubt that you could select competent people to delegate to?

5. Do you dwell on past delegating mistakes—the interns who didn't show up, the employee who made lots of mistakes—as a justification for doing everything yourself?

6. Has anyone ever called you a "control freak," a "micro-manager," or someone who has to do everything yourself?

7. Are you a perfectionist to the point that you're rarely satisfied with what you or anyone else achieves?

8. Are you unwilling to delegate the responsibility for an entire job when assigning a specific task?

9. Have you ever fantasized that life could be more pleasant, and you could actually take some time off and not worry about work, if you could just give up doing everything yourself and rely more on others to help you succeed at work?

10. Have you come close to being fired or have you been fired one or more times over the issue of delegating?

If you answered yes to one or more of the above questions, your delegating skills probably need some fine-tuning. Read the rest of this chapter carefully for tips on how to accomplish this goal.

> It always starts with trust. Early on in my career as a teenage classified ad salesman, I respected the fact that once the ad left my hand I had to "trust" the composing room of printers—trust the billing department. Later as publisher of that same newspaper, I carried that sense of trust to our 978 employee-colleagues. Then, as nationwide CEO of all Hearst newspapers, I had total comfort in our local city leadership and the 6,000 employee-colleagues. Some might label that "delegating." I prefer the concept of "trust."

4. **Give clear assignments and instructions.** It's not as easy to explain something to someone else as it sounds. There are those who have a tendency to explain things in such simplistic terms that the listener is insulted. There are others who are so vague and incomplete that it's difficult for someone to grasp what is expected of them. This situation may be complicated by the listener's fear of asking questions and appearing stupid or inattentive. Work hard to strike the right balance between explaining too much to your listener and not explaining enough. Think about what you would need to know if you did not understand how to do what it is that you are attempting to explain. Think back to that time when you were learning, when you were a neophyte.

5. **Set a definite task completion date and a follow-up system.** Establish specific deadlines at the beginning of a project, including several mini-deadlines. In this way you may follow up and check on the job's progress, rather than waiting until the final deadline. This is especially important if you're not yet comfortable with the skill level of the person to whom you delegated this project.

6. **Give credit.** You will inspire loyalty and a wish to serve if you give other people credit for their achievements. Giving credit can be as simple as letting others know about the help someone is giving you when you introduce that person. For example, "This is my assistant, So-and-So. She just finished researching the contact information for all the key marketing directors that we're going to invite to our product launch next week." Credit could be given in a written way, in the front of a report or on the program for the annual meeting where there is a space for acknowledgments. Weekly, monthly, or annual performance reviews are another obvious place to give credit to those people to whom you delegate work.

7. **Delegate responsibility for the job, not just the task.** Only by delegating entire jobs, not just the individual tasks comprising them, will you avoid the monkey-on-the-back syndrome, first espoused in the classic *Harvard Business Review* article by William Oncken, Jr,. and Donald L. Wass, "Management Time: Who's Got the Monkey?" This article showed, step by step, how managers who fail to delegate responsibility in addition to specific tasks eventually find themselves reporting to their subordinates and doing some of their work, rather than vice versa!

DAY
12

DELEGATING OPTIONS

Make a list of the tasks at work you currently delegate and to whom you delegate these responsibilities:

TASK   PERSON TO WHOM IT IS DELEGATED

_____   _____

_____   _____

_____   _____

_____   _____

Now make a list of other tasks that you could delegate and to whom. Weigh the pros and cons of delegating these tasks. If you do decide to assign these responsibilities, consider how you will accomplish this without spending as much time supervising as you would doing the tasks yourself:

TASK   TO WHOM MIGHT I DELEGATE IT?

_____   _____

_____   _____

_____   _____

_____   _____

Dealing with a Boss Who Lacks Time Management Skills

Now let's look at the other side of the equation: If you have had work delegated to you, you may experience certain challenges in managing your new responsibilities and workload that may be caused by a chaotic boss. This section will provide some suggestions for how to better deal with a boss whose time management skills are less than exemplary. Of course you can always hope that your boss will change by reading a book on time management or going to a workshop. However, you can't control whether or not your boss changes. You can, however, improve the situation by working with, not against, your boss's efficiency deficiencies.

Some bosses are workaholics, working around the clock, coming in early, staying late, and often expecting everyone else to put in as many hours. We'll discuss tactics for dealing with workaholic bosses in Day 14. In this section you'll find help for dealing with a boss who's disorganized, a procrastinator, or poor at moving projects along.

IF YOUR BOSS LACKS BASIC TIME MANAGEMENT SKILLS

Sometimes we have the best time management skills in the world but our boss needs a lot of help in this area. Here are some tips for working with a boss who is time management challenged:

- Suggest that the department or company bring in a time management consultant to present a workshop for all levels of employees, including your boss. In that way, your boss won't feel singled out for his lack of time management skills, but will, we hope, benefit from what he learns in the workshop.

- Continue to exhibit excellent time management behaviors that your boss might emulate. Rather than letting your time management skills deteriorate to his level, continue to operate efficiently, even improving your own effectiveness; your boss might take the hint from your positive model and become more like you.

- If your company holds regular skill-building sessions, suggest time management as one of the skills that you will discuss and focus on. If your company or your department doesn't have such sessions, suggest starting them. Include time management as one of the topics to be addressed. Brainstorm how all of you could improve your productivity. If possible, bring in an outside speaker/facilitator to help everyone in attendance, including your boss, to address time management issues in a nonjudgmental, brainstorming, educational, and fun way.

IF YOUR BOSS IS DISORGANIZED

We hope that your boss has an organized assistant who keeps her on a more organized track. But if you're the assistant who's supposed to be organizing your boss, or if your boss's organizational challenges are spilling over into your work, making it harder for you to get things done, consider these suggestions:

- Send your boss important memos or other documents in multiple ways. For example, in addition to sending information as an attached file or imbedded within an e-mail, you could also fax it, hand-deliver, or mail a hard copy to your boss for backup. Since disorganized people tend to misplace or lose things, this increases the likelihood that the key information your boss needs will be available in some format.

- See if a "clean your desk" day could be implemented throughout your department so your boss doesn't feel as if you're targeting his lack of organization. Hopefully, this will allow him to get a better grip on where everything is stored or filed.

IF YOUR BOSS IS A PROCRASTINATOR

We discussed causes and possible cures for procrastination in Day 3. However, that information was intended to remedy your own tendency to put things off. What do you do if you don't procrastinate, but your boss does? Here are some tips:

- Keep tactfully reminding your boss of what his priorities should be, especially as it relates to your own work, so you don't let his procrastination become your problem. In writing or verbally, gently say something like, "When did you say you'd be getting me that revised agenda for tomorrow's meeting?"

- Offer to help so it doesn't look like you're nagging: "Is there anything I can do to help you move along our plans for attending that technology conference next month? Do you want me to find out what information the travel agency needs to get all the plans firmed up?"

- Since procrastination can also provide information, try to figure out why your

DAY 12

WORKING WITH KAIZEN

What if you're reporting to a new boss for the first time? Apply the Japanese concept of *kaizen,* which means, "change for the better" or "continuous improvement," from *kai* ("change") and *zen* ("good"). If you find that a change in your work situation—such as a new boss with a new supervisory style—is not leading to a good outcome, reflect on (1) what's different, (2) how and why it's negatively impacting you, and (3) what you can do to change things, now or in the future, to return to your previous higher level of productivity.

It's human nature to want to please your new boss, but is her way of going about the work setting you and your actions back, way back? It may be helpful to tactfully advise a new boss of what works best for you, based on past accomplishments and experiences. Taking control so you are as productive as possible, without criticizing your boss in a way that makes her resent you, is a challenge, but it's definitely possible and it's definitely in everyone's best interest. Here are some suggestions for accomplishing this feat:

1. Point out that an additional key concept to kaizen is providing feedback in a way that does not place blame. It is blame-free and not negative or disapproving. (No one, especially a boss, wants to be criticized.)

2. However you've been communicating till now, pick a different way to interact when you have this feedback session. For instance, if you always exchange e-mails, set up a phone session. If you always talk on the phone, try meeting face to face. If you always meet face to face, trying instant messaging or sending each other e-mails.

3. Gather all your data from this particular project, in terms of how long each part of the task is taking, and also gather data from one or two previous examples of when you've performed the same or similar tasks under a different boss or with different coworkers or subordinates, and how long the task took that time.

4. Present the data and show your boss, in concrete terms, the difference in productivity among the various situations. How long did it take in situation A to accomplish the same goal compared to situation B? Ask your boss for his or her input so it becomes a discussion about how to achieve better productivity, rather than a lecture.

5. Give your boss an opportunity to share about why he or she has been going about the work and/or supervision in a particular way. Maybe it's a bad habit that he or she wants to change but hasn't had the opportunity to focus on it, till now. Maybe he or she is overwhelmed by too many projects. While you don't want to show up or anger your boss, you don't want to let your boss's poor work habits to negatively impact your own productivity or your professional reputation at the company.

6. End your discussion with an action plan that you both agree on. If possible, make it a written plan. You and your boss resolve to interact in a particular way, with an interim or long-term deadline and with revised work patterns that should lead to a specified outcome (presumably, achieving greater productivity).

7. Set a date when you will communicate again to see if progress is being made in achieving this improved productivity.

boss is procrastinating and see if you can address those issues. For example, is there missing data that needs to be gathered before the annual report can be submitted? Is there ambivalence about a certain course of action that the procrastination is concealing?

If Your Subordinate Needs Help with Time Management

On the surface, it may seem easier to tell someone who reports to you that she needs to improve her time management skills than to guide a disorganized superior. However, it may not be as easy as it sounds. Criticism of any kind has to be handled tactfully and delicately. With time management seen as such a pivotal skill, especially in the United States today, telling someone that he is a poor time manager could be interpreted as telling him that he is a poor worker. Therefore, if you need to critique an employee's time management skills, follow the proper business protocol for any kind of feedback at work—namely, begin with praise. Lead off with an affirmation such as, "Your phone manner is exceptional. I'm always hearing lots of positive comments about how welcome you make all our clients feel when they call for assistance, day or night. That's rare today and it's great that you have that natural ability."

Avoid labeling your employee a poor time manager, a mark that could damage his image with other employees or even with the human resources department. Instead, frame his negative time management behavior in the context of something specific: "You have missed your deadlines for these reports over the last couple of weeks. What do you think

might be behind that?" Avoid putting your employee in the position of defending himself. Instead, encourage him to share with you any information that could be helpful in dealing with this specific situation. For example, perhaps the deadlines were unrealistic to begin with or perhaps he was grappling with competing demands or personal issues of which you were unaware. Had you been privy to this information, you could have delegated some of the work to someone else or modified the deadlines.

If there's a time management workshop that you think your employee would benefit from, consider suggesting that she attend one as part of the job. Offer to pay for the workshop fee as well as any travel costs if the program is out of town and let your employee know that it will be an approved and compensated out-of-the-office workday. Recommend books or articles on time management—either general or on specific subjects, such as goal setting, organizing, or balancing work and personal time.

Perhaps this employee needs you or someone else on your staff to be more closely involved in monitoring her progress so the time issues are detected and dealt with sooner rather than later. Pick a time that you and your employee will revisit this topic to see what progress she has made in dealing with this issue. For example: "Let's meet in two weeks and see how you're doing on that new report that's due in a month."

If it's only recently that your employee's time management skills have taken a major turn for the worse, be sensitive to what might be going on in his life to cause this behavior. Although, ideally, an employee's personal life should not spill over into his job, the reality is that most of us find it difficult to separate the two. There might be a sick parent or child who needs to be taken care of, an upcoming major event like a wedding, depression related to a family member's passing, or a romantic breakup. Without prying into your employee's personal life, let him know that you've noticed a change in his efficiency level. Suggest that your employee get help for whatever it is that's temporarily causing him to perform at a level that is unacceptable before it irrevocably hurts his reputation at the company or causes your department to underperform or lose out on valuable business. If your company offers an employee assistance program, you might suggest to your employee that he consider taking advantage of this service.

BEAT THE CLOCK

1. If you already delegate to others, are there ways you could delegate further and more effectively to boost your productivity? How would you do that?

2. What aspects of your job are keeping you from spending time on those tasks that only you can do? What's holding you back from asking others to work on those items?

3. You might be reluctant to delegate out of fear of dealing with certain potentially unpleasant (but relatively common) situations. To plan ahead, determine how you would deal with the following scenarios, should they ever occur:

- You have to tell your employee that his work needs improvement. How would you go about doing that?

- You have to let go of your employee because business is slow and you don't have the revenue to pay her. How would you tell her?

- You have a big project that needs to be done immediately. How would you ask others if they're willing and able to put in additional hours and days over the next two weeks to meet the deadline?

Making the Most of Meetings

The daily, weekly, or monthly meeting can be a notorious time waster. Yet, if used correctly, it can also save time. For example, you can use meetings to get to the heart of a departmental challenge, brainstorm possible solutions, and come up with a greater number of ideas and concepts more quickly than if each person were working individually. In this chapter we'll explore ways to better conduct and participate in formal meetings, as well as how to help your boss run meetings more effectively, so that you accomplish your goals and move your business forward. We'll also look at ways to deal with informal, one-on-one interactions so that all parties get more out of the experience. Networking enables you to expand your sphere of influence, critical for most businesses and careers. We'll share some tips about how to network effectively.

How to Conduct a More Effective Meeting

Are you in charge of running specific meetings within your organization? Here are suggested guidelines to make the best use of this time and to keep attendees involved and productive:

- Make sure there is a reason for the meeting and that all those expected to attend have been advised, in writing, of that purpose, as well as the time the meeting will start and conclude.

- Make it clear in advance that it's important for everyone to arrive to the meeting on time.

- Stick to the starting time, even if all attendees have not yet arrived. Latecomers will get the point for the next meeting, and those who are on time will not be kept waiting.

- Have a written agenda for the meeting and follow it. Try to include specific times for each presentation or discussion.

- Decide in advance if you, or someone you delegate to, will take notes during the meeting. If you decide to tape-record the meeting, make sure that is acceptable and make provisions for transcribing the tape.

- Keep discussions on topic and control questions that stray off on a tangent; otherwise, your meeting (and you) may start to seem unfocused and disorganized.

A SAMPLE AGENDA

Here's an agenda that was written at the front of the room on a flip chart for a brainstorming/product development day that I recently participated in as one of four invited experts. In addition to the experts, attendees included the product development agency, several executives in the production development division of the manufacturer, and a couple of typical consumers. Notice that even though the agenda only indicates the broad category for each time slot, each break is noted as well as the time for lunch.

MONDAY MEETING

8:30 a.m.	Breakfast
9:00 a.m.	Introductions, objectives, overview of agenda
9:30 a.m.	Expert panel presentations and discussion
10:15 a.m.	15-minute break
10:45 a.m.	Exercise 1
11:45 a.m.	Sharing and feedback about Exercise 1
12:15 p.m.	Lunch
1:15 p.m.	Exercise 2
2:15 p.m.	Exercise 3
3:15 p.m.	15-minute break
3:30 p.m.	Sharing and discussion of Exercises 2 & 3
4:00 p.m.	Exercise 4
5:00 p.m.	Wrap-up
5:30 p.m.	DONE!

- Be certain that, by the end of the meeting, participants have a sense of accomplishment.

- Thank participants for attending and advise them if they will receive a written or oral follow-up. If the same group will be meeting again, announce when and where the next meeting will take place.

- End on time.

HOW TO HELP YOUR BOSS RUN MORE EFFECTIVE MEETINGS

Your boss and meeting attendees will appreciate a well-organized event. Here are some suggestions for better meetings:

- Offer to create a written agenda for the meeting, if your boss has not already done one. Try to make sure an agenda is circulated in advance of every meeting (even if it's just an hour or two before). If an agenda isn't circulated in advance, it will still be helpful to have one available at the meeting, even if you just write out the agenda on a flip chart in the front of the room. If a written version is impractical, at least share the agenda verbally so everyone has the same time frame and goals for the meeting,

- Does your boss tend to get through just a fraction of the agenda at every meeting? Allot specific times to each aspect of the agenda, including start and end times, goals for each part of the meeting, and time for wrapping up. That way it's easy to see just how far off course your boss has wandered if there are twenty projects to discuss, and, halfway through the meeting, you're still on the first one. It will seem less like you're criticizing the boss when you, or someone else, points out that you're behind on the agenda.

- Elect a timekeeper for each meeting so it is someone's job to monitor how much time has elapsed, and to move the discussion along to the next point.

- Based on your past experience, it may be more realistic to break one meeting into two or three meetings with more manageable agendas. By scheduling multiple meetings with specific and achievable goals, it will be easier to keep your boss on track.

Getting More Out of the Meetings You Attend

Do you find that you spend much of your meeting time mentally sorting through the pile of work on your desk—or mindlessly doodling your name while issues irrelevant to your workload are discussed in depth? Here are some guidelines for making the most of those meetings you have to attend:

- In advance of the meeting, set clear goals for yourself. If you're attending at someone else's behest, you may be required to write a report detailing what you gleaned from the meeting. If you do write such a report, keep it simple and concise. Going on for fifteen pages may waste the time of the person who has to read your summary.

- Be on time. Not only does arriving late make you look unreliable and disorganized, but it can annoy the meeting leader and other attendees, who must either wait for you or deal with your interruption.

- If you have something specific to contribute or a pertinent question to ask, by all means speak up. However, avoid

DAY
13

boasting about your work as a way of gaining recognition.

- Rather than interrupt the presenter while he or she is making a key point, take notes during the meeting and ask questions at the appropriate time. You might even consider planning your statements or questions in advance so you can present your ideas or questions as succinctly and tactfully as possible.

- Don't overbook. Leave some extra time after a meeting for networking. You'll be distracted and nervous if the meeting is running behind schedule (and most do) and you're running late for an important business lunch or another meeting that's happening right after in another part of town.

- Avoid hogging the floor. Resist the impulse to talk just because someone's paused or there's a silence. It's not your job to fill the silences.

- Share your insight and wisdom, especially if it's unique and pertinent. It's the people who take risks and let others know who they are who get ahead.

- Avoid looking like you're part of a clique during the meeting. This could alienate others, including the presenter or meeting leader, who may feel left out or question whether or not you're paying attention to the discussion at hand.

- If the goal and/or the agenda for the meeting has been circulated in advance, be sure to review these items. Consider this meeting and make sure you really need to attend. Remember that if you're attending a meeting, you're not doing something else. So unless the meeting is truly necessary, politely decline to participate (if possible). Point out why your presence is unnecessary or redundant and, if applicable, suggest someone else whose presence would be more relevant instead.

- If a meeting's usefulness is over for you and you don't think you'll offend the meeting organizer or the other attendees, politely excuse yourself at an optimum time. It is less offensive to leave during a break or at the end of a presentation. Try to avoid walking out when someone is talking. If you have to leave, it might not be necessary to excuse yourself to the entire group. Figure out who needs to know that you plan to leave, and let that person know. The less disruptive you are in your exit, the better. If it's just a matter of a half-hour or an hour, you might consider trying to stay until the end, so you don't look like you're rushing for the door. Sometimes important networking and communication occurs at the end of a meeting, as people are dispersing.

Dealing More Effectively With Drop-in Visitors

Colleagues who drop by unannounced can be the biggest time savers or time wasters of your day. The loquacious employee down the hall, with whom you just ate lunch for an hour, can be a real drain on your time. On the other hand, greeting a CEO based in another country who happens to be in the office for one day could be the best use of your time that day.

Alas, most drop-in visitors will fall somewhere in between the two in terms of whether their presence is a useful or unproductive expenditure of your time. Here are some tips for cutting short unexpected visits:

- Suggest an action take place while walking toward the door (or, if you work in a cubicle, while moving toward its opening). For example, "Robert, thanks for stopping by and discussing this application with me. I'll get the additional research that you suggested and have it on your desk by Friday. Will that work?"

- Remove extra or especially comfortable furniture, so there's no place for unannounced visitors to sit. If you want a visitor to stay longer, you can store a fold-up chair inside a closet, if you have one, taking it out for welcome guests. Or, cover a chair in the corner of your office with a plant, files, or books; remove these items from the chair to clear a space for a visitor to sit more comfortably.

- Be direct about the pressure you're under and why you need to bring the meeting to a close: "I'd really like to continue this conversation, but I have to get back to the phone calls I promised I'd place before 3."

- Suggest an alternative way to keep the dialogue going, such as "Thanks for stopping by. Let's continue our discussion by phone or e-mail, okay?"

- Leave the vicinity yourself, taking the person with you as you head anywhere else—even to the cafeteria or the bathroom—just to get that person out of your office or cubicle.

- If it's true that you have another imminent appointment, you can certainly state, "I have another appointment that should be arriving any minute now and I need to prepare for it."

- List here any ways of dealing with drop-in visitors that have worked for you in the past and that you could employ again:

_____

_____

_____

_____

Making the Time to Meet

Lifetime employment is rarely guaranteed anymore (except in certain countries, such as France) the way it once seemed to be for some Americans who worked for major companies or government agencies and retired after 30 to 50 years with a gold watch and a pension. So, in addition to your current work relationships, you need to take the time to seek out other connections that might be useful if a job change occurs. That includes joining associations and going to meetings, keeping up on the latest trends by attending workshops and industry conferences, and perhaps even taking continuing education classes at night or on weekends or studying toward an advanced degree. Are you allotting time for these ancillary but pivotal activities? What about joining or starting a group, such as a mastermind group, of likeminded individuals dedicated to developing work skills and expanding their professional networks? These groups could meet in person or in a telephone or teleconferencing format on a weekly, biweekly, or monthly basis.

Some companies build time for socializing into the workday through luncheons or end-of-day gatherings. Other companies sponsor company picnics, retreats, baseball teams, or holiday parties. I've been asked to

DAY
13

speak at such retreats over the years, and the organizers always emphasize that the networking and social opportunities are as important to the attendees as what they will learn from the speakers. For companies whose offices are scattered throughout a state—or even around the country or the world—retreats, training sessions, and conferences can offer employees a chance to initiate and develop relationships.

Improving Your Workplace Relationships

Whether you're meeting with a group of colleagues in a formal setting or working one-on-one with a coworker on a project, how you interact with others impacts your ability to manage your time. The better your workplace relationships, the better able you will be to accomplish goals you have in common and to communicate clearly, effectively, and honestly. You don't have to like everyone you meet. You don't even have to want to work with everyone you meet. But sometimes you have to find a way to get through the day, or the project, with someone who is definitely not your best friend. Here are some techniques to help you improve workplace relationships, especially if you're stuck working with someone you really can't stand:

- Start by looking at your own behavior: Are you consciously or unconsciously doing anything to trigger your coworker's hostile behavior? If so, change yourself first.
- Think back to when you first met this person. Were you completely neutral or did you have a strong positive or negative reaction to him or him right from the

start? If your instant, gut response to this person was negative, you may not even be giving this worker (or boss) a fair shake. Instead, you may be bringing to the relationship your own feelings that have little to do with him or her. By becoming aware of your attitudes, however, it may be easier to give this person another chance.

- Give him or her the benefit of the doubt. Try taking your colleague's point of view.
- If possible, reduce the frequency of your contact with this person, or take some cooling-off time. If you still must deal with this person on a regular basis, gradually scale back the closeness of your relationship, being careful not to hurt his or her feelings by being too obvious about it.
- Listen carefully to each other's side of things. Before you get offended or angry, try to understand the other person's explanation or perspective. There may be facts or extenuating circumstances of which you were unaware that account for a situation you may have misconstrued. Agree to disagree.
- Ask a third party to mediate.
- If your company has a human resources department, try going to them for help.
- Ask for a change in your work situation. If possible, switch to another department.
- If this is someone you like but someone with whom you're having conflicts at the moment, let your coworker know that you care and that the relationship matters to you.
- Use "I" statements to let your colleague know how his or her actions or words affect you. Your goal is not to reject this person, just to get your colleague to stop a particularly annoying behavior.

- Keep it simple. Focus on the one issue that needs work, rather than everything under the sun.

- Avoid getting into a one-upmanship situation. Let the other person "win." Even if you're right and you know you're right, figure out a way to approach this person that minimizes conflict.

- Emphasize your similarities and shared goals, interests, values, or beliefs, rather than creating a wedge by dwelling on your differences.

- Share credit, as appropriate, so that you get labeled a "we"—rather than a "me"—colleague.

USING TIME MANAGEMENT SKILLS TO MANAGE YOUR WORK RELATIONSHIPS

Here are three ideas that you might find helpful in managing your work relationships:

1. **React in the now.** Family, school, and previous work experiences may be influencing how you react (or overreact) to fellow coworkers, bosses, employees, clients, customers, or service providers. Do you have difficulty dealing with authority figures (perhaps due to overly critical parents)? Do you take suggestions from your coworkers or your boss as negative criticism rather than useful feedback? Does your need to be liked lead you to accept whatever someone says or does—even if you disagree—so you don't make waves? Try to react in the now, putting these deep-seated associations behind you that may be negatively affecting your having more positive connections *today*.

2. **Stop making excuses.** For many, time has become just an excuse. Look beyond that excuse and see what's really causing the challenges you're facing—whether they're work-related or people-related. If you are procrastinating about getting together with coworkers, your boss, clients, or customers, view this behavior as providing information. Why are you procrastinating? Are you afraid you'll say or do the wrong thing? Do you want to invite your colleagues or business associates to your home, but find you are too much of a perfectionist to entertain? Are you afraid that you won't have enough time so that everything will be exactly right?

3. **Take time to connect.** Are you mismanaging your work or personal time so you lack the time and energy to socialize, even though you know it's a key element to your success and personal happiness? Make connecting with others a priority, and find the time to foster those connections. While e-mail is fast, it can be counterproductive if it doesn't bring a relationship closer. Nuances are often lost in cyberspace, and hurt feelings and miscommunications can ensue. Don't rely on e-mail exclusively; pick up the phone or, if possible, get together in person.

DAY 13

Tips for Networking Effectively

If you work at home or in an outside office with few or no staff members, getting out and meeting others becomes increasingly important. Interacting with others is key to your mental health so you don't feel isolated and ignored, especially if you're also unattached and living alone. You and your business will also benefit from the ideas and information you gather from others, whether they're in similar or disparate industries.

Why is networking so challenging, especially for those who are used to working in more isolated environments? You may have heard of the comfort zone, that place where you feel most understood and most welcome. As you'll see from Figure 13-1, however, for most of us the comfort zone of relationships—which usually includes you in the center, followed by your family and/or romantic partners and then your closest friends—encompasses a relatively small number of relationships. For success in most businesses, you need to have a very wide sphere of influence, or SOI. This encompasses the relationships that fall outside your comfort zone, namely, your casual friends and acquaintances, as well as your workships. I define *workships* as relationships with colleagues who are not yet

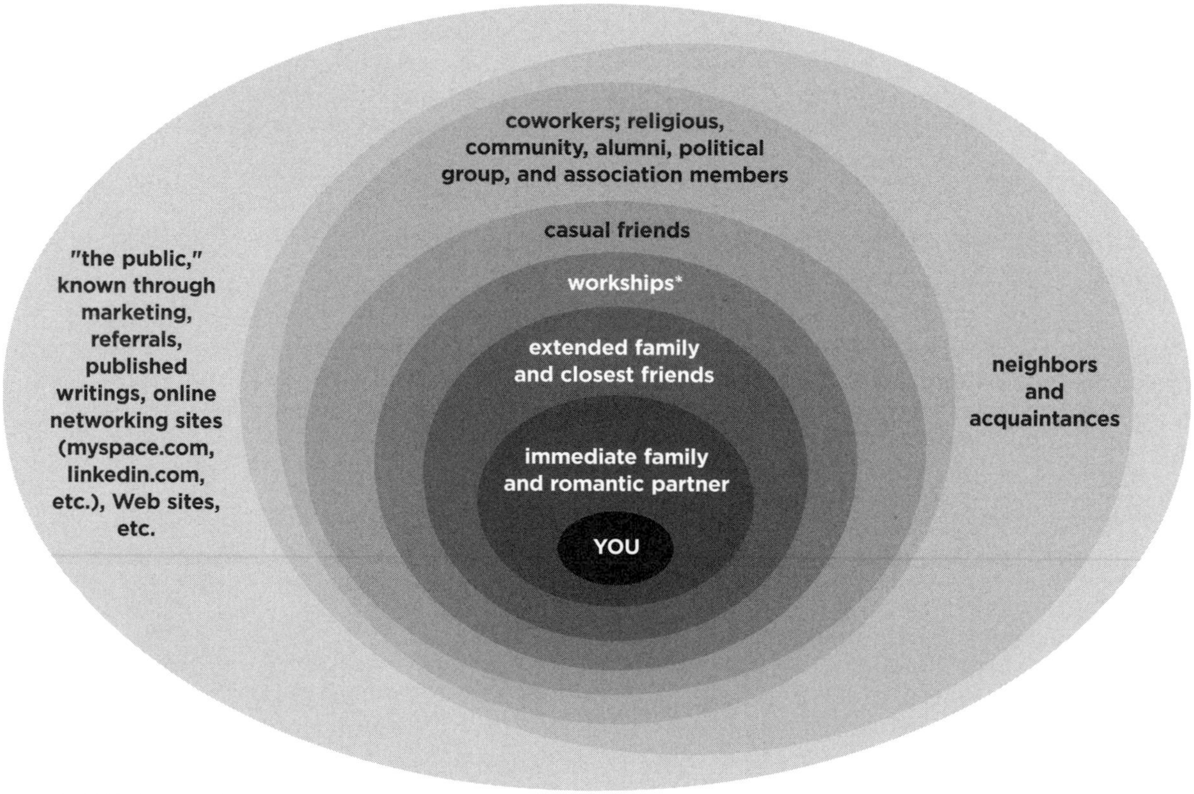

coworkers; religious, community, alumni, political group, and association members

casual friends

workships*

extended family and closest friends

"the public," known through marketing, referrals, published writings, online networking sites (myspace.com, linkedin.com, etc.), Web sites, etc.

immediate family and romantic partner

YOU

neighbors and acquaintances

Fig. 13-1. Your sphere of influence (SOI)
*This illustration shows how your sphere of influence (SOI) extends from yourself to your primary family/romantic partner and friend relationships. In general, as the circle widens, the intimacy level in each relationship diminishes. To succeed in most businesses and careers, you need to constantly expand your SOI. *Note: Workships is a term I use to denote a business- or work-related relationship that is more than an acquaintance but less than a friendship.*

friends, but are more than casual acquaintances. For example, a relationship with a coworker may progress into a workship if you socialize with this person in or out of the office, eating lunch together, going out for a drink after work, or getting together at each other's homes or apartments. Workships can include coworkers, clients, customers, or service providers. Your SOI also includes your extended family. Depending on how large your family is, and how frequently you connect with your siblings, aunts, uncles, and cousins, that sphere can be small or extensive.

Networking enables you to go beyond your comfort zone to create as extensive an SOI as possible. You can attend an event such as a conference, a trade show, or an association meeting, or take a more active role: Help to organize a charity event, teach a course, or offer to be a guest speaker at a class or on a panel.

Next, follow up on any new relationships you form through your networking efforts. Over the years I've observed that there are those who don't take the time to network; they admit that their business suffers as a result. There are others who do make the effort to go to events and forge new connections; however, the way they follow up with those new relationships fails to make the initial networking effort pay off in the way that it should and could.

Paulette Ensign, who runs her own San Diego based company, Tips Products International, is a consummate networker. Over the years, she has found that some networking techniques just don't work for her. Ensign notes: "An almost involuntary exchange of business cards to anyone attending a networking meeting has proven time and again to be a completely useless activity. It's a waste of time, business cards,

energy, and makeup." She does, however, still network—in person, over the phone, and by e-mail. For her, the secret to effective networking is to follow two principles: First, she gets as much information as necessary to determine that someone is indeed "a likely conduit to the people I want to reach." Second, she attempts to be as specific as she possibly can with her request for information.

Ensign shares a recent example of how these two networking principles have worked for her:

> I was invited to contribute to someone else's book about information products. The invitation came from my responding to a query in someone else's ezine. The book was published, and I had some additional communication with the book's author, getting to know her a bit more. I independently decided to offer a full-day public workshop in her city, which is a city I have never visited. I asked if she knew anyone who could help me promote the class there. She offered me two contacts, both of whom are ideal, each in different ways, both of whom are in the throes of now working with me on this. In the meantime, the author and I have only ever communicated via e-mail. We live in the same time zone and have never even heard each other's voice.

Here are some additional tips for more effective networking:

- People are usually more comfortable meeting others with whom they already have some sort of connection, such as a shared membership in an association or a mutual acquaintance. As noted in Day 8, this is what I call a POR—Point of Reference.

- It's always better to have someone call on your behalf first to let a third party know that you're interested in setting up a meeting or an introduction, rather than to cold call. If an acquaintance says, "Call and use my name," try to get him or her to call for you instead; then follow up with your own call to this new connection.

- Sometimes you have to decide between completing a task and taking the time to network. If you decide that your time is not best served attending a function, don't beat yourself up over your decision. Try, if possible, to get an attendee list, and buy tapes, CDs, or DVDs of the presentations you missed, so you have something to share with those who attended the event when you do find time to network.

- Ask someone who is attending to report back to you about the event, so you are as in the loop as possible when you network with this group again, especially if they have regular meetings or regular gatherings.

- Try to have fun when you network. If you enjoy meeting other people and getting to know them, it will show. The outcome of your networking efforts will be more positive than if you're resentful of spending time away from the office or so desperate to make new contacts that you're pushy and short with people.

- You want whoever you meet to know and care about you and your business. That means sharing with that person the essence of what you do, as well as listening and showing an interest in the other person so the interaction is not one-sided.

- Follow up with new people you meet within 48 hours to a week. However, don't pounce on someone so quickly that you look desperate. In your follow-up, if

possible, try to include something of interest to the person you're networking with. It could be a statistic that you've learned that applies to your industry, a reference to a book you're reading, or a movie you've seen that you want to recommend or comment on.

- Take the time to enter any contact information that you receive into your database, along with notes so that you can remember a week, six months, or a year down the road why and how you met someone, and what information you exchanged.

- To be effective, networking should be a continual process, not just something you do once a year, at holidays, or at an annual conference. Although meeting in person is optimal, between get-togethers you can stay connected through e-mail or by phone.

If you're not a fan of attending association meetings or structured events, you can network from the comfort of your home or office at all hours of the day or night. There are several online services, like myspace.com, linkedin.com, and friendster.com, which are based on the premise of expanding one's SOI (sphere of influence) through online connections that ripple into larger and larger spheres. Online networking services are fast, convenient, and often free or low cost. Unfortunately, what you learn about someone online may not be accurate; at times, people misrepresent themselves online. Exercise the necessary caution when dealing with a total stranger. Some services try to link you to new people through mutual acquaintances. Still, make sure to take necessary precautions when beginning a relationship on the Internet.

IS SOCIALIZING A WASTE OF TIME?

According to a 2008 telephone survey of 573 men and women who were employed full- or part-time, socializing was considered one of the four top time-wasters at work. Included by survey participants in the category of socializing was gossiping at the water cooler, socializing not related to work issues, and compulsive talking. The survey was conducted for me by CARAVAN® Opinion Research Corporation.

I wonder if those men and women who labeled socializing as their number-one time-waster at work would consider it in such a negative light if they knew that research has linked having friends at work and socializing to increased productivity and worker satisfaction, as well as lower employee turnover. As William D. Marelich wrote in his article, "Can We Be Friends?" published by *HR Focus*, "The reality is that friendships in the workplace can be quite beneficial, both for the individuals involved and the organization."

My years of research into work and friendship, highlighted in my book, *Who's That Sitting at My Desk?* confirms that having a connection is the first step in forming a possible friendship. What better way to try to connect than to socialize at work, the key place where new friendships are initiated in the post-high school, college, and graduate school years?

BEAT THE CLOCK

1. Consider each and every meeting you're supposed to attend or lead in the next month. Do you have a firm agenda for each one? What can you do to prepare and plan so that each meeting is more effective? Is each meeting useful, or would a phone or video conference call be more effective?

2. Consider your last networking opportunity. Was it enjoyable? Stressful? Successful? Are there any networking events that you could attend in the near future? What are some of the communication techniques you've learned or perfected that you could apply in these new situations to achieve a better outcome?

3. Role-play a typical networking experience with a friend or family member—such as introducing yourself to a total stranger or reacquainting yourself with someone you've met before—to boost your confidence and hone your skills as a networker.

DAY
13

DAY 14

Balancing Your Life and Making Time for Relationships

If you're like most people today, you're completely inundated with work, family matters, personal interests, community concerns, and even volunteer activities. How do you manage it all? What I've learned is that you can't do it all. But you can determine what is most important to you at this point in your life and focus on those relationships and responsibilities, accomplishing more of what counts with less stress. The trick is to strike a balance between work and personal time. In this chapter we'll look at balancing your life—even if you're a workaholic (or you work for one)—as well as looking at how to find and cultivate time for yourself, your romantic partner or spouse, and your children, whatever their ages. We'll also discuss ways to add an extra hour to your day and the value of vacation time and how to plan better for it.

How Balanced Is Your Life?

The vice president of commercial asset management for a North Carolina company acknowledges that the line between work and leisure time has faded as she finds herself working longer hours than ever before. She explains: "I put my kids to bed and then go work on the computer at home, sending e-mails or writing letters, creating my reports."

Pat Schroeder, CEO of the Association of American Publishers, faced similar challenges when balancing her demanding career as a congresswoman with her responsibilities as a wife and mother of two small children. Before she was elected to Congress, she taught at the university level and practiced law part-time; however, upon assuming office she quickly discovered that Congress was a 24/7 whirlwind of activity. After working all week—including many late nights—she would return to her district in Denver on weekends to reconnect with her constituents. As a rule, her family always tried to have dinner together. Schroeder read that National Merit Scholars had dinner with their parents three or four nights a week, so if she were in session late her children would come in and have dinner and do homework up in the office. Looking back on that period, she says her children enjoyed their eventful lifestyle: "Washington during the week. Colorado on weekends. They did better than I did. Mine was the energy problem."

As you can see, there are time demands and scheduling issues associated with every job, from congresswoman to office worker to entrepreneur or freelancer. The trick is to strike a balance between work and personal time—to avoid becoming a workaholic with an out-of-balance life.

The Dangers of Being a Workaholic

In some fields, long hours are par for the course and difficult to avoid, no matter how time management savvy you are. If you're in your internship or residency years at a hospital, putting in 60 to 80 or more hours a week is not unusual; the same goes for those beginning at a corporate law firm. In other businesses, there are deadline pressures—such as getting out a daily newspaper or online publication, a monthly magazine, or working around the clock to make a major deadline—that are consistent or intermittent, but tied to the job. If you're in retail, your hours may be excessive during certain times of the week as well as certain months of the year, such as in the two weeks right before Christmas. By contrast, the workaholic puts in extreme hours each and every day, even when there is no specific deadline pressure. How do you know if you've crossed this line? If you're unsure about whether or not you're a workaholic, take the quiz titled Are You a Workaholic? Then read the discussion of the answers to see how they relate to you.

Workaholism can take a toll, both physically and mentally, since it's difficult for workaholics to keep up the intense pace that they set for themselves. The workaholic's personal relationships may also suffer, as children and romantic partners feel ignored, members of the extended family become distant as a result of neglect, friends are put off indefinitely until the relationships ultimately fade away, and new relationships fail to develop as the workaholic struggles to make time for current relationships.

Fortunately, one of the cures for workaholism is to put into practice the time management strategies detailed in this book.

DAY 14

That's because workaholics tend to be poor managers of their time. Workaholics often struggle with procrastination and other time management issues. Once they do get to work, they don't want to stop—after all, it was so hard to get going in the first place. Learning how to counteract procrastination will help the workaholic (or the reformed workaholic) to begin a job in a timely fashion so there's a greater likelihood of completing the work and moving on to other tasks, such as spending time with loved ones or volunteering in the community.

If You Work for a Workaholic

Even if you're not a workaholic, you may work for one. It's generally easy to identify the symptoms—your boss gets to work excessively early, leaves very late, works at night and on weekends, and everything else in his life, including relationships, takes second place to work. (If you're uncertain if your boss qualifies, retake the quiz titled Are You a Workaholic, applying the questions to your boss.)

The first step is to determine whether your boss is even aware that she's a workaholic. As with overcoming every other addiction, your boss first has to admit that she has a problem. If she needed to work around the clock to get to where she is now—especially if that entailed years of juggling a full-time job, going to school at night, and studying on weekends—it may not be easy to give up those habits, let alone acknowledge that she's a workaholic. However, if you (and the team) can't keep up with her pace or you fear that she is heading toward burnout, stress-related ailments, and possibly even a heart attack, try to help raise her awareness of the situation. For example, if it's eight o'clock on a Friday night and, once again, you and your boss are the only ones still working at the office, you might say, "Wow. Can you believe no one else is around? What time is it, anyway? Eight o'clock already? On a Friday night? What do you say we call it a night and start in again on Monday?"

If your boss says, "No, that's okay, I'm going to keep on working. You go home," at least you can make a graceful exit and help yourself to avoid either an out-of-balance life or burning out. But if your boss expects you to stay and continue burning the midnight oil, consider whether this is a one-time or occasional request, tied to a looming deadline, or a daily or regular pattern that you need to watch out for. If it's a one-time or occasional requirement, it's usually in your best interest to put in those extra hours. (Of course, be careful about driving home so exhausted that you put yourself or others on the road in jeopardy.) Practically every job has that occasional crunch time that requires you to work overtime. But if it's more than once or even twice a week, see if you can discuss the situation with your

boss, without putting your job in danger. Proceed with caution: If you suggest hiring one or more additional employees because the workload is obviously too much for both of you, you could be labeled unproductive or uncooperative. Instead of suggesting hiring additional help, or even outsourcing some jobs so the workload is more manageable, consider staggering deadlines and due dates.

Sometimes others can see clearly negative patterns in your behavior and provide a catalyst for change. I was conducting interviews with high-earning real estate professionals in preparation for my time management talk at their upcoming educational retreat in Dallas. I had played telephone tag for several days with one very successful broker and we finally got to speak by phone on Friday night at around seven o'clock. I asked him if he was a workaholic. He assured me that he had a balanced life. His wife must have heard enough of the conversation on his end to have figured out what I'd asked him, because she called out, loud enough for me to hear, something along the lines of: "You're telling her that you're not a workaholic and here it is seven o'clock on a Friday night and you're doing a phone interview related to work!"

The second step is to look at your own behavior, as well as your boss's, and see what could be changed. Is there anything you could do or suggest to help your boss pace himself better? Perhaps you're agreeing to unrealistically short deadlines in order to yes your boss, and then working around the clock in a desperate effort to make those deadlines. Could creating more realistic deadlines help your boss (and you) to work at a diligent but healthy pace? How about suggesting that your boss start taking a one-hour break for lunch (if he doesn't take a lunch break), and getting away from his

DAY
14

desk—whether that means going to an outside restaurant, eating in the company cafeteria, or using the time for exercise. Also look at your own habits and see if there's a way to streamline your productivity so you get more done without staying late. As an alternative to staying late at the office, especially if you have a long commute, you might offer to keep working once you get home or over the weekend. However, this should be only on an as-needed basis. If it becomes a regular pattern, you have allowed your boss to remake you in his own workaholic image.

Let your boss know that you're worried about what his work habits might be doing to him. Since workaholics often use work to numb the pain that they associate with relationships or other activities, knowing that someone cares about him beyond work might help to open the door to considering how to face and overcome this work addiction.

Finally, know that reporting to a workaholic boss does not mean that you're lazy or underperforming, because you are putting in the required hours (and then some). If you work for a workaholic, you have to accept that she may expect you to replicate that behavior. Figure out what is reasonable and what is so extreme that you would be risking your health and your other commitments—such as your relationships or outside interests—if you allowed yourself to fall into these habits. If the atmosphere is unpleasant because your boss is a workaholic and she will not or cannot change, consider looking for a new job before you turn into a workaholic yourself.

Adding an Hour to Each Day

When I was conducting a recent workshop on time management, I asked the development officers and administrative assistants in the group if they had any suggestions for accomplishing more at work. A man replied, "Add an eighth day to the week." I jokingly asked, "Should it be a leisure day or another workday?" He wanted it to be another workday.

If you added a sixth workday to the week, would you get more done? Or would you just be more exhausted from having to wait another 24 hours to get to your leisure time, traditionally the time we use to replenish ourselves before the workweek recommences?

An alternative to actually adding another day to the workweek is to shift how you go about your work, and how you manage your time, so you not only feel as if you had an extra hour at your disposal but you actually do have it, because you're getting so much more done in less time. Furthermore, if you could find an extra hour each day—a gift, if you will, that you can use for work or for leisure—that adds up to an extra day of accomplishments each week, without having to actually expand the workweek in practice.

LOOK AT YOUR OWN BEHAVIOR

Could creating more realistic deadlines help your boss (and you) to work at a diligent but healthy pace?

15 WAYS TO ADD AT LEAST ONE HOUR OF PRODUCTIVE TIME TO YOUR WORKDAY

1. Put a sign on your door that reads DO NOT INTERRUPT FOR ONE HOUR. Indicate the beginning and end of this hour-long period.

2. Cut down on time-consuming telephone tag by finding alternative ways to communicate, such as by e-mail, instant messaging, fax, or cell/mobile phone. Whenever possible, let others know what times you'll be available for phone calls and ask others to let you know what is a good time to reach them, so you don't waste time fruitlessly trying to communicate with each other.

3. Wake up an hour earlier. (But be careful not to become sleep-deprived. The average sleep requirement is six to eight hours daily, although there are, of course, individual variations.)

4. Go to sleep an hour later. (Once again, make sure you're still getting enough sleep for you.)

5. Take a 15-minute catnap to replenish yourself and refuel your mind, so you can continue to be productive, work longer hours, or get to sleep later.

6. Shop by phone or via the Internet as much as possible; this will save an hour or more that you might have spent commuting to a store, sitting in traffic, or standing on line waiting to be served.

7. Shorten your commuting time by traveling or commuting during off-peak or non–rush-hour times, when traffic jams are less likely. Use your commuting or travel time productively by listening to books or professional magazines on CD or on your MP3 player. Use a tape recorder to document your thoughts for an upcoming presentation or writing assignment, or as a verbal version of a journal. (We'll discuss more ways to make effective use of your commuting time later in this chapter.)

8. Have a list of your frequently called business and personal phone numbers readily accessible, so you don't waste time trying to locate missing phone numbers.

9. Delegate or outsource nonpriority tasks to others, including family members (such as your spouse, your children, or your retired parents), hired help, additional assistants, or nonpaid interns.

10. If you work at home, put a clock in every single room—including your bathroom(s), kitchen, and office—and by each phone, to keep track of time, so you don't spent too long on nonpriority calls. This practice will help you to maintain your time awareness even while getting ready for appointments. Make sure each clock is accurate and that batteries are replaced so the time is reliable.

11. Use a portable phone or a headset so you can complete other tasks that do not require your full concentration, such as home or office filing, or retrieving pages from the fax machine, while you're on a personal or business call.

12. Learn how to read faster. Take a course in speed-reading.

13. Prioritize your key goals each day, and say no to nonpriority tasks or activities. This will free up your time and improve your focus on what really counts.

14. Cut down on time spent on errands or performing regular tasks. Have monies that are owed to you credited to your account; use automatic bill paying, so you no longer have to write out checks each month, especially for monthly bills, such as your mortgage or rent payment, your car payment, and your electricity bill. Set up a secure Internet component to your bank account, enabling you to at least check the balance in your bank account, eliminating the need for in-person trips to the bank; some Internet accounts even provide for electronic deposits or withdrawals.

15. Use time spent waiting for your doctor, dentist, or any other appointments to catch up on your reading—whether it's business-related or for your own edification or enjoyment. Carry around that novel or business book you're reading during your spare time so you can grab it when those extra moments occur.

Why Balance Saves You Time As It Improves Your Productivity and Your Relationships

As noted above, maintaining a balanced life is usually the sign of someone who is productive and efficient. In addition, engaging in non-work-related activities and reconnecting in a positive way with friends and family helps you to refuel, so you return to work refreshed and revived. (Remember all the benefits of taking a break discussed in Day 3?)

Having a balanced life also increases the likelihood that you'll be more interesting to be around. You're far more likely to bore people if all you talk about is your work. Making time for your personal relationships, as well as for hobbies, sports activities, and attending social or cultural events, sends out a clear message at work and in your personal life that you're in control of your time. A balanced life also contributes to a longer and healthier life; non–work-related activities may reduce stress, helping you to be more resilient in the face of day-to-day work pressures. Here are some tips for maintaining balance in your life:

1. Wondering if you have a balanced life? Ask those who depend on you—such as your children, your spouse, your parents, or your friends—if they feel you have enough time for or with them. (If a child is unable to speak yet, of course you'll have to look for nonverbal cues that he feels he's getting enough attention.)

2. Ask yourself how much time each day you take for yourself. If your answer is "none" or "less than 30 minutes," you need to work on the balance in your life.

3. Is there a difference between your weekdays and your weekends? If your week is one huge blur, consider making more of a distinction between your work and leisure days and evenings.

4. Make time for your friends who live far away, scheduling events weeks or even months in advance, if

necessary. It's usually better to have a plan to get together, even if you have to reschedule as the time draws nearer. That's preferable to failing to see each other for months or years because you've simply lost track of time.

5. Retake the Are You a Workaholic? quiz and consider what your answers say about you (or your loved ones).

Getting More "Me," "We," and "Us" Time

Part of having a balanced life is having enough me time. "Me time" refers to whatever you need for yourself, whether that means time alone or time to pursue hobbies, special interests, community service projects, or any other activities that you enjoy besides those responsibilities and activities you have to do for your job or for your family members. Why is this so important?

ON YOUR OWN: "ME TIME" BENEFITS AND GOALS

What are some of the reasons you need "me time"? List the benefits to you of carving out me time for the things you enjoy, such as taking a bath, writing in your journal, meditating, doing yoga, and so forth, each day:

1. _____

2. _____

3. _____

Imagine that I could wave a magic wand and you suddenly had at least one hour a day that was now your official "me time." (Don't worry now about the logistics of how you'll make this happen, whether you need a baby-sitter for your children, a caregiver for an aging parent, or a way to delegate some of the work that's piled up, to which you haven't gotten.) Write down the top three ways you would spend this "me time." Make sure you pick activities that you truly enjoy, not things you think you should want to do, so that these goals motivate you:

1. _____

2. _____

3. _____

If you're having trouble coming up with one—let alone three—ways to spend your "me time," that's okay. Think back to the last time you did something completely frivolous, whether it was last month, last year, or five years ago. Was it going to the movies? Playing squash or tennis with a friend? Getting your nails done? Going to a concert on a work night? Going out to dinner? If necessary, write down activities that you've imagined doing but have never tried. Fill in all three possibilities on the blank lines above. By concretizing your "me-time" goals, you will increase the likelihood that your "me time" will become a reality.

First of all, time to yourself helps reduce stress (which bolsters your immune system's ability to fight disease, keeps you from stress eating, and promotes your ability to be a better listener, parent, spouse, worker, and friend). Second, especially if you're parenting young children who require you to be alert and aware of their every move, it makes parenting more fun. That's because you'll be less likely to be resentful that all your time is spent taking care of others and doing what everyone else wants or needs to do. Having fun at some time during the day, even briefly, in ways that you relish makes you more effective overall. That doesn't mean that you don't genuinely enjoy reading to your children or taking them on a nature walk. But make the time to read a novel or short story for yourself, even if it's for 15 minutes a day, or to play tennis or participate in a group exercise class with other adults.

For some working parents, the idea that they are not only entitled to some "me time," but that it also can make them better parents, can be very liberating. I am reminded of the relief expressed by one of the attendees at my Finding More "Me Time" workshop, when I shared that concept with her and the rest of the group. She was a married physician who was working part-time and parenting three young children. Previously she thought she might have to put off having a moment to herself until all the children were grown up!

WAYS TO CARVE OUT "ME TIME"

1. Commit to a set amount of "me time," either daily or weekly. Recognize that this time is crucial for you as well as for your children and your spouse, and that it will reduce your stress level, help you to operate more efficiently in all areas of your life, and make parenting more fun.

2. Select one or more specific ways to spend your "me time," such as walking or jogging, luxuriating in a bubble bath, learning a new language, sorting through old photos or organizing digital photos into a scrapbook, taking a course one night a week, or going for a massage. Establishing a concrete target is more effective than setting a more general or vague "me time" goal.

3. Group chores and errands together so you shop for groceries once or twice a week, not daily, and prepare meals in advance so you can freeze and reheat them, as needed. Shop by phone or over the Internet as much as possible, so you save time going to stores or standing in line.

4. Wake up an hour earlier or go to sleep an hour later. (But don't let yourself become sleep-deprived or you'll risk falling asleep at the wheel or in a meeting.) If necessary, take a 15-minute catnap to replenish yourself so you'll accomplish more.

5. Ask a trusted family member or friend, such as your spouse, a parent, or a sibling, to help with child care so you can arrange for "me time." Alternatively, you could hire a baby-sitter or attend an exercise class at a health club that offers baby-sitting services.

FINDING "WE TIME"

Your second wish has been granted: You now have "we time." For starters, how do you define *we*?

We could refer to you and your significant other—your date, your romantic partner, your spouse, you and a friend, or you and your child. This is a "you plus one other person" goal, such as making the time for physical intimacy with your romantic partner or getting together with your closest friend for a weekly cup of coffee. (Finding "us time," or time for you plus two or more people, will be discussed in the next section.) So what are the three top ways you want to spend your "we time"? Below are a series of exercises to help you set goals for spending time with the special people in your life.

GOALS FOR TIME SPENT WITH YOUR ROMANTIC PARTNER

You don't want to take your romantic relationship for granted. By making time for each other and making your romantic relationship a priority in your life, you and your partner are more likely to beat the odds, unlike couples whose relationships falter and end. Below, list the top three activities you and your romantic partner enjoy together.

LONG-TERM GOALS

1. _____
   _____
2. _____
   _____
3. _____
   _____

SHORT-TERM GOALS

1. _____
   _____
2. _____
   _____
3. _____
   _____

Treat every day as if it's Valentine's Day; it shouldn't be just once a year that you fuss over your partner!

DAY 14

GOALS FOR TIME SPENT WITH FRIENDS

Now apply the same philosophy to your friends. If you take your friends for granted, you run the risk of their finding other friends with whom to connect. Sure, you can send an e-mail telling your friend how busy you are, or call to say "we'll get together soon." But if the "soon" turns into weeks, months, or even years, your friendship will fade. Deep friendships take time to sustain. Use the space below to note the ways that you like spending time with three of your closest friends. Try to list at least one activity you enjoy together in person (as opposed to chatting on the phone or e-mailing).

FRIEND #1 _____

1. _____

2. _____

3. _____

FRIEND #2 _____

1. _____

2. _____

3. _____

FRIEND #3 _____

1. _____

2. _____

3. _____

FRIEND #4 _____

1. _____

2. _____

3. _____

FRIEND #5 _____

1. _____

2. _____

3. _____

GOALS FOR TIME SPENT WITH YOUR CHILDREN

I include a separate category for "we time" you spend with each of your children individually, because that's a different kind of time and emotional commitment than that reserved for all your children together, or your children and their friends. Time with your son or daughter could include watching a favorite TV program together, going to a ball game, or going out to lunch. Below, list ways you already enjoy spending time with your young child, teen, or adult child. List additional goals for how you would like to spend your time together. You might even want to ask your child, teen, or adult child what activities he or she would enjoy doing with you. Your child's interests may have changed quite a bit if it's been a while—perhaps even years—since you spent a lot of time together.

CHILD/TEEN/ADULT CHILD _____ (NAME)

ACTIVITIES WE ENJOY DOING TOGETHER:

1. _____
2. _____
3. _____

MY CHILD/TEEN/ADULT CHILD'S SUGGESTIONS:

1. _____
2. _____
3. _____

CHILD/TEEN/ADULT CHILD _____ (NAME)

ACTIVITIES WE ENJOY DOING TOGETHER:

1. _____
2. _____
3. _____

MY CHILD/TEEN/ADULT CHILD'S SUGGESTIONS:

1. _____
2. _____
3. _____

Even if you only do one of these "we" activities with your child occasionally, such "we time" is important for both of you, whatever your child's age.

FINDING MORE "US TIME"

In addition to time spent alone or individually with the special people in your life, you also need to allow for "us time" for your immediate and extended family, as well as for socializing with your friendship network. This "us time" involves you and a number of friends, getting together as a group. These friends may also be friends with each other, or they may only be connected through their friendship with you.

GOALS FOR "US TIME"

What are your favorite ways to spend "us time" with your family and your friends? Use the space below to list those activities. You may include activities you currently take pleasure in as well as those pursuits you would like to get involved in.

"US" IMMEDIATE FAMILY TIME

1. _____
2. _____
3. _____
4. _____

"US" EXTENDED FAMILY TIME

1. _____
2. _____
3. _____
4. _____

"US" FRIENDS TIME

1. _____
2. _____
3. _____
4. _____

Vacation Time

Vacation time—whether it's a long weekend, a full week or two over the summer, or ten days spread out throughout the year—offers an opportunity for you to reconnect with family, your romantic partner and friends. It can even offer another dose of the "me time" that you seem to be lacking, due to the intense competing demands of your family, your job, and your other responsibilities. And ideally, when you return to the office, you are replenished and motivated to work hard until your next vacation.

It's great to be able to decide on a Friday that you'd like to go away for the weekend on a mini-vacation, or to decide on June 1 that you'd like to get a two-week rental in Martha's Vineyard during the first week of August. However, for many of us, planning a vacation requires weeks or months of decision making because a number of other people are involved—bosses, coworkers, spouses, children, and the like—and it's often necessary to book far in advance with airlines, hotels, or resorts, especially during the most popular vacation times. In addition, you may need to make accommodations for pets or dependent elders to be cared for in your absence.

What about spontaneity? Of course it would be a real treat to be spontaneous, especially about vacation time. Who wouldn't love to take a spur-of-the-moment trip to Europe or round up the family on a Friday and just take off to the mountains for a three-day weekend? Those spontaneous vacations are great goals and dreams, and airlines and online travel services make those last-minute vacations even more appealing by sometimes offering spectacular discounts if you wait until the last minute. But, for most of us, that kind of a drop-every-thing-and-go planning just doesn't work. If you have to coordinate the schedules of one or more working parents and school-age children, you'll have to make a commitment to a specific week or two for your vacation; otherwise, another year may go by without your taking any time off at all.

There is no one way to plan short breaks or long vacations. But if you have not been taking vacations on a regular basis, or you have not had any "dream" trips till now, it's time to reconsider how you and your family have gone about your vacation planning.

USING YOUR VACATION TIME

For starters, answer these questions:

I get _____ weeks of vacation each year.

I plan to use that vacation this year during these weeks: _____.

I will make formal plans for this vacation during _____.

DAY
14

VACATION PLANNER

TYPE OF VACATION (CHECK ONE)

_____ Extended (one week or longer, usually the annual vacation)

_____ Mini (less than one week; usually an extended weekend of three to four days)

_____ Weekend (from Friday night or Saturday morning through Sunday night, returning to work by Monday morning)

_____ One-day (a one-day trip, whatever day of the week it falls on)

DATES

_____ (specific dates planned)

_____ alternative date(s), if preferred dates are unavailable

DESTINATIONS

List destinations in order of preference, with #1 being the most desirable:

1. _____

2. _____

3. _____

MODE OF TRANSPORTATION TO THE DESTINATION

_____ car

_____ train

_____ plane

_____ boat

_____ other (fill in)

_____

BUDGET: ESTIMATED COSTS:

Transportation _____

Hotel _____

Number of rooms _____

Meals _____

Entertainment _____

Any frequent flyer, rewards points, free companion tickets, or programs available for this vacation?

_____ Yes   How many?_____

_____ No

What are the requirements/restrictions on redeeming the points and/or free tickets?

_____

Passport fees _____

Miscellaneous

_____

_____

_____

Name of travel agency and contact information (if any)

_____

_____

_____

Websites or company contact information and/or Web sites for reservations

_____

_____

_____

Making the Most of Your Commuting and Travel Time

Another great way to gain time—time that you may use for yourself or spend with those who are important to you—is to make more effective use of your commute or travel time. Practically everyone who works has to deal with commuting and travel time. Even if you work at home, for yourself or for a company through a telecommuting arrangement, there may be times when you have to travel, locally, nationally, or internationally, for your job. Luckily, there are some ways to reduce your commute and make the time you must spend commuting more enjoyable and productive.

Try to commute during off-peak hours so you avoid the usual rush-hour hubbub. (The only potential downside to this strategy is that there are usually more trains and buses, and more expresses, during the rush hours.) You can employ the same technique when you're driving to and from work or business appointments. As much as possible, choose times that minimize the likelihood that you'll be stuck in rush-hour traffic. You can save anywhere from 30 minutes to an hour or two by carefully timing your car trips and appointments.

Ditto for air travel. While the duration of the flight may not vary, the time spent traveling to and from the airport, as well as clearing security or customs, may be severely reduced if you choose non–rush-hour times for your trips. If you have the option of arriving somewhere an hour early, and having a leisurely cup of coffee or getting an extra hour of work done before everyone else arrives, that's a far better alternative to sitting in traffic or squeezing into a packed subway car during rush hour.

Of course, many people have little control over when they need to be on the road or the rails. If you have to commute during rush hour, make the most of that time. I remember how I used the time during my rush-hour commute from my apartment in Queens to my job in midtown Manhattan to learn enough conversational German to help me through an upcoming business trip to Berlin, Munich, and nine other German cities. Although the trip took only 14 minutes by bus at off-times, in the height of rush hour the trip could take almost an hour. Years later, I still remember some of the German phrases that I taught myself during those daily trips.

COMMUTE DURING OFF-PEAK HOURS

As much as possible, choose times that minimize the likelihood that you'll be stuck in rush-hour traffic. You can save anywhere from 30 minutes to an hour.

DAY 14

TIPS FOR MAKING THE MOST OF COMMUTING OR TRAVEL TIME

- If you use public transportation, or you're in a car pool and you're able to read while someone else does the driving, bring a book along for pleasure reading or for work-related research, or bring other reading materials, including newspapers, magazines, or newsletters related to your job.

- When traveling by air, whenever possible fly direct rather than taking one or more connecting flights.

- Bring along your laptop computer and work on the train or plane.

- Listen to books on tape or CD if you're commuting. (If you're driving, make sure this activity doesn't interfere with your concentration.)

- Write in a notebook or journal or talk into a tape recorder to record your thoughts for correspondence, or creative or professional writing.

- Daydream, think, strategize, plan, fantasize, imagine.

- Commute with others, whether personal acquaintances or colleagues, using the time to connect.

- Bring a video iPod or a portable DVD player, and watch TV programs or movies you didn't get to view the night before. Use a headset so you don't disturb other commuters.

- Pursue a hobby, such as knitting or sewing (being careful not to hurt yourself or other passengers, especially if there's a sudden stop).

- Use the time to learn a foreign language or to gain an even more detailed understanding of how the software you use works by reading the manual—things you don't seem to have time for during your days, evenings, or weekends.

- Bring along the booklets that accompany equipment, such as digital cameras, video-cameras, or office equipment like a computer, printer, or scanner, and read those booklets from cover to cover if you never seem to find the time to read that literature.

- If you're a student, use the time to read, review, or study.

- Observe what is going on in the world—how people are dressed and how they interact with each other—taking yourself outside of your own myopic world.

Daily Time Log: Day 14

In the next chapter, the Conclusion, you'll be reviewing what you have learned in *Work Less, Do More,* as well as how you are now using your time. Therefore, in preparation for tomorrow's review, please fill out the following Daily Time Log for today, Day 14. If possible, fill it out as you go through your day, rather than retrospectively.

DAILY TIME LOG: DAY 14

TODAY'S DATE: _____   **DAY OF THE WEEK:** _____

TYPE OF DAY: _____ (Work? School? Leisure?)

TIME	ACTIVITY

Begin with the time you wake up:

_____   _____

_____   _____

_____   _____

_____   _____

_____   _____

_____   _____

_____   _____

_____   _____

_____   _____

_____   _____

_____   _____

_____   _____

_____   _____

_____   _____

_____   _____

_____   _____

_____   _____

DAILY TIME LOG: DAY 14, *continued*

TIME   **ACTIVITY**

End with going to sleep:

_____   _____

_____   _____

_____   _____

_____   _____

_____   _____

_____   _____

_____   _____

ADDITIONAL NOTES:

_____

_____

_____

_____

_____

_____

COMMENTS (Try to notice if there are any periods when you are especially alert, or particularly tired, as well as any peaks of efficiency, times of heightened concentration, and periods when you pay better attention to details. At what times are you better or worse at working with people—both in person and over the phone?)

_____

_____

_____

_____

_____

_____

_____

BEAT THE CLOCK

1. Devise comprehensive "me time," "we time," and "us time" plans for the upcoming month. What activities will you want to explore? When and how will you get input from your family members, romantic partner, and friends about their "we time" or "us time" preferences? If you have dependent children or elders, what provisions can you make to allow yourself adequate "me time"?

2. Where are you going on your next business trip? How could you make your trip more effective for your job in terms of the timing or the pre-trip preparations? Would including a friend, your spouse, or your entire family on your business trip work? Would it help or hinder the business part of your trip or provide a vacation opportunity if you rarely or never take a vacation?

3. How do you commute to work? Have you timed the various commuting options to see which one is the most efficient and effective for you? If you have not reconsidered the way you commute, take the time to do it now. What's changed since you first started this method of commuting, in terms of the time you leave or the type of transportation that you use? Are there other options you have not recently considered that might be time savers, such as carpooling?

4. Look ahead to the rest of this year, next year, and the year after that. What are your vacation dreams and goals for this time? What do your romantic partner and/or family want to explore during your vacations? Take the time to sit down and discuss these ideas. Ask each family member to create a wish list of vacation goals. For those family members who are too young to write down their own goals, help them to write things down or to create pictures to illustrate their goals. What steps will you need to take to make those vacation dreams come true?

DAY
14

CONCLUSION

Assessing Your Progress and Looking Ahead

Now let's review what you have learned over the previous 14 days and discuss some additional ideas that will help you to accomplish more, faster and more effectively, in your work and leisure time. This will reinforce, as well as expand on, the lessons of this book. Also, since business has become increasingly global, we will explore time management issues you may face if you take a job (or start a business) where you interact with clients and colleagues around the world.

Taking Stock

It's time to assess the changes you have made in how you handle your time. First of all, look back at the benchmarks you set for yourself in Day 1—your own personal indications that you were managing your time more effectively. Write them down here again:

_____

_____

_____

_____

_____

_____

Now review the log you made yesterday. Look over when you woke up, what you did, when you got to work, what you accomplished at work, any breaks you took, phone calls you placed, projects you worked on, meetings you led or attended, how often you checked e-mail throughout the day, when you finished work, and what you did at night.

Compare that log to the one you filled out on the very first day. How do they differ? Are you spending less time distracting yourself by checking e-mail? Are you now grouping similar tasks together, placing phone calls when you have time in your schedule to do so, rather than interrupting other priority tasks to place a call? Do you see evidence that you have better concentration? Did you have any time yesterday to think, plan, strategize, and brainstorm, so you were not just rushing from activity to activity, client to client?

Look at the barometers that you were going to use to measure your time management improvements. Applying those measurements, consider yesterday. Consider what you've accomplished at work in the last 14 days. How would you rate your productivity on a scale of 1 to 5? How about compared to before, especially if you compare your productivity yesterday, on Day 14, or the day before, Day 13, to your productivity when you started out, on Day 1, or Days 2 or 3?

Putting Found Time to Work for You

We've all heard the expression "found money." Well, this is what I call *found time*. Found time is time that is now yours to use wisely, time that you used to take for granted, assigning it a low priority as minutes, hours, maybe even days were consumed without having something concrete to show for that time. If, after you've completed this two-week time management makeover, you still feel as though you have more to do than time to do it in, you may need to uncover these hidden times.

Look at your time logs. What times during the morning, afternoon, evening, or weekend are you idle? Decide how you can use these idle times to your advantage. For example, you could use the time you spend waiting for the bus or the half-hour you spend waiting in someone's office to plan, dictate, write, or read. Creating found time might entail waking up a little earlier, or going to bed a little later, or blocking out a certain number of hours on the weekends.

Your Time Management Horizon

One of the themes of this book is how change—both predictable changes that we all go through, and unpredictable changes, such as emergencies, changes in job responsibilities, or projects that are forced upon us—affect how we manage our time. At every stage of our lives there are unique time concerns, and those pulls change as we progress through the life cycle, from our earliest years through the school years, from working as a single person to working as part of a couple with or without children, to working as an older adult, to deciding how to spend your time as a retiree. Each stage has time issues. Let's examine some of those stages, and how improvements in time management might enhance those years.

THE PARENTING YEARS

If you're like most parents, your schedule is at least partially dictated by your children's time commitments. Of course, it's entirely possible to travel once you have children—remember the example of business owner Victoria Sutherland, who managed to spend an entire month in Bermuda with her husband and her teenage (homeschooled) son. For most, however, the parenting years must be a children-first stretch of time, lasting well into the kids' late teens. That does not mean that you must forgo "me" or "we time." As discussed in the previous chapter, finding a way to take care of all the family's needs, not just those of the children, is key to everyone's enjoying, not resenting, the parenting years.

As anyone who has gone through the difficult decision about whether to return to work or to stay home full time or even part-time can attest, there are a wide range of issues to consider, from economics and lifestyle concerns to deciding how to balance parenting and working to time issues. Some parents simply prefer to be around adults most of the day, rather than taking care of infants or children. Other parents, for

economic reasons, have to work. Perhaps even more important than whether or not you decide to remain employed outside the home when children are in the picture—by choice or by economic necessity—are the ways that parenting affects how you manage your time. For example, if you were used to working until 7 p.m. every night before you had children, you may want to get home by 5:30 so you get to spend at least one or two hours a night with your children before they go to sleep. How do you accomplish more during your workday so you're able to leave by 5? Although not an ideal solution, if you want to get home in time for a family dinner at 6, you might take home the work you were going to do at the office, retreating to your home office or working on your laptop in the bedroom from 9 to 11, after the kids are asleep.

You may also have to reorder your priorities, with the result that relationships you once had time to maintain at night or on weekends, you now squeeze in during rare free moments. For example, while you once got together with certain friends for dinner or at parties, perhaps now you meet for a quick lunch, if you work in the same city. Don't make your entire lives about your children or one day, before you know it, the children are grown, away from home, and you and your spouse will realize that you haven't done anything together since your courtship days.

Work Less, Do More is about making choices and shifting priorities and demands to accommodate where you are in life. What I hope I have taught you in this book is not a rigid plan but skills that can be applied to whatever ongoing or new challenges you're facing. Newborns or dependent children are parenting responsibilities that require you to shuffle time management goals and make tough choices. Caring for aging or sick parents is another predictable challenge that will affect time management at work and at home.

THE RETIREMENT YEARS

Few like to think about it, but the golden years, the senior years, or whatever you want to call the years after work, may for some last as long, or longer, than the more structured working years. The comment that I have consistently heard from retired seniors is, "I'm so busy now I don't know how I ever found the time to work!" Yes, some really are busy, and they're good busy, doing part-time paid or unpaid work that they love, pursuing hobbies or new interests that are all-consuming, traveling, and spending time getting to know their spouses, children, extended families, and friends better. But for others, especially those who are plagued with health problems, these retirement or postworking years can be tough, particularly if they never got the hang of managing their unstructured leisure time during the previous working or childrearing years.

My grandmother worked as a seamstress after my grandfather died and her three children had grown up and left home. When I started spending more time with her, she had been retired for many years. She didn't handle her seventies or eighties well. Sadly, most of her friends had either relocated to Florida or had died. Especially as her health deteriorated, my grandmother's time alone weighed on her. I used to jokingly tell her that my freelance lifestyle was actually preparing me for retirement; unlike most people, who work 9 to 5 for someone else, I was used to making my own hours and creating my own structure.

That is my best piece of advice to anyone who is retired and in those postworking years, whether you were a full-time home-maker who never had an outside job or someone who worked 70 hours a week: Create and follow a schedule, at least a couple of days a week. Set specific goals for yourself, for projects, for exercise, for reading and other leisure activities, and for socializing. If you don't create a schedule, it's too easy to fall into the trap of watching too much TV and becoming a shut-in, especially if you have to give up driving a car in an area where there is limited public transportation. If you're single and alone, it's easy to begin feeling isolated and lonely.

Creating a schedule helps to bring order into the potentially disorganized days of the postworking adult. Even if you were a stay-at-home parent while your children were growing up, your children's school and after-school schedules, as well as your spouse's work schedule (if you were married), gave a structure to your days and weekends. Now, with your children grown and work behind you, it's up to you to create a structure for yourself.

Eighty-one-year-old Nat Swann is an excellent example of someone who fills his days with regular and fulfilling activities. Swann, a married retired physician, now works part-time as a medical advisor. He is also completing his second book, a novel, and he plays golf several times a week. He eats lunch those days at the golf course as a way to socialize as well. The key is that he has a routine and a schedule that he tries to follow for his writing, his part-time work, and his physical activities. As Dr. Swann shared with me in an e-mail: "My retirement has allowed me to accomplish things I never had time to do during 35 years of concentrated practice. I won't say I'm 'driven' but I get bored if I'm not going at full gait."

By crafting a master plan for your retirement years, you can ensure that this time is blessed and precious, rather than squandered or plagued by boredom and isolation.

Doing Business Internationally: Time Management Concerns to Keep in Mind

If you do business internationally over the Internet, or if you travel extensively for business, there are time-related considerations that you need to bear in mind so you avoid potential clashes with your international colleagues. Even the way certain time-related behaviors are viewed can vary from culture to culture. For example, a young woman from Japan who is a Manhattan-based coordinator for a Japanese TV program shared with me that in Japan, "A workaholic who spends too much time on work will be praised" but in New York, people might consider such behavior to be a problem and accuse this person of "not fulfilling his own life."

Below are some useful guidelines for doing business with someone in China, Romania, Mexico, Germany, or any other country.

OVER THE INTERNET

- Find out if there are any holidays or vacation times you should know about that will prevent your international colleague from responding to your e-mail. Some countries, like all of the Scandinavian countries, France, Italy, and Germany, have one or more months over the summer when businesses are closed, so you should not expect a prompt reply to any of your correspondence or voice-mail messages during that time.

- Don't assume the person to whom you're writing has a high-speed Internet connection, especially if he or she is traveling internationally or relying on an Internet café, which may lack high-speed access. What that means is that attached files or downloads may take a very long time to access. If that is the case, you might want to paste material within the body of the e-mail, rather than sending that material as an attached file, or consider faxing or mailing long documents.

- Attitudes toward time differ internationally. If you're too pushy with those who are more relaxed about deadlines or time pressures, you can alienate them and even cause the business relationship to rupture or end. As a 64-year-old American publisher and consultant who conducts business internationally notes: "Time is treated more subjectively and abstractly in other countries and it is not a source of anxiety. The well-being of individuals and families has precedence over time."

CONDUCTING BUSINESS IN PERSON

- Know what is expected in each country where you travel for business. For example, working overtime and attending dinner with clients is de rigueur in Japan.

- Is entertaining at home acceptable in the country where you are doing business? It might be more common to meet for business at a restaurant. This could actually be a time saver, since you would avoid making the preparations that would be necessary if you were to host a dinner party or business gathering at your home.

- Age and socioeconomic factors may be more of a factor in attitudes toward time than nationality. For example, an older person may place a greater emphasis on trust and building a relationship through a face-to-face meeting than a younger client, who may prefer to handle business as quickly as possible and restrict contact to the phone or e-mail whenever possible and appropriate.

While there are various factors to consider when conducting business internationally, the reality is that the time management issue you're facing may have more to do with a particular company or individual and little to do with cultural differences. A business colleague in Germany pointed out that one's experience with a particular company may simply be a question of whether or not an office is especially efficient and responsive. As she notes: "There are companies that seem to have a similar approach and seem to be efficient depending also on how well they are equipped technologically and then there are companies where everything takes ages."

A BASIC ORGANIZING PRINCIPLE

Teaching young children the basic organizing principle of assigning everything its own place and returning an item to its place after removing it will take those children far in helping them to organize their own space as they mature into teenagers.

Passing the Torch: Teaching Time Management Skills to Your Children

Time management is a skill that parents can teach their children from the earliest years, first by example and then by creating household or academic expectations for their children and teens to apply to their daily activities.

THE EARLY YEARS

During the earliest years, parents organize their infants' lives. As early as the toddler years, it's possible to start teaching children the concept of sorting by category—for example, you can teach them to sort clean clothes by color or to put all the same kinds of toys in one container and other kinds of toys in a different one.

Teaching young children the basic organizing principle of assigning everything its own place, and returning an item to its place after removing it, will take those children far in helping them to organize their own space as they mature into teenagers.

Preschoolers don't respond to time as a cerebral or vague concept but rather as a sequence of events that mirrors its passage: First you wake up, then you brush your teeth, then you get dressed, then you have breakfast, then you go to preschool, then you get picked up by Mommy or Daddy, then it's time to go home.

Even though young children don't get a lot of homework, helping them to understand the concept of doing their homework first, before they play, can help to prevent them from acquiring a lifelong habit of putting off what has to be done until the last minute, or procrastinating.

I taught a four-week course on time management to fourth graders that was part of a "college for kids" program offered by the local community college. I was impressed with how well the students assessed their own organizational habits. When asked to respond to the statement "I have a 'to-do' list every school day" with "yes," "sometimes," "rarely," or "never," nine students answered "yes," one "sometimes," one "rarely," and four "never." Even by fourth grade, many of these students were thinking about organizational and study skills issues. Another question they were asked was, "If I had more time I would . . ." One girl responded, "go clean my closet," followed by "make my bed." Other responses from students included "clean my room," "do my homework," "read books," and "do a project." (However, this class wasn't filled with time management prodigies: Typical answers also included "watch TV," "play with my friends," and "go to a ball game.")

Giving your child a chore chart is a great way to teach delegating and organizing, as long as there is enforcement and reinforcement of the duties that are assigned. Either buy or create a chart indicating everyone's responsibilities. Some chores will be performed regularly; other tasks will be rotated. For example, this week it's Sally's turn to tie up the newspapers with string for recycling day; next week it will be Amy's turn, and the following week it will be Carl's. However, Sally, Amy, and Carl—ages six, nine, and ten, respectively—are expected to make their beds, brush their teeth, replace the cap on the toothpaste, and put their clothes in the hamper daily.

THE MIDDLE SCHOOL YEARS

For some overprogrammed middle school children, time is so parceled out among competing activities that these preteens seem headed toward burnout. By contrast, other preteens may start experiencing motivational challenges with their schoolwork, spending a disproportionate amount of time on leisure activities and too little time on studying, reading, and extracurricular school-related activities. Achieving balance is a goal, even as early as the middle school years, if not sooner. That balance should include a healthy mix of friends, family, community and volunteer pursuits, and extracurricular activities, as well as exercise, sleep, and relaxation.

When their children reach the middle school years, many parents who stayed home full-time with the children now consider their children independent enough for the stay-at-home parent to return to work. Although middle schoolers may seem mature enough to make their own decisions about how they will spend their time, they still need after-school supervision. Some seem to need one or both parents' help with schoolwork and studying for tests. Other parents encourage their children to take more direct responsibility for their studies, uttering the refrain, "Did you do your homework yet?" rather than personally helping the child to study for tests.

THE TEEN YEARS

During the teen years, time is one of the ways that the struggle to become independent plays out. Giving a teen a curfew helps her to structure her school and leisure time and reminds her that her parents and other authority figures still control her time. As teens start to drive, how they handle their own time becomes a measure of their maturity. It becomes harder for parents to discipline their teens about using time wisely; this motivation has to come from within. Tardiness or procrastination may become strategies used to gain negative attention, or to reflect ambivalence toward activities that are unpleasant, as much for the teen as for the adult. These are important years to continue reinforcing the value of being organized, meeting deadlines, prioritizing responsibilities, and setting goals.

As teens face the formalized testing necessary for most college admissions and students are divided into a range of classes based on their aptitude and grade point average, study skills and habits need to be seriously addressed. For some who need help, tutoring by peers or paid tutors is a welcome option and is usually time and money well spent. For others, attending summer school, taking additional classes, or transferring to another school that might better serve the teen's special needs, even if that means taking extra time to graduate, might be a good choice. Such extra instruction can address the teen's low school achievement, which is often as much a reflection of how time is spent on schoolwork as it is a reflection of a student's abilities and achievements.

Getting More Out of Each Experience

In their textbook *Health, Illness, and the Social Body,* sociologists Freund, McGuire, and Podhurst put it this way: "Control over time—our own or other people's—is a form of power. . . . Those with more power have more control over time."

Fortunately, learning time management techniques can actually give that power to anyone, regardless of his job or status at a company, because time management gives people time control. Proactively taking control of your time includes addressing the big picture—goal setting, prioritizing, and delegating—as well as managing day-to-day concerns, such as dealing with paperwork, eliminating clutter, and filing.

Effective time managers make everyone feel as though he or she is the only concern that they have at that moment (even if they are actually juggling five, ten, or dozens of other people or projects).

There is a feeling of being centered within each of us, a place where intellectual and creative work is nurtured and developed. It is usually necessary to have that concentration to create and work effectively. If your work or personal life lacks that centeredness, find a way to create it.

I recommend that you reread parts of this book, or the entire book, at different times in your career. You are reading it now, applying it to where you are at this moment. But if you get a promotion and your job function changes, if you progress from a single worker to a married executive with small children, or if you transition from one type of work environment to another—for example, moving from a major corporation to a smaller business where you have to do more for yourself—consider retaking this two-week makeover, so that you may address and work through any new challenges you may encounter. This is also true if there is a move, a beginning or ending of a major personal relationship, or physical challenges that you need to address.

21 Top Time Management Ideas

Here are some additional ideas, as well as several key suggestions presented earlier in *Work Less, Do More:*

1. Prioritize. It's not just a question of getting something done quickly and efficiently but making sure that what you're doing is what you should be addressing in the first place. Figure out what you need to do to succeed; focus your energies on just those actions, and say no to everything or everyone that distracts you.

2. As the $1 million+ top earners at a major commercial real estate company shared with me, when I asked for their time management secrets of success: Avoid doing between 9 and 5 what you can do between 5 and 9.

3. Plan, plan, plan, but be flexible enough to allow for urgent and pivotal changes to your plans.

4. Spread your net wide; don't waste time waiting for any one possibility when you could be generating more business or getting things done more effectively by taking advantage of multiple options. Learn to know when you need to deal with someone exclusively and when such restriction is unproductive and unnecessary.

5. Leave some free time every day in case there is a crisis or a new urgent priority you have to address. Don't overbook! (Especially at the end of a meeting, leave some free time for connecting and networking with other meeting attendees or leaders, if possible.)

6. See filing and paperwork as part of your job, not something you'll do when you finally get around to it.

7. Delegate to get more done in less time. When possible, delegate tasks, not relationships. Do what you do best and delegate to others those tasks that they do better, or those items that will bore you because your mind and talents are underutilized.

8. Periodically reevaluate your technology. (You don't just have to wait until something breaks down to replace it.) Are you up to date, or do you need to replace or upgrade any equipment? Not only may newer equipment be faster and better, but it may even cost less than the now antiquated versions you bought two, five, ten, or more years ago. How proficient are you on your equipment? Do you need additional training on your hardware or software? Are you making time to read any useful instructions or operating guidelines that will save you time?

9. Create and maintain your database of contacts, disciplining yourself to enter in new names, addresses, contact information, and the date and context of your initial meeting with each of these contacts as soon as possible after your introduction, whether over the phone, via e-mail, or in person. Consider purchasing a contact management software

program or a scanning device specifically designed to help you enter the data from business cards in a user-friendly format.

10. Take periodic breaks every day. This practice will help to improve your pacing and cut down on your stress. Make the most of your leisure time: Take vacations once or more throughout the year. If your weekends or other time off is not satisfying you, you might need to put some more time and energy into a leisure time plan.

11. Create realistic (attainable) deadlines and stick to them. However, if it becomes clear that a deadline cannot be met, either because it is unrealistic or because other projects or responsibilities have become priorities, let everyone know as soon as possible so that they can make adjustments in their schedules and any related marketing or sales commitments as well.

12. Time management is an ongoing process, not a static one. Revisit each and every section of this book when there are any changes in your work or personal life. Reapply what you learned to those changes, adjusting your time strategies accordingly, so that you can always say that you practice the pivotal life management principles of *Work Less, Do More*.

13. Back up your work often—even get backup equipment so that if your computer, printer, or scanner breaks down you have an alternative system available to you to save time, especially when you're in a deadline crunch. (Back up in multiple ways: Use a Zip disk, a second computer, or a memory stick; e-mail your work to yourself as an attached file; enlist a commercial service to which you can send your work over the Internet; or print out a hard copy.)

14. Review, reread, correct.

15. We re-create externally the chaos we feel internally. Hence, to get rid of clutter, or to cut down on distractionitis, look inside yourself to its cause.

16. Developing improved focus and concentration will allow you to immerse yourself in projects or relationships. If you consider yourself to be spread too thin, see what low-priority tasks or relationships you're able to reschedule or put off temporarily or longer.

17. While filing, organizing, and sorting through papers takes time, you will reap the benefits in time saved searching for things. In addition, you'll avoid the stress of feeling as if you're drowning in paper.

18. Observe what effective time managers do. Emulate their successful strategies, but also design your own systems that work for you.

19. Having enough time is a perception as much as a reality. In addition to meeting the demands of your boss and family members, you have to define what it takes for you to feel,

each day, that you have made optimum use of your time. Avoid using "I don't have enough time" as an excuse. Look beyond that cliché and probe what's really going on. You might be surprised that others find it refreshing when you start offering reasons besides lack of time for your choices. However, if you truly are hard pressed for time, especially if you're experiencing deadline crunches at work or you're on overload from family demands, don't be ashamed or afraid to say so.

20. Enjoy every task, every moment, and every relationship to the fullest. This moment is all you—or any of us—have. If you enjoy each and every moment completely, it will add up to a fulfilling life. Don't wish time away. Learn from all your experiences—even the negative ones—

so you can apply those lessons to what you say and do.

21. If you really want to get more out of each and every day, reach (and maintain) your healthy weight and exercise regularly. The increased energy that you feel, and your improved stamina, will help you to go about your everyday tasks with a quicker step. By taking control of your diet and exercise regimen—which can reduce stress, burn excess calories, and increase your endurance—you can add years to your life. Thus, you will give yourself the greatest productivity makeover—and gift— of all: more time!

Thank you for joining me on this 14-day productivity transformation. Now continue to make it a daily part of your life!

LIST OF WORKS CITED

Brod, Craig. *Technostress: The Human Cost of the Computer Revolution.* Reading, Mass.: Addison-Wesley Publishing Company, 1984.

BusinessWeek. "Smashing the Clock." December 11, 2006. Cover story.

Cockerham, William C. *Medical Sociology.* 10th edition. Englewood Cliffs, New Jersey: Prentice-Hall, 2006.

Davis, Sampson, George Jenkins, Rameck Hunt, with Lisa Frazier Page. *The Pact.* New York: Riverhead Books, 2002.

Drucker, Peter. *The Daily Drucker.* New York: HarperBusiness, 2004.

Freund, Peter E. S., Meredith B. McGuire, and Linda S. Podhurst. *Health, Illness, and the Social Body: A Critical Sociology,* 4th edition. Upper Saddle River, N.J.: Prentice-Hall, 2003.

Gardner, Chris, and Quincy Troupe. *The Pursuit of Happyness.* New York: HarperCollins/Amistad, 2006.

Goforth, Candace. "Tuesday is most productive day of week, statistics show." Knight Ridder/Tribune News Service, January 29, 2002, published in the *Akron Beacon Journal.* Posted online at: http://www.ohio.com.

Hallowell, Edward M. "Overloaded Circuits: Why Smart People Underperform." *Harvard Business Review on Managing Yourself.* Boston, MA: Harvard Business School Press, 2005, pages 21-41.

Kolberg, Judith. *Conquering Chronic Disorganization,* 2nd ed. Decatur, Ga.: Squall Press, 2007.

Lakein, Alan. *How to Get Control of Your Time and Your Life.* 2nd edition. New York: Signet, 1989.

Marelich, William D. "Can We Be Friends?" *HR Focus,* August 1, 1996, Vol. 73.

Mehrabian, Albert. *Silent Messages,* 2nd ed. Belmont, Calif.: Wadsworth Pub. Co, 1980.

Mitchell, Margaret. *Gone With the Wind.* Preface by Pat Conroy. New York: Scribner's, 2007.

National Institute of Mental Health. "Attention Deficit Hyperactivity Disorder." Available at: http://www.nimh.nih.gov/publicat/adhd.cfm#cause, revised 2006. First printed in 1994 and reprinted in 1996. Revised by Margaret Strock.

National Study Group on Chronic Disorganization (NSGCD), "What is the definition of chronic disorganization?", http://www.nsgcd.org/resource/faqs.phpl

O'Meara, Stephen James. "Keystroke Performance." *Odyssey*, April 2000, volume 9, page 4. (Articles about the results of Cornell University's Allan Hedge's study on the productivity benefit of taking breaks.)

Oncken, William, Jr., and Donald L. Wass. "Management Time: Who's Got the Monkey?" *Harvard Business Review* (November–December 1974): 75–80.

Rubenstein, Joshua S., David E. Meyer, and Jeffrey E. Evans. "Executive Control of Cognitive Processes in Task Switching." *Journal of Experimental Psychology: Human Perception and Performance* 27, no. 4 (2001): 763–797.

Sandberg, Jared. "Rise of False Deadline Means Truly Urgent Often Gets Done Late." *Wall Street Journal* (January 23, 2007), available at http://online.wsj.com/public/article_print/SB1169493746183999.html.

Statham, Anne, and Ellen Bravo. "The Introduction of Technology and Resulting Stress in the Workplace: How Do We Plan?" Paper originally presented to the Third Annual Women and Work Conference, Graduate School of Social Work, University of Texas at Arlington, May 1986, 29-page typescript.

Tracy, Brian. "5 Steps to Setting Goals." *Personal Excellence* (November 1997): 5.

Wheelis, Allen. *How People Change*. New York: Harper & Row, 1973.

Winter, Arthur, and Ruth Winter. *Brain Workout*. New York: St. Martin's Press, 1997.

Yager, Jan. *Creative Time Management*. Englewood Cliffs, N.J.: Prentice-Hall, 1984.

_____. *Creative Time Management for the New Millennium*. Stamford, Conn.: Hannacroix Creek Books, Inc., 1999.

_____. *Making Your Office Work For You*. New York: Doubleday, 1989.

_____. "Permanent Delegation." *Exec* (Spring 1995): 78–81.

_____. *Who's That Sitting at My Desk? Workship, Friendship, or Foe?* Stamford, Conn.: Hannacroix Creek, 2004.

_____. "Working Smart in Your First Job." *National Business Employment Weekly*, Spring 1992, pages 15, 17.

RESOURCES

Associations, Organizations, and Government Agencies

NATIONAL ASSOCIATION OF PROFESSIONAL ORGANIZERS (NAPO)

http://www.napo.net

National association for professional organizers, established in 1985, with numerous regional chapters. Members offer hands-on help to residential and business clients, including organizing, time management coaching, seminars, and workshops. Educational programs include an annual conference. Sponsors local events on organizing in celebration each January of Get Organized Month.

NATIONAL RESOURCE CENTER ON AD/HD

CHADD (Children and Adults with Attention-Deficit/Hyperactivity Disorder)
8181 Professional Place, Suite 150
Landover, MD 20785
http://www.help4adhd.org

Government-sponsored information clearinghouse, funded through a cooperative agreement with the Centers for Disease Control and Prevention.

NATIONAL STUDY GROUP ON CHRONIC DISORGANIZATION (NSGCD)

4728 Hedgemont Drive
St. Louis, MO 63128

http://www.nsgcd.org

Educational association affiliated since 2005 with NAPO (National Association of Professional Organizers), providing information on those who are chronically disorganized for the public and for organizing professionals.

APPENDIX OF BLANK TIME LOGS AND WORKSHEETS

DAILY TIME LOG: DAY _____

TODAY'S DATE: _____   **DAY OF THE WEEK:** _____

TYPE OF DAY: _____ (Work? School? Leisure?)

TIME   **ACTIVITY**

Begin with the time you wake up:

_____   _____

_____   _____

_____   _____

_____   _____

_____   _____

_____   _____

_____   _____

_____   _____

_____   _____

_____   _____

_____   _____

_____   _____

_____   _____

_____   _____

_____   _____

_____   _____

_____   _____

_____   _____

_____   _____

DAILY TIME LOG: DAY _____ *continued*

End with going to sleep:

_____   _____

_____   _____

_____   _____

_____   _____

_____   _____

_____   _____

_____   _____

ADDITIONAL NOTES:

_____

_____

_____

_____

_____

_____

_____

_____

_____

COMMENTS (Try to notice if there are any periods when you are especially alert, or particularly tired, as well as any peaks of efficiency, times of heightened concentration, and periods when you pay better attention to details. At what times are you better or worse at working with people—both in person and over the phone?)

_____

_____

_____

_____

_____

_____

_____

DAILY TIME LOG: DAY _____

TODAY'S DATE: _____   **DAY OF THE WEEK:** _____

TYPE OF DAY: _____ (Work? School? Leisure?)

TIME   **ACTIVITY**

Begin with the time you wake up:

_____   _____

_____   _____

_____   _____

_____   _____

_____   _____

_____   _____

_____   _____

_____   _____

_____   _____

_____   _____

_____   _____

_____   _____

_____   _____

_____   _____

_____   _____

_____   _____

_____   _____

_____   _____

_____   _____

_____   _____

_____   _____

_____   _____

End with going to sleep:

_____ _____

_____ _____

_____ _____

_____ _____

_____ _____

_____ _____

_____ _____

ADDITIONAL NOTES:

_____

_____

_____

_____

_____

_____

_____

_____

COMMENTS (Try to notice if there are any periods when you are especially alert, or particularly tired, as well as any peaks of efficiency, times of heightened concentration, and periods when you pay better attention to details. At what times are you better or worse at working with people—both in person and over the phone?)

_____

_____

_____

_____

_____

_____

_____

LANDLINE/OFFICE PHONE LOG

CALLS RECEIVED AT WORK

TODAY'S DATE: _____

DAY OF THE WEEK: _____

TIME	WHO CALLED	HOW LONG DID CALL LAST	PURPOSE OF CALL
_____	_____	_____	_____
_____	_____	_____	_____
_____	_____	_____	_____
_____	_____	_____	_____
_____	_____	_____	_____
_____	_____	_____	_____
_____	_____	_____	_____
_____	_____	_____	_____
_____	_____	_____	_____
_____	_____	_____	_____
_____	_____	_____	_____
_____	_____	_____	_____

CALLS RECEIVED AFTER WORK (AT HOME)*

TODAY'S DATE: _____

DAY OF THE WEEK: _____

TIME	WHO CALLED	HOW LONG DID CALL LAST	PURPOSE OF CALL
_____	_____	_____	_____
_____	_____	_____	_____
_____	_____	_____	_____
_____	_____	_____	_____
_____	_____	_____	_____

*You may prefer to log only those calls you receive at work here, and to address calls received at home on another day, if at all.

LANDLINE/OFFICE PHONE LOG

CALLS PLACED AT WORK

TODAY'S DATE: _____   DAY OF THE WEEK: _____

TIME	WHO CALLED	HOW LONG DID CALL LAST	PURPOSE OF CALL
_____	_____	_____	_____
_____	_____	_____	_____
_____	_____	_____	_____
_____	_____	_____	_____
_____	_____	_____	_____
_____	_____	_____	_____
_____	_____	_____	_____
_____	_____	_____	_____
_____	_____	_____	_____
_____	_____	_____	_____
_____	_____	_____	_____

CALLS PLACED AFTER WORK (AT HOME)*

TODAY'S DATE: _____   DAY OF THE WEEK: _____

TIME	WHO CALLED	HOW LONG DID CALL LAST	PURPOSE OF CALL
_____	_____	_____	_____
_____	_____	_____	_____
_____	_____	_____	_____
_____	_____	_____	_____

*You may prefer to log only those calls you receive at work here, and to address calls received at home on another day, if at all.

CELL PHONE LOG

TODAY'S DATE: **DAY OF THE WEEK:**

CALLS RECEIVED

TIME	WHO CALLED	HOW LONG DID CALL LAST	PURPOSE OF CALL

CALLS PLACED BY CELL PHONE

TIME	WHO CALLED	HOW LONG DID CALL LAST	PURPOSE OF CALL

INTERNET TIME LOG

TODAY'S DATE: _____   **DAY OF THE WEEK:** _____

TYPE OF DAY: _____ (Work? School? Leisure?)

TIME	INTERNET TASK*	LENGTH OF SESSION	PURPOSE	WHAT I SHOULD HAVE BEEN DOING INSTEAD
_____	_____	_____	_____	_____
_____	_____	_____	_____	_____
_____	_____	_____	_____	_____
_____	_____	_____	_____	_____
_____	_____	_____	_____	_____
_____	_____	_____	_____	_____
_____	_____	_____	_____	_____
_____	_____	_____	_____	_____
_____	_____	_____	_____	_____
_____	_____	_____	_____	_____
_____	_____	_____	_____	_____
_____	_____	_____	_____	_____
_____	_____	_____	_____	_____
_____	_____	_____	_____	_____
_____	_____	_____	_____	_____
_____	_____	_____	_____	_____
_____	_____	_____	_____	_____
_____	_____	_____	_____	_____
_____	_____	_____	_____	_____

*Note: The task might be e-mail, surfing, research, for example.

TO-DO LIST

Here's a very simple to-do list that includes space to write down up to ten tasks.

TODAY'S DATE: _____   **DAY OF THE WEEK:** _____

	TO DO	COMMENTS	DATE COMPLETED
1.	_____	_____	_____
2.	_____	_____	_____
3.	_____	_____	_____
4.	_____	_____	_____
5.	_____	_____	_____
6.	_____	_____	_____
7.	_____	_____	_____
8.	_____	_____	_____
9.	_____	_____	_____
10.	_____	_____	_____

WHAT'S YOUR PRIORITY?

How do you know what your priorities should be? It will help to ask yourself these questions every single day:

1. What is the #1 project I have to do today? _____

2. How am I going to do it? _____

3. How will I know when I'm done? _____

4. How will I reward myself for doing it? _____

5. What is the #2 project I have to do today? _____

6. Can I juggle multiple projects simultaneously, or do I have to complete one task at a time and/or delegate some or all of the work to others? _____

ACTION! STRATEGY WORKSHEET

For a discussion of the ACTION! System, refer to Day 4: Prioritizing: Using the Action System for Optimum Productivity

Project or Task: _____

A (Assess): _____
_____
_____

C (Control): _____
_____
_____

T (Target): _____
_____
_____

I (Innovate): _____
_____
_____

O (Organize): _____
_____
_____

N (Now!): _____
_____
_____

ASSIGNMENT/PROJECT SHEET

Set up a system for keeping track of your assignments or projects. You can buy tracking sheets at the office supply store or make your own on the computer. Here's a simple project tracking sheet that you might find useful.

TODAY'S DAY AND DATE: _____

Client Name: _____

Title: _____

Company: _____

Address: _____

_____

Phone: _____

Cell phone: _____

Fax: _____

E-mail: _____

Website: _____

Preferred way to communicate: _____

Referred by: _____

Project: _____

Date assigned: _____

Deadline/due date: _____

Length/type: _____

Fee and/or rate: _____

Budget: _____

Expenses: _____

Letter-agreement and/or contract signed: _____

Project submitted on: _____

Follow-up: _____

Outcome: _____

Notes: _____

_____

_____

ACKNOWLEDGMENTS

Beginning with the first all-day time management seminar that I offered at Sacred Heart University in 1984, I want to thank the thousands of men and women, boys, girls, teens, and college students who have attended my time management workshops over the years. Over the last two decades, I've interviewed CEOs, CFOs, vice presidents, real estate brokers, fundraisers, executives, writers, artists, students, entrepreneurs, managers, administrative assistants, computer programmers, account executives, mental health professionals, paralegals, lawyers, publicists, editors, actors and actresses, agents, working parents, stay-at-home moms, stay-at-home dads, writers, small business owners, entrepreneurs, administrative assistants, sales representatives, and others. I want to express my gratitude to everyone throughout the United States and the world—especially Australia, Japan, Denmark, England, India, the Netherlands, Taiwan, New Zealand, and Germany—whom I interviewed in person or by phone, or whom I surveyed or coached on time management and related issues. Whether you are named in this book or you wished to remain anonymous, your valuable input has been pivotal.

Thanks especially to George Sheldon, a fellow writer and member of ASJA (American Society of Journalists and Authors), who was kind enough to get the word out that Sterling Publishing Co., Inc., was looking for a time management expert to write a new book on that topic, and for passing my name and credentials along to his agent, Robert (Bob) DiForio of D4EO Literary Agency. I would also like to thank my caring, hardworking, and detail-oriented editor at Sterling, Meredith Hale; her enthusiastic boss, Editorial Director Michael Fragnito; project editor Isabel Stein; and former CEO and Publisher Charles Nurnberg, who envisioned a need for a new book on time management. Other thanks are due to a multitude of publishing professionals, including Marilyn Kretzer, Toby Ernst, and Toula Ballas for their help in selling the foreign rights, as well as Caroline M. Brown and the Sterling publicity department for their assistance in getting the word out to the media about *Work Less, Do More.*

I want to thank Vince Poscente, Bob Danzig, Ed Peters, Suzanne Vaughan, Ronald Brown, Richard Laermer, Paulette Ensign, Victoria Sutherland, Mary Ellen Lepionka, Pat Schroeder, Barbara Hemphill, Julian Block, Nat Swann, Abby Marks Beale, Chuck Scott, Katherine Humphrey, Shirley Cheng, Dara Tyson, Brian Zumbano, Peggy Stautberg, Bob Dickson, Mike Toth, J. Kirby Best, Christine Hartline, Fran Silverman, Terry Nathan, the late Jan Nathan, Lisa Krebs, Evelyn Lee, Ramona Creel, Debbie Williams, Barry Izsak, Jon Chakoff, Richard Quinney, Katie Davis, Steve Cone, Alison Ravenscrost, Jim Pritchert, Linda Marsa, Marilynn and Dick Smith, Lucy Hedrick, Denise Marcil, Barbara Lowenstein, Michael LeBoeuf, Glenna Salsbury, Matthew B. Kiger, Don Gabor, Marie Raperto, Julie Jansen, Nella G. Barkley, Simon T. Bailey, Richard Laermer, Carole Copeland Thompson, Cammy S. Bourcier, Tonia Port, Sandi Givens, Marie Farrugia, Donna Hanson, Nina Sunday, Lorna Patten, Robyn Pearce, Catherine Palin-Brinkworth, Peter A. Turla, and Jane Covner, among others. Janet Ulrich of CARAVAN® Opinion Research Corporation went beyond the call of duty in her assistance when I was crafting the question I commissioned them to ask in their semi-weekly omnibus survey on behalf of this project. A heartfelt thanks to my responsive NSA Business Coaching mastermind group: Julia, Yvonne, Gail, Tom, and Michael.

Thanks to my loving husband and best friend Fred, our terrific sons Scott and Jeff, my mom, Glady Barkas, my mother-in-law Mary, my sister, Eileen, my brother-in-law Dick, my aunts Jo, Peggy, and Alice, my sisters-in-law Karen and Becky, my nieces Vanessa and Courtney, my nephews Sky and Ariel, my cousin Phyllis, and the rest of my extended family. Thanks also to my understanding friends Joyce, Mary, Judy, Gail, Ginny, Paula, Suzanne, Elia, Joseph, Sharyn, Jennifer, Nona, Arlynn, Sue, Rob, Sheila, Art, Anette, Marilynn, Abra, Colin, Rhonda, Pat, Annette, Betsy, Richard, Marcia, Ib, Bebbe, Kathy, Bob, Monica, Steve, Linda, Charlie, Karen, Howard, Debbie, Ruth, Rob, Rande, and Franka for being there for me.

ABOUT THE AUTHOR / HOW TO REACH DR. JAN YAGER

Jan Yager, who holds a Ph.D. in sociology from The City University of New York, has been conducting time management workshops since 1984, when her first book on time management, *Creative Time Management,* was published and subsequently translated into Japanese. Her second book on time management, *Creative Time Management for the New Millennium,* published in 1999 and translated into Russian, Indonesian, and Japanese, has led the author to speak about time management, or conduct workshops or seminars on it, throughout the United States and internationally. A prolific writer, Jan is the award-winning author of 26 books, translated into 20 languages, including *Who's That Sitting at My Desk? Workship, Friend, or Foe?, Making Your Office Work for You, Business Protocol, Effective Business and Nonfiction Writing, Career Opportunities in the Publishing Industry, Road Signs on Life's Journey, Friendshifts®, When Friendship Hurts,* and others.

In addition to graduate work in art therapy at Hahnemann Medical College, Dr. Yager received a master's degree in criminal justice from the Goddard College Graduate Program and a B.A. in fine arts from Hofstra University. She has taught sociology, criminology, and writing courses at several universities and colleges, including Penn State, Temple University, St. John's University, and, most recently, at the University of Connecticut.

A work and relationship expert and coach, she is interviewed often on TV and radio shows or quoted in magazines, newspapers, or online publications, including *The Oprah Winfrey Show,* the *View,* the *Today Show, Good Morning America,* the *Early Show,* National Public Radio, BBC radio, CNN, the *New York Times,* the *Wall Street Journal,* the *Independent on Sunday,* the *Toronto Star, Parade, Time,* and Forbes.com. Jan is a member of NSA (National Speakers Association), ASTD (American Society of Training and Development), NAPO (National Association of Professional Organizers), Women's Media Group, and other professional associations.

A recipient of a prestigious Alumni of the Year Award in 2006 from The City University of New York Graduate Center, Jan practices what she preaches as the working parent to two sons and wife to husband Fred, a writer, communications consultant, and producer who ran Merrill Lynch television for seven years. Together the Yagers have coauthored two novels, two nonfiction career books, and several screenplays.

If you wish to hire Jan Yager (the former J.L./Janet Barkas) as a speaker or workshop leader, contact your favorite lecture bureau, including:

- Leading Authorities, Inc. (www.lauthorities.com)

- Authors Unlimited (www.authorsunlimited.com)

For coaching or media inquiries, send an e-mail query to yagerinquiries2@aol.com, or write to Dr. Jan Yager, P.O. Box 8038, Stamford, CT 06905-8038 USA, leave a phone message 24/7 at 1-212-560-5638, or send a fax to 1-203-968-0193. For more information, visit www.drjanyager.com.

INDEX